Understanding Karl Rahner
Volume 5

A Pattern of Doctrines

Part III

Understanding Karl Rahner
Volume 5

A Pattern of Doctrines

Part III: A Man of the Church

George Vass

Sheed & Ward
London

ISBN 0–7220–9354–3

Published in Great Britain in 2001 by
Sheed & Ward Limited
4 Rickett Street
London SW6 1RU

Production editing, design, typesetting, from author's disks: Bill Ireson

Printed and bound in Great Britain by Biddles Limited, Guildford and
Kings Lynn

Contents

Preface

Presenting a summary of Rahner's ecclesiology is not an easy task. The whole of his theology, including (as I hold) his philosophical foundation, is geared to the service of the Church. He tried to explore and explain our faith in contemporary terms. It is not, therefore, a freelance theology owing nothing to the believing community, and there are no theological themes without significance for understanding the Church. Such qualities must of course be true of the work of any dogmatic theologian – or, to use the term now more generally preferred, of any systematic theologian – beyond the denominational divide. Karl Barth, indeed, was insistent that his monumental work be called *Church Dogmatics*, in this respect differing from his eminent predecessor F. Schleiermacher.[1] A Roman Catholic theologian must take the same stance, and that is the reason for my attempt to make clear from the outset that my project, 'Understanding Karl Rahner', should be a dialogue with his thought from within the Church to which we are both happy to belong.[2]

The main difficulty, however, which delayed both the expository parts and my own reflections on Rahner's ecclesiological thought was the extent of his writing with explicit reference to the Church. Well before the Second Vatican Council, and especially in its wake, Rahner tackled again and again topics concerning the basic constitution of the Church and wrote and lectured about particular questions which emerged concerning the idea of the Church in theory and practice. The Table of Abbreviations provides a short survey of these various topics. An added source of difficulty was the obviously repetitious nature of his essays and articles (most of them transcripts of his public lectures) which nonetheless contained ever-new insights into his developing thought. In presenting them I have tried to cover the whole of

Rahner's ecclesiological writing and thus exposed my book to repetitions. My only excuse is the already well-known complexity of Rahner's thought. Identical topics illuminated from different angles, together with verbatim quotations from the English translations of his works, have made this volume bulkier than the preceding four. Indeed, contrary to my original plan, I have to leave his sacramental theology and eschatology to a following volume. These two aspects nevertheless belong organically to Rahner's doctrine of the Church.

Personal factors of ill-health and teaching engagement delayed my work, and I apologise both for postponing the treatment of these topics and for the lapse of time between the fourth and the present volume. I could not keep abreast with the ever-growing secondary literature on Rahner, nor could I put to use the recent republication of his works and manuscripts by my colleagues in Innsbruck, Rahner-Archive, an enterprise not in view while the theologian was still alive. Readers of my fifth volume have to be satisfied with the material already published and translated. I have never thought, and still do not believe, that most of Rahner's occasional writings are, or ever will be, normative for contemporary Roman Catholic theology. Their exceptional value, to my mind, lies elsewhere: instead of being a Church-Father of the twentieth century, he is a stimulus for those generations who grew up in the tradition of neo-scholasticism, and an incentive to theologians writing and publishing in modern circumstances. His thought encourages confrontation or dialogue; it inspires a rethinking or extending of his own insights. There should never emerge a Rahnerian school of theology which reverences each and every word of the master. I was happy to know him in person, and I know he would have been the first to resist such an approach.

In this volume, therefore, I continue the method, particularly, of Volumes 3 and 4 (as suggested by the title *A Pattern of Doctrines*) with regard now to Rahner's thought on the Church. The only difference is perhaps that the expository parts endeavour to consider almost all of his essays of ecclesiological importance, and that my Comments and Questions more often than not represent a theology for which I am alone responsible. The Rahnerian inspiration for these should be obvious even when they contradict, correct and extend his thought.

Nonetheless, Rahner's genuine love for the Church (expressed often by the ill-chosen words such as 'churchmanship' or 'churchliness') has certainly excited my growing admiration. I could detect a man of the Church behind every word he wrote about our Christian communion. Indeed, his ecclesiology is a genuine witness to the Church.

Before I submit this volume to the judgement of the reader, I would like to finish on a personal note. I have spent now more than twenty years away from an English-speaking environment and academic fraternity. My command of the language of my preference is accordingly impaired. I needed the help of friends correcting my own writing; their style, or even their attitude to a foreigner writing in English has left a mark on my work. Not everyone has the talent of a Joseph Conrad for assimilating a for-eign tongue to perfection and no academic writing can avoid using the auxiliary products of non-English literature. That must excuse my references to works written mainly in German and perhaps the occasional Germanic constructions that have escaped the attention of my correctors.

Without these long-suffering advisers and friends the present volume could not have been submitted to print. My sincere grat-itude is due first of all to Mrs Alison Wilson, B.D. London, a theologian in her own right, and to my lifelong friend Fr Peter Hackett, SJ, with whom, as an undergraduate of Heythrop College, I shared the laborious preparation of our finals in theol-ogy. I gladly acknowledge some degree of co-authorship, even though they would not agree with many of my own positions. Theology is done by constant dialogue and this is perhaps the only value of my own work on Karl Rahner's doctrine of the Church.

GEORGE VASS
Innsbruck
October 2001

Table of Abbreviations

Karl Rahner's books, articles, essays, collaborations and other publications were published over a period of 40 years. They amount to some 4,000 works in German, English and in other languages.

Those of his works frequently quoted in this book (and some works by other authors with whom he collaborated) take the form of single key words, abbreviated to save space; for example, 'Piety', *Dynamic*, 'Membership'. A major source quoted is Rahner's *Theological Investigations* (*TI*), the English translation of the original German, *Schriften für Theologie* (*ST*); thus, 'Piety' was published in both editions (*TI* 5, *ST* V).

Where articles written earlier were gathered and published later in a single edition, or in a series of editions, similar abbreviations are employed; for example, *Handbook*, 'Hierarchy', *Commentary*.

I also use key words for works by other authors (for example, Tanner, Bonhoeffer, Egan) and acronymic abbreviations for standard works (*AAS*, *CIC*) and so on.

AAS

> *Acta Apostolicae Sedis*, Rome (1943 and 1966)

'Aspects'

> 'Aspects of the Episcopal Office' in *TI* 14, pp. 185ff (= *ST* X, pp. 430 ff) (1972)

'Assent'

> 'Assent to the Church as She Exists in the Concrete' in *TI* 12, pp. 142ff (= *ST* IX, pp. 479ff) (1968)

'Authority'

> 'Authority' in *TI* 23, pp. 61ff (*ST* XV, pp. 326ff) (1987)

Bonhoeffer

> Dietrich Bonhoeffer, *Sanctorum Communio: A Theological Study of the Sociology of the Church*, Vol. 1, Minneapolis, MN (1998). The English translation of Bonhoeffer's *Werke*, Vol. I, edited by Eberhard Bethge and others, published in Munich (1986).

'Certainties'

> 'Does the Church Offer any Ultimate Certainties?' in *TI* 14, pp. 47ff (= *ST* X, pp. 286ff) (1971)

'Charismatic'

> 'Observations on the Factor of the Charismatic in the Church' in *TI* 12, pp. 81ff (= *ST* IX, pp. 414ff) (1969)

'Changeable'

> 'Basic Observations on the Subject of Changeable and Unchangeable Factors in the Church' in *TI* 14, pp. 3ff (= *ST* X, p. 241) (1971)

'Church as a Subject'

> 'The Church as a Subject of Sending of the Spirit ' in *TI* 7, pp. 186ff (= *ST* VII, pp. 183ff) (1955/56)

'Church of Saints'
  'The Church of Saints' in *TI* 3, pp. 91ff (= *ST* III, pp. 111ff) (1955/56)

'Church of Sinners'
  'The Church of Sinners' in *TI* 6, p. 259 (= *ST* VI, pp. 307f) (1947) 'Church's Responsibilty'
  'The Church's Responsibility for the Freedom of the Individual' in *TI* 20, pp. 51ff (= *ST* XIV, pp. 248ff) (1979)

CIC
  Codex Juris Canonici, Rome (1923 and 1983)

Commentary
  Commentary on the Documents of Vatican II, K. Smyth (ed. and trs), London (1966). The English translation of *Ergänzungsband, Vol. 1*, Rahner's extensive commentary on the 'Dogmatic Constitution of the Church' in *Lumen Gentium*, pp. 105–97, published as a supplementary volume in *Lexikon für Theologie und Kirche*

'Consecration of the Layman'
  'The Consecration of the Layman to the Care of the Souls' in *TI* 3, pp. 263ff (= *ST* III, pp. 313ff) (1936)

'Consecration in the Church'
  'Consecration in the Life and the Reflections of the Church' in *TI* 19, pp. 57ff (= *ST* XIV, pp. 113ff) (1976)

'Crisis of Authority'
  'The Teaching Office of the Church in the Present-Day Crisis of Authority' in *TI* 12, pp. 3ff (= *ST* IX, pp. 339ff) (1969)

'Diaconate'
  'On the Diaconate' in *TI* 12, pp. 61ff (= *ST* IX, pp. 395ff) (1968)

Dynamic

> *The Dynamic Element in the Church*, London (1964). First published as 'Prinzipien und Imperative' in *Das Dynamische in Der Kirche*, Freiburg-im-Breisgau (1958), pp. 14–37

Egan

> *Faith in a Wintry Season*, H. D. Egan (ed.), New York, NY (1990)

'Episcopacy'

> 'Pastoral-Theological Observations on Episcopacy in the Teaching of Vatican II' in *TI* 6, pp. 361ff (*ST* VI, pp 338ff) (1965).

'Episcopate'

> 'The Episcopate and the Primacy' in *Quaestiones Disputatae*, Vol. 4, London (1962). The English translation of *Episkopat und Primat*, Freiburg-im-Breisgau (1961), as published earlier (1956/57) in *Stimmen der Zeit* 161.

'Faith and Doctrine'

> 'The Faith of the Christian and the Doctrine of the Church' in *TI* 14, pp. 24ff (= *ST* X, pp. 262ff) (1971)

Foundations

> *Foundations of Christian Faith: An Introduction to the Idea of Christianity*, W. V. Dych (tr), London (1978)

'Freedom'

> 'Freedom in the Church' in *TI* 2, pp. 89ff (= *ST* II, pp. 95ff) (1959)

Glaube

> *Glaube in winterlicher Zeit: Gespräche mit Karl Rahner aus den letzten Lebensjahren*, Dusseldorf (1986)

Handbook

Vols. I and II. *Handbuch der Pastoraltheologie: Praktische Theologie der Kirche in ihrer Gegenwart,* Freiburg-im-Breisgau (1964)

Hearers

Hearers of the World, R. Wall (tr), London and New York, NY (1969). The English translation of *Hörer des Wortes,* Freiburg-im-Breisgau (1963).

'Hierarchy'

First published as 'Verus Pastor, Vom Sinn der kirchlichen Hierarchie' in *Über das bischöfliche Amt,* Karlsruhe (1966), pp. 65–81. This essay, in pamphlet form, was also published in Freiburg-im-Breisgau under the title, *Vom Sinn des kirchlichen Amtes.* Throughout, I quote from the former publication

'I Believe'

'I Believe in the Church' in *TI* 7, pp. 100ff (= *ST* VII, pp. 103ff) (1954)

'Infallibility'

'On the Concept of Infallibility in Catholic Theology' in *TI* 14, pp. 66ff (= *ST* X, pp. 305ff) (1971)

'Interpretation of the Dogma'

'The Interpretation of the Dogma of the Assumption' in *TI* 1, pp. 215ff (= *ST* II, pp. 239ff) (1951)

'Jus Divinum'

'Reflections on the Concept of *Jus Divinum* in Catholic Thought' in *TI* 5, pp. 219ff (= *ST* V, pp. 249ff) (1962)

'Kritik'

'Kritik an Hans Küng. Zur Frage der Unfehlbarkeit theologischer Sätze' in *Quaestiones Disputatae* 54, Freiburg-im-Breisgau (1971)

'Lay Apostolate'
>'Notes on the Lay Apostolate' in *TI* 2, pp. 319ff (= *ST* II, pp. 339ff) (1955)

'Lehramt'
>'Magisterium and Theology' in *TI* 18, pp. 54ff (= *ST* XIII, pp. 69ff) (1978)

'Magisterium'
>'Magisterium' in *SM*, Vol. 3, pp. 351–8. The English translation of *Sakramentum Mundi*, under 'Lehramt', Vol. 3, pp. 177–93 (1978)

Meditations
>*Meditations on Freedom and the Spirit*, London (1977)

'Membership'
>'Membership of the Church according to the Teaching of Pius XII's Encyclical *Mystici Corporis Christi*' in *TI* 2, pp. 1ff (= *ST* II, pp.7ff) (1947)

'Mysterium Ecclesiae'
>'Mysterium Ecclesiae' in *TI* 17, pp. 139ff (= *ST* XII, pp. 482ff)

'Office'
>'The Episcopal Office' in *TI* 6, pp. 313ff (= *ST* VI, pp. 369ff) (1963/64)

'Official Teaching'
>'What the Church Officially Teaches and What the People Actually Believe' in *TI* 22, pp. l65 (= *ST* XVI, pp. 214ff) (1981)

'On *Humanae Vitae*'
>'On the encyclical *Humanae Vitae*' in *TI* 11, pp. 263ff (= *ST* IX, pp. 276ff). First published in *Stimmen der Zeit* 182 (1968), pp. 193–210.

'Past and Present Forms'
> 'Past and Present Forms – Dogmatic Considerations: Bishops' Conferences' in *TI* 6, pp. 369ff (=*ST* VI, pp. 432ff) (1962/63)

'Pastoral Ministries'
> 'Pastoral Ministries and Community Leadership' in *TI* 19, pp. 73ff (= *ST* XIV, pp. 132ff')

'Piety'
> 'Dogmatic Notes on Ecclesiastical Piety' in *TI* 5, pp. 336ff (= *ST* V, pp. 379ff) (1961)

'Pope and Bishops'
> 'The Relationship between the Pope and the College of Bishops' in *TI* 10, pp. 50ff (= *ST* VIII, pp. 379ff) (1967)

'Position of Woman'
> 'The Position of Woman in the New Situation in which the Church Finds Herself' in *TI* 8, pp. 75ff (= *ST* VII, pp. 351)

'Priesthood'
> 'The Point of Departure in Theology for Determining the Nature of the Priestly Office' in *TI* 12, pp. 31ff (= *ST* IX, pp. 366ff) (1968/69)

'Priestly Existence'
> 'Priestly Existence' in *TI* 3, pp. 239ff (= *ST* IX, pp. 366ff) (1942)

'Priestly Image'
> 'Theological Reflections on the Priestly Image of Today and Tomorrow' in *TI* 12, pp. 39ff (= *ST* IX, pp. 373ff) (1968/69)

'Priestly Ministry'
> 'How the Priest Should View his Official Ministry' in *TI* 14, pp. 202ff (= *ST* IX, pp. 448ff) (1969)

'Priestly Office'
>'The Point of Departure in Theology for Determining the Nature of the Priestly Office' in *TI* 12, pp. 31ff (= *ST* IX, pp. 366ff) (1969)

'Sinful Church'
>'The Sinful Church in the Decrees of Vatican II' in TI 6, pp. 270ff (= ST VI, pp. 321ff) (1968)

'Situation'
>'On the Situation of Faith' in *TI* 20, pp. 13ff (= *ST* XIV, pp. 23ff) (1980)

SM
>*Sacramentum Mundi*, Vols. I–VI, Bangalore (1975f). The English translation of *Sakramentum Mundi*, Vols. I–IV, Freiburg-im-Breisgau (1968f)

'Structure'
>'On the Structure of the People of the Church Today' in *TI* 12, pp. 218f (= *ST* IX, pp. 519ff) (1970)

'Synod'
>'On the Theology of Pastoral Synod' in *TI* 14, pp. 116ff (= *ST* X, pp. 358ff) (1969)

Tanner
>*Decrees of the Ecumenical Councils*, Vols. I–II, N. P. Tanner (ed.), London and Georgetown, Washington DC (1990)

A Pattern of Doctrines

Part III: A Man of the Church

Introduction: The 'Wintry Season' of the Church

Anyone who has read the previous four volumes in this series should already have a good idea of Karl Rahner's theoretical concept of the Church. However, any analysis of his writings about the Church would have to go beyond theory and, indeed, whilst one cannot expect anything basically new, a major part of 4,000 titles published in forty years betrays his practical concern for the Church.[1] They reveal Rahner as a man of the Church.

Vorgrimler's introduction to the life and thought of Karl Rahner gives an outstanding account of the biographical side of the theologian's activity.[2] It is a feature which I, in turning to Rahner's ecclesiology, cannot ignore. At almost every stage of his life, Rahner faced the problem of the contemporary Christian; he tried to project a more palatable image of the Church for modern man, whether inside or outside her fold.

From the beginning, Rahner dreamt of the Church's future life and role in a post-Christian society. This dream seemed to have come true when, in 1959, Pope John XXIII announced the general Council, Vatican II. This was, in many ways, a turning point in Rahner's life, a *Zäsur* as he often called it. In the years after the Council, accepting innumerable invitations to read a paper or give a lecture on its various aspects, he turned into a 'wandering scholar', spreading abroad and arguing the great achievements of Vatican II. Interviewed by outsiders whose interest was aroused, under the crossfire of questions by people who found themselves at loggerheads with the Church, or who were anxious to maintain her pre-conciliar splendour, Rahner became the man in constant *Gespräch*. Almost all his utterances had a significance 'for the shape of the Church to come'.

1

At this stage I shall refer to one aspect of Rahner's last years which brought me into closer contact with his life. Living in the same community at Innsbruck, I had only an inkling of what was in the interviews Rahner gave during the last years of his life, and which were later documented by P. Imhof and H. Biallowons.[3] They can be regarded as the 'table talk' of a theologian which merge into the testament of a man of the Church.

The title of these interviews, *Glaube in winterlicher Zeit*, is significant: whether Rahner coined the phrase, or borrowed it from elsewhere, he speaks of a 'wintry season', a 'winter time' of the Church. He explains what he means by this: whilst one cannot fail to see the 'restorative' tendencies which prevail in the wake of Vatican II, one can speak of another divide (another *Zäsur*) impeding the full application of the Council or impairing its achievements. Rahner mentions several of these. Curiously enough, he refers repeatedly to one in particular: since Vatican II the Church has ceased to be a narrow European Church with missionary export to other continents; she has become at last what she was meant to be – a truly *catholic* Church embracing the whole globe. Rahner asks, Has the Church lived up to this ideal? Or, has she remained, at least in Europe, in a mood of anxiety and defensive resignation? That the latter appears to be the present situation, suggests Rahner's epithet 'wintry'.[4]

It is obvious that winter for Rahner does not mean the end of the Church.[5] He will try to find remedies, project strategies to introduce a new springtime, but behind all his practical suggestions an unconditional love for the Church asserts itself. In any case, this love for the Church is deeply rooted in Rahner's experience of God.

Once asked by a student how can we love the Church, Rahner replies with another question:

> Can you love Christ? Can you say, 'I stake my life and death on my faith in Jesus Christ, crucified and risen; that by this faith I am to be saved and sanctified'? If you can say this . . . then one could also say that you have accepted the Church.'[6]

The love for 'mother' Church which, as Rahner puts it, is 'the mediator and the guarantee of his life in union with God' is implied in our basic Christian experience. It is an experience not only of a transcendent God but of his irrevocable acceptance (*Zusage*) of mankind, and therefore of the self. One can be born into Christendom, be 'indoctrinated' by the Church and take her teaching for granted; yet one comes nearer to her if, in full awareness one accepts her message about the world, about man and God. But to be a Christian in a truly 'ecclesial' sense means that the Church is interiorized: our love for her becomes a necessary and valid constituent of our Christian faith. The Church must belong to the very core and content of our existence, of our conduct.[7]

This is why Rahner is unable to sympathize with an 'exodus' from the Church – a phenomenon that began to afflict the Church of central Europe during his last years. Although he tries to be charitable towards those who leave the Church,[8] he finds the question whether one should leave the Church painful: *Es macht mich verrückt*, ('It makes me mad,').

Rahner's answer to the question, Why am I *still* in the Church? is another question: 'For me as a believer it is in the last analysis meaningless. What can the word "still" mean here? It is like asking whether I will "still" live in this pitiable twentieth century.'[9]

This riposte is most relevant. Love for the Church is existentially rooted not only in one's explicit faith in God, but also in one's concrete human life. For the person who believes in and loves the Church, her reality is God's ultimate and irrevocable self-commitment to mankind.[10] Indeed, for Rahner, it is in the Church, that he can perceive the word of the crucified and risen Lord: 'In the absolute power of my love I have given myself to you for all eternity.'[11] God's commitment to us solicits our commitment to him. In the light of this human commitment in faith all discrediting experiences of the visible Church are but passing phenomena which can (at most) have a secondary significance. And even where this explicit faith is missing an inkling of the Church's reality is given in the 'unbeliever's implicit commitment' to neighbour.

However, this basic humanism[12] cannot substitute for the full reality of the Church nor excuse one's separation from her. For human love goes beyond the confines of a merely material and temporal aid. In fact, its most noble act is the enabling of one's fellows to listen to the gospel and to experience God's love for mankind.

For whosoever:

> . . . respect and love the other as someone addressed by the message of eternal life, they have already established the foundation of the Church. A private love of neighbour remains, in a certain sense, intimate, yet is not full and total love at all.[13]

Although the Church is entailed in faith and one's love for her in human conduct to mankind, it must come to an explicit commitment.

Rahner's faith in and love for the Church was a most *critical* commitment. It was a trait which accompanied him throughout his life; he always held criticism an obligation arising from the love for his Church.[14] Even as an old man, he was capable of being upset by the slightest shortcomings of his own Church. Some of his works, before they were censured by Rome, reflect this.[15] When, in the year of his death (1984), Rahner was asked about Rome's conduct, he compared his situation with that of one of his evangelical colleagues:

> A Protestant exegete like E. Käsemann can certainly threaten to leave the regional Protestant Church in Germany without thereby ultimately contradicting Protestant theology. For a Catholic Christian, priest, and theologian something corresponding to this is *a priori* unthinkable! The latter has an 'absolute' relationship to his Church. But obviously one can also express one's criticism in the Church . . . therefore . . . criticism is legitimate and necessary, and, as criticism, looks for public exposure.[16]

This passage was introduced by Rahner with a modest admission of having been a Catholic theologian always absolutely faithful to the Magisterium. Yet this absolute faithfulness has never prevented him from re-thinking its positions. His was not a blind obedience (*ein Kadavergehorsam*): he criticized not only the way and life of the Church, her rulings, her hierarchy,[17] but also her doctrine. For, apart from explicit definitions, the Church can and indeed has erred:

The Teaching Office of the Church can err and make a statement which can be criticised or reformed . . . Catholic theologians not only can, but must, criticise statements which have not been defined and must find ever new and deeper interpretations for the already formulated dogmas. On this level there is and must be almost unlimited [*grösstte*] freedom'.[18]

Every statement is within the scope of the hierarchy of truths. For Rahner, this was a matter of course – not only in the sense that there are primary and secondary statements of faith, but that even among those explicitly defined there is a gradation in the obligation to consent. The very substance of Christianity is and remains the experience of God *and* the conviction that we are all called in Jesus Christ to accept God's self-communication to mankind. Anything over and above this commitment in faith is open to further research, to renewed interpretation and to ever new ways of expression. Only on this foundation can we 'believe the Church' and obey her teaching.[19]

It is therefore not surprising that Rahner raises critical points against the Church's actual rulings; against the rigidity of her stance in ethical and doctrinal matters; against her failure in implementing and living out the achievements of Vatican II. Rahner's eyes were ever open to ways of reforming the Church which he loved.

To take some random examples. The official Church should be less 'clerical' and the divide between the ministry and laity should shrink: both are responsible for the affairs of the Church.[20] Was it not fundamental to Vatican II? Of course, this appeal to co-responsibility can, on the one hand, be misused by ultra-progressives; but, on the other hand, it has not as yet been exploited by the post-conciliar Church.[21] Elsewhere, Rahner complains that the collegiality of bishops – a real achievement of the decree on the Church – is not reflected in the synodal conventions of world episcopacy. Instead, Roman centralism is on the increase and the bishops have but a limited role.[22] According to Rahner, the new Code of Canon Law was a slight improvement on the earlier 1919 Code, but the opening to dialogue (presupposed and introduced by the Council's decree on religious freedom) has not yet come into its own.[23] Instead, a number of official documents have been produced regulating the ethical conduct of Catholics.

In a 1981 interview Rahner asks where there is to be found an encyclical confronting contemporary atheism:

> I have been told recently in Rome that the popes have published encyclicals about the rosary, about the veneration of the Sacred Heart, about indulgences, about the sacrament of penance, etc. But have we got an encyclical about contemporary atheism? Not that I know of! And such a document would be more important.[24]

Unlike Küng, Rahner is against the convocation of a third Vatican Council. He holds it inopportune until a 'change of mind' – even in official circles – can take place. He presupposes, of course, that such a change of mind has begun to formulate itself in the Church, as it were, 'from below'.[25] Although he is not in favour of the full democratization of the Church on the pattern of modern democracies, he can envisage the appointment of bishops with a juridically ordered participation of priests and laity.[26] He could envisage a more liberal attitude of the official Church as regards ecumenical intercommunion;[27] as regards the validity of Anglican orders;[28] as regards the ordination of women to the ministry;[29] as regards the ordination of a non-celibate clergy;[30] as regards family planning.[31]

One gets the impression from these last dialogues that, from beginning to end, Rahner anticipated 'the shape of the Church [he wished] to come'. It is as if he were living in a Church that is building herself up from her grassroots:

> The Church in the future will consist of a network of small base communities. These, of course, will have to be organically bound together. They must have some commonly shared features [*Gemeinsamkeit*] as maintained by the bishops. There will have to be a pope. But a great deal will be quite different from what it is today.[32]

This also belongs to Rahner's vision of the Church of the future which, apart from reasserting her past treasures, is in the sobriety of her present already planning her future. He demands within the present Church a serious theological *futurology*.[33]

These random remarks of an old conversationalist raise certain questions: Are we dealing with a thoroughly liberal theologian of the Roman Catholic Church? Or, was Rahner, as he himself confesses, a modest teacher of the faith – however with courage for sensible change in the Church? Was he the theologian who, whilst retaining the concepts of an orthodox ecclesiology, prepared the way for a new one?

Chapter 1

Foundations of an Ecclesiology

Apart from his book *Foundations of Christian Faith*, Rahner never produced a systematic treatment of the Church. The nearest he came to it was his introductory essay to the first volume of the *Handbuch der Pastoraltheologie*.[1]

However, before becoming involved in the *Handbook*, Rahner's basic insights about the Church had crystallized. So, we can speak about an ecclesiology in advance (see 1.1) which was subsumed by the transcendental method that Rahner employed throughout; this explaining the Church as entailed in man's dynamic effort to reach beyond himself for the basic idea and, what is more, the reality of the Church, is implied in the concrete existential relationship between God and mankind (see 1.2).

It is this aspect of Rahner's ecclesiology with which I shall resume my dialogue with Karl Rahner in my comments and questions (see Chapter 2).

1.1 Ecclesiology in Advance: Some Early Insights

Rahner is at his best in his short meditations. It is in these that the combination of personal churchmanship with the insights of the professional theologian is most apparent. In the first period of his writing – that is, roughly up to the beginning of Vatican II – we find two important articles in which his scholarship is well demonstrated. However, for the time being, I shall leave these aside and turn to some shorter publications in which certain aspects of his later ecclesiology can be detected. In these publications, up to the announcement of the Council, the committed Catholic and theologian appears to have been affected by certain

difficulties of the faithful which Rahner makes his own and in
attempting to answer them foreshadows his later theological
approach to the Church. The problems concerning the Church at
that period are still – perhaps in another key – our difficulties in
the present 'wintry season' of a post-conciliar era.

1.1.1 The Word of God and the word of the Church

'Dogma and dogmatic definitions are always a scandal.'[2] This
remark apropos the definition of the Assumption in 1950 which
was not universally welcomed: many Catholics, especially in
Northern countries, found it difficult to share the rejoicing at its
solemn announcement. Already, in 1951, Rahner had attempted
to explain the meaning of the dogma,[3] but here he appears to be
tackling the difficulties it raised: 'It seems to be asserting almost
too much.'[4] Nonetheless, he is ready to plead for its acceptance:
in the words of the Church, God's own truth is mediated to us.
Rahner's question is, therefore: What is the attitude which we
ourselves must adopt in order to hear such a message aright?[5]

He suggests that *the* first thing is not to examine the content of
the message – especially if it does not suit our expectations.[6] And,
what is more, if the human mediators propose something to us
which, in itself, does not seem to be important, unless for pious
ears, we should still face up to it. For it is pronounced 'in an
objective sphere outside ourselves'. This 'sphere' is the Church
where we stand and one should 'believe the Church'. We, the
believers, are, so to put it, in an ecclesial circle.

For us:

> The Church is the object of our faith and, in a mysterious manner,
> at the same time the dimension in which it [the faith] exists. In
> this dimension alone is it possible to have anything like the full-
> ness of Catholic faith?[7]

There are, therefore, two complementary aspects of this faith:
one believes in the message and then in the Church as founded by
Jesus the Christ, or the other way round: 'On the basis of his faith
in Christ the believer includes the Church in his faith in such a

way that it immediately becomes the direct medium and rule of faith as such.'[8] In a later article, 'Piety',[9] Rahner was to analyse the exact nature of this belief in the Church, but at this point he seems to be more interested in the question as to *what* our faith in Christ concerning the Church implies. The question as to *how* this entailment can be explained will derive from his later theology. For its application to the Church, I shall call it 'transcendental ecclesiology'.

Rahner's reasoning in 'I Believe'[10] foreshadows this approach: our faith in Christ refers us to God's objective and saving presence through Christ's cross, as it is realized in time and space by his Spirit. That this is a real factor in the world ('however much it may be hidden') is brought home to the believer in an apprehensible and palpable way by the mediation of the Church: 'This means that the Church . . . is God's eternal compassion and his Body, as it exists in space and time.' In other words, Rahner speaks of a mysterious presence as well as of a reality we can here and now experience.

Later, in the same article, he continues:

> . . . both aspects . . . are . . . inseparable yet distinct. Considered as the sphere of grace in this sense, and simultaneously as an historically apprehensible entity, the Church is the sole dimension in which . . . anything like the phenomenon of Catholic faith is possible at all.[11]

Referring back to the initial question of a dogmatic pronouncement, Rahner is ready for his conclusion: 'When we speak of the word of Christ we mean a word as it exists upon the lips of the Church authorised by Christ. It is because she utters it that it is proved to be his word.'[12]

The insight behind this argumentation is obvious: Rahner envisages the Church on the pattern of the Incarnation. For, according to the Chalcedonian ruling, just as in Christ the divine and human come to an unmixed oneness, so it is with the presence of grace and the visible society of the Church. These elements (grace and visible society) are different (unmixed) yet one and the same. Indeed, just as the working of grace is incarnational so, *mutatis mutandis*, is the mystery of the Church (so to put it) a continued incarnation of the Word becoming flesh. Christ's words take flesh in the words pronounced solemnly by the Church.

This incarnational principle will characterize at least Rahner's early ecclesiology.

The analogy of the Incarnation, however, cannot be applied literally to the nature of the Church. The Word made flesh has become a living subject in Jesus of Nazareth. Can it be said that the life of grace, as rendered present by the Holy Spirit, is 'incarnate' in the Church? An affirmative answer could be called an 'hypostatizing' of the Church; it would mean that the first living subject of which God's efficacious word takes hold is the Church. Rahner comes very near to this view, when he states: 'The life of God . . . is first bestowed upon her and then upon the individual in her.'[13] The Church as a fellowship has a certain priority over and above the individual faithful: she is not only the sum total of those who believe, she is 'more'.

In 'The Church as the Subject of Sending the Spirit', Rahner writes that for him, the Church

> . . . is nothing else than the further projection of the historicity and of the visibility of Jesus through space and time, and every word of his message, every one of its [the Church's] sacramental signs is, once more nothing else than a part of the word in its earthliness, with which the Spirit has united itself indissolubly since the day on which the Logos became flesh.[14]

Although in this 1955 article Rahner does not suggest that the Spirit takes flesh in the Church, there still remains a difference between the Church as quasi-subject and the individual subjects who believe. He speaks of the Church as if she were a 'moral person' who is responsible for her words pronounced under the power of the Spirit. It is in this sense that the Church is 'more' than the sum total of her individual members.

Whilst, of course, this does not mean that the individual in the Church is not responsible for what he or she believes, ultimately a person's beliefs have to conform to the belief of the Church. For 'faith is only completely and truly possible in the community of the faithful, in the Church'.[15] From this it follows that what one believes is not merely a subjective matter: it takes place in the Church 'the only objectivity,' as Rahner paradoxically puts it, 'that can be achieved in faith is the subjectivity of the Church.'[16]

Rahner's incarnational approach to the Church would suggest that the Church as a quasi-subject stands in relationship with the individual subject of the believer and vice versa. Both Church and believer are responsible for the proclaimed word of faith *viz.* the faith confessed to and to be existentially accepted. If we take this statement literally we may reckon with a tension between the Church and the individual believer. This tension may develop into a conflict or may be understood as a blind obedience of Catholics to the authentic representatives of their Church; a problem inherent in our attitude to the teaching of the Church which will characterize Rahner's lifelong activity as a churchman.

At this early stage, however, Rahner did not envisage such a conflict. Rather, he understood this tension as an opportunity for dialogue. For the individual who believes with the Church can, in spite of his or her commitment to the Church, uncover human shortcomings in those who officially pronounce the Church's teaching. He or she can point out gaps in the information on which their arguments are based; can criticize as well as praise the Church on account of what she teaches.

At this time, Rahner's personal difficulties with the official Church – and his *ad hoc* criticisms of Church affairs – are not yet formulated nor yet the many words with which he will attempt to defend the Church's teaching, exposed as it will be to vehement attacks within and without her own fold. These will belong to the, as Rahner calls it, 'wintry season' of a post-Vatican II era.

Prior to this, his interest is, I believe, more theoretical. Rahner's is an unconditional trust in the guiding presence of God's Spirit; the Church is a continual Pentecost – the place where the Spirit is continually poured out. And this allows men and women to become committed members, yet accountable for what they actually believe; members, humble yet daring in action; obedient yet conscious of their responsibility; adhering to the Church's past yet working for her future.[17]

It would, however, be false to affirm that Rahner was blind to the shortcomings of the official Church. He insists on the responsibility of those who speak in her name: they cannot twist the truth of God's word into error. And criticism of the Church on the part of individual believers has always to reckon with the human element which is part and parcel of the Church's nature. Indeed,

Rahner is more than aware of an underlying sinfulness in the Church.

1.1.2 Church of sinners: Church of saints

Rahner's preoccupation with the Church's teaching, as we saw it in 'I Believe' (1954), was preceded by one of his very first essays in *Stimmen der Zeit*. Published in 1947, 'The Church of Sinners'[18] struggles to understand the Church in her very human reality. It speaks about a Church and her sinful members and stresses over and above her incarnational and sacramental reality. The Church can be sinful, because her members are sinful. To assert the contrary, would be heresy. Yet Rahner goes a step further. The body which is made up of frail human beings shares the sinfulness of its members: the Church, though holy in herself, can in 'her manner of acting' fall into sin without impairing her basic sanctity.

To clarify this dialectical statement, Rahner appeals to a pattern of thought connected with, yet different from, that of the Incarnation. The Church is basically a *sacramental* reality. For just as the sacraments *objectively* effect the sanctification of the individual, even when in the sinful recipient the *subjective* fruitfulness of grace fails, so is the Church objectively a sacramental sign. She is efficacious in herself for everyone. The sinful member, whilst he or she subjectively fails to receive the fullness of the Church's redeeming grace, shares her holiness in an objective way.[19] Hence the sinner always remains a member of the Church:

> In a certain sense the Church is a basic sacrament [*Ursakrament*]: in her case we must make a distinction between her visible appearance as a body in so far as this is a sign of grace, and this visible appearance in so far as it is a reality filled with grace, and accordingly also between a [merely] 'valid' and a 'fruitful' membership of the Church. The sinner has the first kind of membership, but not the second.[20]

This sacramental analysis of the nature of the Church, although in a modified form, will characterize Rahner's ecclesiology.

Taken together with its 'incarnational' background, as outlined above, it is a safeguard against a hypostatizing tendency.

In applying, however, this sacramental pattern to the nature of the Church, Rahner will have to point out a difference. The Church as sign does not refer to any particular grace (as, according to Trent, do the seven sacraments) but to Christ's redemptive work in the world, in its whole and *completed* reality. What Rahner understands by this completed reality is only insinuated here. It becomes more obvious in an article published after Vatican II, which deals with exactly the same topic, although in a different context.[21] The change of title from 'The Church of Sinners' to the 'Sinful Church' is itself significant. Whereas the former was cautious in affirming that the Church can fall into sin (that is, be in need of forgiveness), the latter speaks of a sinful Church: the Church herself is in need of repentance and forgiveness. Was it not encouraged by the repeated admission on the part of the Council that the Church is in need of continual reform?[22] Would it not follow from this that the Church, as one Body, is at the same time the holy and the sinful Church: *simul justa et peccatrix*? This is not a merely external juxtaposition, not even a dialectic between her sinful and her holy members (as it seems to have been in the earlier article). Sinfulness and holiness are stated of the one and the same subject, the Church; holiness, because

> ... through Christ and his victory upon the cross there is given to redeemed humanity as a whole, and therefore above all to the Church, not only the *possibility* of salvation, but by his grace which is *in fact victorious* there is given and manifested the *realisation* of this possibility.[23]

Rahner must here be referring to the *eschatological* victory of Christ, as being applied first of all to the Church as whole. It is a kind of predestination by means of an efficacious grace made visible in Christ

> ... a predestination, since the Church is preserved by God, antecedently to the actual behaviour of her members, from falling away from the grace and promises of God in any fundamental and essential way. Hence the Church is [even subjectively] *sancta.*[24]

Thus the Church, anticipating her eschatological fulfilment in the *future*, is *now* the efficacious sign of redemption realized in this world. This redemption, which effects the Church's fundamental holiness, is shared by all her members called to final sanctification – even if they happen to be sinners. Theirs is a state of 'already and not yet' a truly eschatological situation.

Just as the appeal to the Spirit extended Rahner's incarnational approach to the Church, so now is the eschatological an extension of his sacramental pattern as applied to the Church. Later, it will be summed up by an expression, characteristic of Rahner: the life of the members is grounded on the 'ultimate acceptance' (*Zusage*) of God. This motif reappears in 1955 in 'The Church of Saints' where, about to argue for the veneration of the saints in the Roman Church, Rahner appeals to the Church's consciousness of her own holiness:

> The proclamation of her own holiness is an eschatological statement of faith and not merely a kind judgement of history which condescends not to overlook the good which 'after all' exists over and above everything ugly.[25]

The canonization of the saints from among the multitude of 'saints' in a biblical sense is the Church's self-realization of what she really is: the *una sancta*.

It is this ultimate and eschatological acceptance (*Zusage*) by God which, in Rahner's view, distinguishes the Church not only from the synagogue of the Old Testament, but also from any other human association. In underpinning this view the pneumatic motif comes to the fore: 'The Church is always something more than an association, more than a "juridical Church" and confessional organisation, because the Holy Spirit has indissolubly united himself to her.'[26]

Hence, both sinfulness and holiness are inalienable characteristics of the Church. And these qualities pertain not only to the official Church; the corporate subject of these qualities is the Church as a whole. Sin and grace coexist all the way through and holiness is shared out to the hierarchy and to the 'charismatics' in her fold.[27] So is the Church: holy and sinful alike.

§§§§§§

In the last two sections about Rahner's articles, I have tried to give samples of his different approaches to the nature of the Church. These are developed like variations on a theme in an orchestral work. The incarnational and pneumatic, the sacramental and eschatological points of view will be permanent elements in his ecclesiology. These will soon be extended by another, anthropological, motif. To say only that the Church, owing to the Incarnation is a proto-sacrament of an objectively redeemed mankind seems 'lopsided', unless one can point to a basic desire for *de facto* belonging to her. The Incarnation and the sacraments are God's signs for mankind: symbols through which God realizes his redemptive presence. But is not our human life such that, by its very nature, we are bound to live with this sacramental sign of the Incarnate, that is, with the Church? Presence asks for encounter. And Rahner makes room for this encounter in one of his most theoretical early articles about the membership of the Church.

1.1.3 The members of the Church

The most substantial essay in Rahner's early publications, 'Membership', is an apparent defence[28] of *Mystici Corporis Christi* one of the encyclicals published by Pope Pius XII. 'Membership' was published in the same year as 'The Church of Sinners' and followed in 1948 by other essays touching upon the Church, her ministry and her organization.[29]

No doubt these smaller essays reflect Rahner's thought in 'Membership'; it is to be noted that, two years before his death, Rahner expressed his misgivings precisely as regards this essay.[30] Nonetheless, it contains valuable insights for the future development of ecclesiology and enables us to see Rahner's method in interpreting an important text of the Magisterium.[31]

'Membership' confronts us with a dilemma. On the one hand, to say that Church membership depends on a valid baptism which initiates the recipient into the community of Catholic faithful, is not enough. It would raise the questions: What about those who, without visible baptism, but having more or less conscious desire for baptism and the Church (*votum baptismi* or *votum ecclesiae*) obtain the grace of Christ's salvation? Are they not members of the Church? What about the once baptized and lapsed members who by heresy or schism separate themselves from the body of the Church and are expelled? Are they too not members of the Church? On the other hand, to say that Church membership can be decided merely on the internal and externally unverifiable fact of whether or not one is justified, militates against the Roman Church's constant teaching, namely that sinners, too, are members of the Church.[32]

Now, Rahner tries to steer between these two extremes. Church membership must, on the one hand, be manifest and visible, just as being baptized is. The import, however of this 'visibility' is not the material fact of having received the sacrament of baptism, but rather the connection, the visible link with the Church as a whole. He refers to the would-be members of the *primordial* sacrament which is the Church. On the other hand, Rahner emphasizes man's inner attitude, his free decision already under the influence of grace, and requires from members faith in a quasi-ecclesial fellowship (*fides et communio ecclesiastica*). Both, visible link and inner commitment, are decisive factors for membership, even if this introduces a certain stratification: belonging is not uniform, but is, as it were, staggered, since it is realized in various degrees in a Church which comprises a wider range of people than her actual and official members.

This solution is, according to the interpretation of Rahner, at least permitted if not suggested by *Mystici Corporis Christi*, the wording of which leaves room for further development. The encyclical (which is not an infallible doctrinal pronouncement) repeats the hitherto traditional teaching on membership. In doing so, it points out a basic principle of importance: the visibility of the Church and the visible nature of her membership. To neglect this, its (according to Rahner) essential message

> . . . would turn the Church into a purely inward pneumatic community of love. This, however, contradicts . . . the incarnational principle of Christianity according to which God was made flesh and attached his grace to the concrete historical here and now of human realities.[33]

This denial of a merely spiritual character of membership implies a basic conviction which Rahner is not going to alter to the end of his life: God has not left man free to choose how to find his own way of salvation; its precondition is at least an explicit societal relationship to God which, however *de facto*, consists in relationship to and fellowship with Jesus the Christ.[34] Salvation is within, or at least related to, the one and *visible* communion of the Church. It is, first and foremost, this incarnational principle that decides the membership of the Church.

Rahner is, however, aware that *Mystici Corporis Christi*, according to the letter, leaves much less scope for Church membership than that which he proposes as the document's essential message. Hence, he undertakes the laborious task of going beyond its literal teaching without contradicting its essence. He states first that the Pope does not say that there is no salvation outside the established Roman Catholic Church.[35] Theological tradition, as rooted in the principle of *extra ecclesiam nulla salus*, does not require such a narrow understanding. In Rahner's opinion, what tradition requires for the salvation[36] of any non-Catholic is merely a *conditional* necessity to belong to the Roman Church.[37] Therefore, if the encyclical's teaching is in accordance with this tradition, the theologian has the right to add the qualification of *conditional necessity*, even if this qualification is not explicitly mentioned in the text of the encyclical itself. What in fact this conditional necessity implies, and the text states, is that salvation is more *secure* for those who are actual members than for those in whom God's mercy works for final salvation in an unfathomable way. This latter statement presupposes the fact

> ... that besides the simple and straightforward membership of the Church, there are other and looser ways of belonging to Christ and to the Mystical Body of our Lord which reaches concrete form in the Church.[38]

From this, of course, it would follow that the encyclical does not simply identify the biblical and traditional notion of the Mystical Body with the established Roman Church. There is, as Rahner understands *Mystici Corporis Christi*, a 'material' and not 'formal' identity between the Mystical Body in its biblical sense and the Roman Catholic Church. Hence, theologians have to differentiate between simple membership and the apparent non-members (even non-believers) whose 'orientation'

(*Hinordnung, Hingewiesenheit*) towards the Church can be assumed.[39] We are at the origin of Rahner's later view on the 'anonymous Christian'.

Although a very similar view will be adopted by Vatican II,[40] I do not believe that Rahner in 'Membership' sufficiently explains how an implicit orientation can be taken for a *visible* relationship to and connection with the *visible* Body of the Roman Church. What he lacks here is his, now familiar, 'transcendental approach' which, presumably, was then not yet worked out. Instead, he applies here the analogy of sacramental theology, as already noted in his minor publications of the same period.

Just as the notion of sacrament can be described from two aspects, so can the concept of the Church and the individual member's visible belonging to her. In describing the sacraments, one approach concentrates on the validity of a sacramental rite without paying much attention to its purpose, namely the interior grace produced by it. There can be (as we have seen above) valid but unfruitful sacramental acts. In these the rite, the visible sacred sign is, as it were, an instrument in God's hand for the sanctification of the recipient. Traditional theology calls this aspect *sacramentum tantum*. We can, however, concentrate on the fruitfulness of the sacrament and speak of the grace of justification which it effects: the *res tantum*. The unity of these, indeed the complete reality of a sacramental act, is realized when not only the sign, but also the corresponding grace are present in the recipient. This aspect is called *res et sacramentum*. Thus, the mere sign of baptismal washing and the corresponding grace of justification will be united in the indelible sign of the recipient's effective membership in the Church.

It seems to be likewise with the proto-sacrament which is the Church. Her nature, too, can be approached from different angles. I can describe her bodily nature as a mere sign – for instance, in a juridically determinable form without having regard to the presence of Christ and his grace in her. On the other hand, I could describe the Church as the incarnate presence of Christ.[41] The two extremes – Christ's presence in the visible form as a mere sign and his justifying grace alone – when taken together, comprise the Church's entire reality.[42] If now one of these two, the mere sign or its spiritual effect, is present there is a valid reference to the Church.

Rahner's attempts at extending the scope of Church membership leads him, as I have said, to stratification: members in full
communion with the Church (baptism and justifying grace);
members without one of these marks. So, Rahner can ask the
question, concerning people who are not yet fully members of
this visibly constituted Church but have obtained the grace of
justification: Are they not still members of the Church? Or, to put
it another way: Is not their 'graced' state due to a visible sign of
their belonging *in some manner* to the Church? For the whole
reality of the Church is wider than its defined bodily appearance:
'It is the effective sign of unity between God and the world
through grace.'[43] When this grace happens to be present in a justified person, then his or her engraced state points to its source,
to the membership of the one and holy Church, without which
salvation in a Christian sense is not possible. But this one and
holy Church does not coincide with the juridically defined
Roman Catholic Church. Rahner writes:

> The justified person who belongs [or is 'referred'] to the Church
> without being a member of it, belongs 'invisibly' to the visible
> Church by grace and has a 'visible' relation to this Church, even
> when this relation is not constituted by baptism or by an exter-
> nally verifiable profession of the true faith.[44]

Anyone reading Rahner's argumentation on the question of
this 'visibility' will find it obscure. In his effort to keep his
answer grounded in the Pope's teaching, he will anticipate, to a
certain extent, his main philosophical and theological insights.
First, he concentrates on the meaning of *votum ecclesiae*, admit-
ted by the encyclical: if one is not a member of the Catholic
Church, but somehow desires to be one (*votum*), then a quasi-
membership can be assumed. But how can the visibility of this
votum be established, if even the justified non-Catholic person is
not aware of it?[45] The theory of *votum ecclesiae* alone is not sufficient. Hence, Rahner will appeal to man's free but obligatory
choice of belonging to the one humanity which is more than the
sum total of the individual. This awareness, for Rahner, is tanta-
mount to an obediential potency (*potentia oboedientialis*).[46] He
will appeal to the relationship of the free person to his or her

material and existential situation (to the person's 'nature' as Rahner puts it here) as comprising this overall unity; to the real transfiguration of this situation by the historical presence of the Incarnate[47] who raises the former into what will later be called the 'supernatural existential'. He will also anticipate his cosmic and anthropological Christology:

> When someone totally accepts his concrete human nature by his decision of free will . . . his free action gains an expression [that is, visibility] which is at the same time also an expression of the proper supernatural salvific will of God.[48]

From the last sentence it is but a short step to affirm that this expression has a quasi-sacramental nature, hence it is a *'quasi-visible'* sign referring, if not to this concrete Catholic Church, then to the Church which is the 'people of God':

> For the *whole earthly reality* which we call the Church . . . does in fact, have a meaning only as an *effective sign* of the unity *of the world* with God through grace.[49]

For 'whole earthly reality' substitute 'people of God' and you have, instead of the narrow Pian sense of the Mystical Body, the wide meaning of the people of God of Vatican II. For 'effective sign' substitute 'visibility' and you have a (quasi-visible) relationship of the non-Catholic justified person to the Church of Christ: that person is now 'orientated' (*hingewiesen*) towards her. Finally, for 'unity of the world' substitute 'unity of mankind', into which our free and personal entry is obligatory. Thus you embrace every justified man and woman as at least a potential, or rather anonymous, member of the one and only Roman Catholic Church.

With this, however, I have overstepped the confines of Rahner's early article on the membership of the Church. In presenting his underlying ecclesiology we could see, on the one hand, his effort to remain true to the papal document and, on the other, his free interpretation. Rahner's 'Membership' essay, besides bringing into play the various elements of his early and later writings on the Church, had at the time an ecumenical significance and was a step towards his later view on the salvation of our 'unbelieving' brethren. It broke through the narrow-laced confines of *Mystici Corporis Christi* towards a wider notion of the Church and her membership. Admittedly, Rahner's speculative efforts to point out a certain 'quasi-visibility' in those who are only 'referred' to, whilst not officially belonging to the *una sancta* are not altogether convincing. They will gain in clarity, when he applies his transcendental method to the notion of the Church.

1.2 'Transcendental' Ecclesiology: The Church and Human Freedom

What I understand by 'transcendental' ecclesiology one should already be able to guess. Presupposed always is an experience which contains infinitely more than its actual content. Thus, if in our concrete situation and by our free act we accept God's word and his forgiving grace, we are implicitly referred to the Church. Rahner's idea of the Church derives from experience being concomitant with grace as God's self-bestowal, of revelation achieving its peak in Jesus the Christ. It is an experience in some way inscribed in the very 'performance' (*Vollzug*) of man's free action. This is how, it seems, Rahner overcomes the oddity of his 'Membership' essay, where a quasi-visibility was ascribed to those who are not officially members of the Roman Catholic Church. Rahner's ecclesiology is transcendental as well as anthropological.

1.2.1. The Church as entailed in human freedom

Rahner's transcendental approach to the Church was already hinted at in *Hearers*,[50] and it remained the underlying guideline for his later statements about her, especially during and after the Council. There are two opposite but complementary poles from which the implicit experience of the Church is approached. First, man's transcendental experience of God seeks to become concrete and categorial; it strives to express and objectify itself in worldly realities and, above all, in social relationships. Second, it is assumed that God's self-communication has a dynamic tendency to 'incarnate' itself in worldly realities in which the presence and power of grace become tangible and, for its beneficiaries, objectively certain and assured. According to the first line, Rahner can say that whenever man approaches God he is implicitly accepting the Church. Conversely, God in approaching man will do so by means of what can be termed the Church. At the meeting point of these two 'approaches' man discovers his true self in an achieved freedom and he will be *de facto* related to the Church.

As early as 1959 Rahner had anticipated this approach: for example, in 'Freedom'.[51] His thesis is that the Church is the sacramental sign of human freedom. To underscore this bald statement, Rahner subjects the concept of freedom to a transcendental analysis.[52] Just as knowing, so is a free act finite yet open to an infinite horizon: whether it is exercised as a choice or as indifference. That is, abstaining from engagement in the alternatives, freedom is condemned to an 'impasse'. Either it is shackled by its finite possibilities or it chooses to remain aloof in abstaining from them. Either way, opting for or abstaining from, a choice has to be made.

Hence the main question for Rahner: What is the correct object of freedom which solves the dilemma of its finitude? How is freedom freed? His answer is obvious:

> If God is to be . . . the very object of our freedom which alone makes us free, then this freedom would neither consume itself internally in its own emptiness when it withholds itself, nor would it deliver itself to the slavery of the finite when it gives itself.[53]

This statement, however, is only a postulate, unless the liberation of freedom becomes a divine gift, a grace of the Pneuma – the 'liberating freedom of our freedom': the grace of the Spirit 'frees our freedom'.

One should not, however, forget that freedom is a human act embedded in man's concrete situation. Hence, this divinely initiated process of liberation in our concrete history is a redemptive freedom. This means, according to the above mentioned incarnational principle, that God's free action towards man is manifested in the Logos who became flesh. Therefore: ' . . . this spiritual freedom of our freedom is established by the very act of

God freely present in the flesh of Christ himself as a sign in this world, and is grasped and made our own as present in this sign.'[54] This freedom of our freedom is then made accessible and is applied to us in Jesus who sends us his liberating Pneuma.

From this, deduction (or rather adduction) to the Holy Spirit it is but an easy step to the Church. If Christ is the sacrament of our freedom, the Church is its continuation. If Christ's liberating presence became tangible in the Pneuma, it is the Church as a community which goes on to signify and to effect this God-given freedom. Thus:

> The Church is the quasi-sacramental tangible element, and the historically visible factor of the redemptive liberation of the freedom of man. In so far as she is, or rather has the Pneuma of God she is, or has freedom . . . Where the Lord's spirit is, there is freedom.[55]

Rahner in a way spiritualizes man's freedom and thereby makes it a proper theological notion in the order of grace. It is not something merely natural. The Church, as the guardian even of the natural order ' . . . would then . . . defend and regulate in its ordered exercise and in its different fields in which such freedom is useful.'[56] Therefore, as Rahner concludes, the Church is the indispensable existential place of our freedom.

This early approach to the notion and role of the Church still reflects the analyses of the *Hearers*.[57] In later years Rahner's theology of freedom, although retaining its transcendental bases, will be more concretized. The notion of the Church, as entailed in freedom, will be expressed in the context of interpersonality based on love of neighbour. Rahner will be more and more convinced that freedom is not 'a mere capacity of choice between objects given *a posteriori*'.[58] It is not simply a matter of take it or leave it and be free. Freedom only exists because there is spirit in man – understood as transcendence towards God. For freedom comes from God and is directed towards him. God, the infinite being, is its horizon. Hence it is true ' . . . that we meet God everywhere in a most radical way as the most basic question of our freedom, in things of the world and (in the words of Scripture) above all in our neighbour.'[59]

Therefore, this ubiquitous encounter with God does not occur in the empty space of transcendentality. To act freely requires confrontation with categorically defined objects of choice in man's ongoing history.[60]

And this limited sphere of history is pre-eminently represented in meeting with other human freedoms – in encounter with a thou:

> The transcendental opening out requires a categorial object, a support, as it were, so as not to lose itself in empty nothingness; it requires an intramundane Thou. The original relationship to God is . . . love of neighbour.[61]

With this he presupposes that intersubjective communication is a *sine qua non* of our freedom's transcendental thrust towards God, and that it belongs to man's social nature. It is this love of neighbour which will become the basic act of morality.[62] In and through love of neighbour one participates in the universal order of salvation. Through it one can hear and freely obey the word of God. Rahner speaks of a solidarity as founded on neighbourly love.[63] And this intercommunicative solidarity will then be regarded as conditional on God's self-communication mediated to mankind through the historical man Jesus the Christ. And in the 'thou' one not only experiences God and Jesus, but also the Church. This intramundane thou is the ground on which the transcendental idea of the Church can be built.

If we now turn to the seventh chapter of *Foundations*, where Rahner introduces his ecclesiology, we find a similar reasoning. Although he never abandoned the transcendental categorial scheme, in *Foundations* Rahner concretizes it in interpersonality as based on love of neighbour.[64] His overall thesis is that Christianity must be constituted as Church – it belongs to the religious existence of man as such, regardless of the actual shape of the organized Church of everyday experience.[65] However, any religious experience presupposes the self-communication of God to mankind.[66] If now God communicates himself to mankind, he does so according to the nature of man's self-experience which is social and interpersonal. From this would follow that man is an ecclesial being and Christianity is, by its very nature, an ecclesial religion.[67]

This implicit ecclesiality of human nature hinges upon man's experience of interpersonal love. More precisely, it is founded on the ultimate success of neighbourly love which is 'sacramentally present in the Church'.[68] Of course, Rahner is aware that the Church is not to be equated with love of neighbour as supported by the love of God. The salvation of the individual remains and is a matter of human freedom and decision, for which every Christian has to take responsibility 'in the loneliness of his own conscience'.[69] But if this 'lonely decision' is positively taken for neighbour and thus for the (transcendental) Church, then it will be evident that ' . . . the most real thing about the Church is precisely the liberation of man and of human existence into the absolute realm of the mystery of God himself.'[70]

This 'yes' to the Church, as entailed in the exercise of human freedom is, as it were, avowed both anonymously and explicitly in unreserved acceptance of neighbour in love. It is the condition on account of which man, whether or not he 'believes the Church', is basically an ecclesial creature.

1.2.2 'We believe in the Church'

The 'transcendental Church' is a reality experienced in everyday life. It is entailed in our existential affirmation of God. Nevertheless this latency tends to become explicit: our faith in God will lead us to a belief whose object is the concrete Church. In 'Piety', his relatively early (1961) essay, Rahner apparently presupposes a somewhat different concept of the Church. He speaks here as dogmatic theologian and tries to define what kind of faith corresponds to the Church.

The key question is: Could it be said that we believe *in* the Church, just as we believe in God? Or, do we confess the Church just as *another* object of belief? To restate the question: Is belief in the Church a primary step on one's way to the full acceptance of faith guaranteeing its content as a kind of self-verification? Or, is rather the Church asserted with many other tenets in the wholeness of our faith – that is, just another object of belief? To put it more practically: Do we believe in the gospel because we believe in the Church, or do we believe in the gospel and therefore also in the Church?[71] In the first case one would attribute an absolute, and in the second a relative, value to the Church. Rahner's first option seems to be for the latter.

But lest we misinterpret this relativity of the Church, we must follow Rahner's whole argument. He, indeed, attributes an all-important role to this 'other object of belief'. Why the Church is not its primary object, *a credere in Ecclesiam*, is simply the fact that she is implied in God's redeeming action towards mankind:

> She is the Church of Christ, precisely by reason of the fact that God's forgiving grace has taken hold of human beings like ourselves . . . and has fashioned them into the Church.[72]

It is in this way that the Church is 'just another object of our faith.' Therefore, it cannot be said: 'We believe *in* the Church – *credimus in ecclesiam*.'[73] This formula would imply a personal relatedness, an engagement of the believer with the reality of another person.

This other person, as we have seen in Rahner's analysis of faith is God alone.[74] Belief in God means not a knowledge 'about something'; in faith we reach beyond ourselves, transcend ourselves and so pass beyond reflection and any 'mediation' which may ground our belief. Believing in God, we do not reflect on ourselves to make sure of the correctness of our belief, but 'find the courage to hold onto the reality itself (which is a person)'. Furthermore, belief in God is enabled by God alone, it is supported and effected by the reality of the one who is the primary object of faith: God makes the act of faith possible and supports it so that it becomes that which is in very truth the ground human faith.[75]

This position, however, does not make the Church a negligible quantity. On the contrary, belief in God makes the believer aware of the presence of the Church as something to be concretely experienced. By this Rahner means the:

> . . . wider congregation of believers, not merely as the messenger and guarantor of an . . . individual faith, but as the subject to whom the 'individuum', who experiences his historical finiteness even in his faith, entrusts his faith.[76]

In this quasi-definition of the Church, Rahner expresses the Church's concrete mediatory role which seems to be necessary in order that the 'self-communication of God can be accepted even more radically in a subjective sense'.[77] Thus, for the believer, the Church becomes 'an object of faith, because he or she believes in God'.[78]

With this, we seem to be back at Rahner's 'transcendental' ecclesiology: the Church as an object of our belief is entailed in our faith in God – an experience within experience. At this stage, however, it would be more appropriate to say: faith in God is due to a *fides explicita*, whereas for the believer the Church is first a *fides implicita* in his or her explicit faith in God. It is on this ground that Rahner speaks of 'believing the Church' instead of 'believing in the Church'.

When, however, this implicit belief becomes explicit, it can be equally said: 'Faith comes through the Church and the Church through faith.'[79] The two experiences are interrelated: the one who has the faith believes in the gospel, because he or she believes in the Church; or, one believes in the Church because one had already surrendered oneself to God's word in Jesus the Christ.

This surrender is not altogether impersonal. For explicit faith is always

> . . . surrendering of one's faith into the faith of the believers in general and taking this as the norm of one's faith. . . . [It is] always also faith which from the outset inserts itself in silent obedience into faith of the Church.[80]

This is why ecclesiological piety has often hypostatized 'mother' Church. But dogmatic theology soberly warns us that the Church is not a person. She cannot, like the individual, be conscious of herself, cannot justify herself, she cannot decide. She is not even the hypostatized *we* of all believers. Faith *in* the Church can only be used in a figurative sense, however much she is trusted and loved in our piety. Neither the believer nor the man or woman outside the Church can have faith *in* the Church. Yet an individual can have an attitude of trust and love towards the persons who make up and *form* the Church. The believing neighbour can be, in trust and love, the immediate object of piety – or, more precisely, in encounter with believing individuals in the union of all believers.

But, as we already know, such neighbourly love transcends itself:

> Hence, someone who loves the individuals in their irreplaceable uniqueness loves them also in their mutual unity which is the Spirit of God, and he consequently loves them also as the Church.[81]

The proviso is, of course, that this mutual trust and love between humans is implicitly or explicitly empowered by the grace of God.[82] Such a concrete trusting and loving encounter can be the objectification of man's transcendental tendency towards the Mystery of God. And this objectification is – in a sense – the transcendental Church as believed explicitly by the faithful and implicitly by the outsider. Whereas, for the explicit believer this objectification of a commonly shared faith *constitutes* the Church, for outsiders in encounter with explicit believers, the Church will be a sacramental sign of salvation.

This statement implies that the Church as an object of faith is enabled to be and is concretely formed by the faith of the community. She would not exist if she were not believed at all. She exists on account of man's belief, and God who effects the grace of faith will thus preserve the Church.[83]

'Transcendentally', therefore, the Church is basically in an encounter with human persons – should this take place between believers or between believers and unbelievers. For

> . . . the unbeliever is the neighbour, the relative, the human person on whose honesty, reliability and decency one must rely just as much as on the corresponding qualities of one's fellow believers.[84]

Rahner trusts that the unbeliever is not outside God's universal salvific will: that in him or her, as in the believer, the grace of God is at work. He sees in unbelievers, people 'who do not know what they really are – deep down in their conscience.' Hence, he accepts them as anonymous Christians: encounter with them does not constitute the Church in faith, but rather projects her as the visible 'vanguard' of a church invisibly in formation in order to become the *Church*.[85]

This encounter between the Church 'inside' and the anonymous Church 'outside' will bind the Christian to mankind as it really exists in its destination to supernatural grace. And, what is more:

> The Christian of today and tomorrow will see and experience the Church as the genuine representation of the nature of man as planned by God, as the sacrament of grace which – precisely because it is offered to everyone – presses towards its sacramental, historical appearance, even where the sacrament is not yet present and which precisely in this way is never absolutely identical with its effective constitutive sign, but rather promises . . . that it is powerfully at work everywhere.[86]

Although in 'Piety' Rahner presupposes people who actually 'believe the Church', he does not forget her transcendental concept. God's saving grace of faith is such that it realizes itself in the Church (that is, in and through those who 'believe the Church') – and man's encounter with his neighbour transcends to (objectifies itself in) a sacramental presence of God's grace for the whole mankind which is the Church. Man's transcendental thrust is about to become categorical in the visible Church. This categorical concreteness is a ' . . . historical objectification of man's absolute depth-of-being as open to God's grace.'[87]

The concrete history of the Church is the objectification of man's transcendental experience of grace.[88] And this objectification, the Church, is within the communitarian history of mankind. As Rahner will put it in a later essay, the whole history of the world culminates in the history of salvation and this latter transforms itself into the history of Christianity and of the Church.[89]

As we saw, the transcendental disclosure of the Church, even if it happens in an anonymous way, is indispensable. It is presupposed by every human being who in his or her own history experiences God, his grace and his saving presence. Because one believes in God, one also believes the Church. It is, however, true to say that for those who explicitly commit themselves to the Church ' . . . because they believe the Church, they believe in God'.[90]

1.3 Doctrinal Ecclesiology: The Irreversible Sign of Salvation

As early as 1960, Rahner became involved in a new enterprise, the nature of which was somewhat unusual for a dogmatic theologian. He projected a plan for a monumental presentation of Pastoral Theology. It may be that the success of his collection of essays published in 1959 under the title *Sendung und Gnade*[91] provided the motivation for bringing together a team which was to elaborate and present crucial questions regarding the Church's practical action in the contemporary world. To do this, however, presupposed a clear-cut vision of the Church, which he saw as having a specific task to perform in the world. Pastoral Theology was to be grounded on the theoretical doctrine of ecclesiology.

Despite initial difficulties on the part of his chosen collaborators, Rahner's plan for the *Handbook* was realized: the *Handbuch der Pastoraltheologie: Praktische Theologie der Kirche in ihrer Gegenwart* was published in five volumes at Freiburg-im-Breisgau between 1964 and 1969, to be followed by a voluminous Lexicon in 1972.[92]

Rahner's own contributions to this monumental work are, to my mind, the most characteristic specimen of his thought on the Church. Though intended to be pastoral or practical, his concise summaries in the *Handbook* are, in fact, the basis of a doctrinal ecclesiology. They are not easy reading. Chapters such as *Grundwesen der Kirche* (on the basic nature of the Church) and *Die Träger des Selbstvollzuges der Kirche* (on the subject of the Church's 'performance'[93] in the world) and their like are hard enough to understand even in a merely doctrinal context. All the more difficult are they for a theologian of practical bent.[94]

Yet Rahner's scheme for the whole of the *Handbook* was accepted, and discussions began in order to decide the correct starting point. This was in fact the 'definition' of the Church along with the existential task she has to fulfil in the world. For pastoral theology is nothing else than the 'performance' (*Selbstvollzug*) of the Church grounded in an 'existential' ecclesiology.[95] But even such an ecclesiology needs to be defined on a theoretical level: What is the Church in her very essence?[96]

1.3.1 On defining the Church

The answer to this question in its basic perspectives seems already to have been decided at the preparatory stage: the 'definition' of the Church was not to be arrived at from the rather narrow sense of *Mystici Corporis Christi*: the Church is more than her juridical confines. Instead, Rahner's anthropological approach seems to have triumphed when the publishing team of the *Handbook* agreed upon the main elements to be taken into consideration. Man as the personal recipient of divine revelation (the hearer of the word!) whose nature was raised through his encounter with Jesus the Christ, would be the starting point. Furthermore, man is to be considered in his social and interpersonal nature and in his concrete history which tends to its eschatological fulfilment. Thus, the Church is the 'unity'[97] of those people who have in one way or another accepted God's self-communication in Christ Jesus and the Spirit and who, in their ongoing communitarian history reflect the union which exists among the three persons of the Godhead.

The elements of this initially debated definition have been crystallized in the second part of the first volume of the *Handbook*, composed by Rahner himself:

> The Church is the socially legitimated fellowship (or communion) of people in which through faith, hope and love the eschatologically fulfilled revelation of God (understood as his self-communication) in Christ becomes real and true and as such present to the world'.[98]

Now, apart from its anthropo-theological prelude this 'definition' of the Church seems to reach its climax in her function: the Church's *raison d'être* is to 'make present'. Although the first part contains the strictly doctrinal elements of Rahner's ecclesiology, the second, more functional, half seems to belong to the first: he 'defines' the Church in her function.[99]

Rahner uses two words to characterize the Church: she is a

fellowship (*communio*) as well as a society (*Gemeinschaft* and *Gesellschaft*). Though I shall, in due course, dwell upon the connotations of these two words, here it is enough to note that for Rahner both aspects seem to be required to describe the Church adequately: the fellowship (*communio*) of believers becomes Church in their legitimate social (cultic, juridical and sacramental) togetherness. The Church is where persons 'engraced' by God's self-bestowal exist.

To expand his 'definition' Rahner introduces two other aspects of importance. The Church as a whole is both the fruit of (*Heilsfrucht*) and the medium (*Heilsmittel*) of salvation. The first means that the Church is a kind of fellowship in which God's self-communication is (in some way) already accepted and that this acceptance is the work of God's victorious and efficient grace. By means of this, the ecclesial fellowship becomes a visible society in history. The Church as the fruit of salvation is the 'arrival' the *Angekommenheit* of God's self-bestowal. But, at the same time, the Church is a medium: she mediates in her confession that Word which God has entrusted to her (which is a word of acceptance, on God's part) for the whole world, including her believing members. The Church is and functions as God's *Zusage*, his commitment to the world.

We have now extracted the strictly theological implications of Rahner's 'definition'. He speaks of a concrete historical reality: that is, something 'categorial' which is in process towards its own fulfilment. Nonetheless Rahner's – what I have called – transcendental ecclesiology is still, at the back of his mind. For his 'definition' presupposes that salvation is meant for every man and woman in all the dimensions of their humanity (especially in their historical and social nature). Hence, every human being, in one way or another, shares God's irrevocable *Zusage* and mankind's acceptance of it. Rahner's 'definition' should always be seen in this framework.

However, precisely from this transcendental viewpoint, it is more difficult to see that God has in and through the Church 'invaded' history, that he is no longer only the transcendental ground of our history, but is present to our time and space. And this is exactly what Rahner is about to affirm ' . . . the history of God's self-communication is committed to the historicity of its creatures'.[100]

In order to state this, Rahner had to appeal to two facts. First, God's self-communication has become a definite and irrevocable fact: in and through Christ, God has already accepted the world and by this it has entered into the last phase of its history – God's deed in Christ is eschatological. Second, reflection on this self-communication of God, in which the Church is disclosed, is not man's work: it is due to the same self-communication of God in grace.

In other words, Rahner appeals to a Christological fact and to grace in order to ground the very being of the Church. In Rahner's own language: Where the 'history' of God's transcendental self-communication achieves its peak in the event of Jesus the Christ and this is accepted in the faith of a 'categorial' human society, then we have the Church in distinction from the synagogue of the Old Testament, and from any other human associations. The Church is embedded in the ongoing history of human knowing and freedom, because she anticipates the end of the same history. In this way the Church is a historical *a priori*.[101]

1.3.2 The 'existential' being of the Church

This attempt to define the Church's being, as she is in herself, is only the first step towards her more existential or functional description. It is a Church whose task is to 'present'. What she has to present and how it is done seem to be implied in the above 'definition'. For Rahner, essence and function cannot be adequately distinguished. The Church is basically identical with what she is supposed to do. Her very presence is in itself already a representation. The Church is not just an institution which helps people to salvation (*ein Heilsmittel*): she is salvation 'incarnate' and, as such, the presence of God on earth (*Heilsfrucht*). Thus, the sacramental character of the Church belongs to her very being.[102]

The first and obvious thing which the Church is supposed to present is God himself as he really is, namely, the Mystery that communicates itself in Jesus the Christ. If, however, Jesus is the sign of God permanently accepting mankind then the Church in her turn is the sign of mankind's accepting the Mystery of God. Hence the first 'performance' (*Selbstvollzug*) of the Church is to open man to this absolute Mystery. But it also means that the Church should be the congregation of those who are in permanent revolt against any 'absolutes' other than God. Her action is a revolt deposing man's idols.[103] At the same time she should be aware that in her faith in and confession to Jesus the Christ she presents the Mystery which is beyond the horizon of human reason and can only be accepted in faith, hope and charity. In proclaiming this faith, the Church presents God to the world.

The second thing to be presented by the Church goes even further: the Church is the way in which this Mystery has been manifested to mankind. God is the Mystery, not just a puzzle which can once for all be resolved[104] and he remains ever a mystery, even in his self-manifestation. Yet in Jesus the Christ he gives himself away as eternal *truth*. The presence of God in the Church is the 'speaking out' (*das Ausgesprochensein*) of the Mystery in the *Word* which has once for all occurred in the manifestation of the *Son*. Hence, the foremost 'performance' of the Church is that she presents, points to the the truth of God in which he has communicated himself to the world. As such she is the fruit of salvation (*Heilsfrucht*). But, at the same time, the Church is the communion of those who not only hear and believe in God's truth but also confess and pronounce it in the world. As such she is the medium of salvation (*Heilsmittel*). It should be noted that by truth Rahner does not mean here any verbalized proposition, but basically the Word made flesh. Nor does he mean by the 'performance' of the Church any privileged class in the Church confessing and pronouncing the truth, but 'all the faithful' who in and through their confession to and proclamation of the truth become the Church in an *indefectible* way.[105]

God the Mystery in his self-communication gives himself away not only in the mode of truth, but also in that of *love*. This second way is rooted in the fact that, in faith granted by God's grace to the ecclesial communion, this truth of the Word has already been accepted in corresponding human love. In this mode of self-communication, God remains as incomprehensible as he ever was, yet now accepted as loving and forgiving Mystery cherished and loved by the Church.

Hence, the Church is the communion of those who have accepted God's love (Church = fruit of salvation) and pass it on to the whole of mankind (Church = medium of salvation). The two aspects of this 'performance', acceptance of God's love and passing it on, constitute the existential being of the Church. And it is on this ground that the Church is 'holy' because as a whole she can never fall away from the victorious and eschatologically irrevocable love of God. The subject of this 'performance' is again the whole of the Church embracing both the sacramental ministry and the deeds of neighbourly love of each and every member of the Church.

It is now easy to see what lies behind Rahner's scheme of speaking about the Mystery's twofold self-communication and its presentation to the world by the Church. The ever incomprehensible Mystery is the Father, his self-communication in truth is the Word made flesh, whereas its taking root as *love* as accepted in an ecclesial communion is the Spirit. It recalls Rahner's thesis on the coherent unity of the immanent and economic Trinity[106] and, parallel to Vatican II's teaching, connects the doctrine of the Church with the mystery of the blessed Trinity.[107] The Church is rooted in this mystery, on account of which she herself, as she is and in the way she lives, shares in the very Mystery of God, one and three.

1.3.3 The functions of the Church

The twofold way of God's self-communication as truth and love determines the very being and the basic 'self-performance' of the Church: she is the presentation of the Mystery in the world. From this we can work out *how* she should function, how she should perform her task. Rahner sums up in six points, what he calls, the 'properties' of this function. I paraphrase and discuss these six points, (a) to (f), in what follows.

(a) The Church should always be aware that she stands for an incomprehensible Mystery which she has to announce to the world. It would be a mistake for her to step into God's place and act as his representative (*Statthälterin*) on earth. This would be incompatible with God's Mystery which the Church reflects and has to make known.[108]

On the contrary, the historical progress of the Church's action (*wachsender Selbsvollzug*) in the world should emphasize the mysteriousness of the God whom she proclaims. Her existence is due to the fact that through her mediation this divine Mystery is made present. She mediates this presence, but in her mediation she herself, in her visible form, remains present.

(b) From this follows another property of the Church's function. She proclaims God's presence as a sacramental sign in which the reality of the sign as well as the One signified are contained. The Church is the proto-sacrament of God's self-communication.

At the time of writing this chapter in the *Handbook*, Rahner used the term *Ursakrament*; in its basic meaning, the term was the language of Vatican II in its decree on the Church.[109] The concept of the proto-sacrament had already been elaborated by Rahner in *The Church and the Sacraments*.[110] In calling the Church 'a sacrament' Rahner had to face the difficult question: How does the Church differ from the Incarnate who is also the permanent sign, as it were, another proto-sacrament of God's engracing presence among his people on earth? Furthermore, the meaning of the *Ursakrament* Church has to be distinguished from the sacramental practice of the Roman Church. It is not identical with the administering of single sacraments.

This is why Rahner hastens to add that *Ursakrament* is used in an analogous sense. Christ as God and man is *tout court* the proto-sacrament, because in his person the signified reality and its effective sign, as well as its acceptance on behalf of the whole of mankind, are identical. The Church is not in this way the *Ursakrament*: with regard to Christ, she is on the receiving end – the Church is not goal and fulfilment of salvation in the same sense as Christ is: the Church is not the permanent source of salvation for all eternity. Thus, it would be a mistake simply to transfer Christ's attributes to the Church.[111] All the same, there is an analogy between the 'two' proto-sacraments which Rahner explains more daringly in *The Church and the Sacraments*. He affirms that the Church is the continuation, the ever permanent sign (*das Gegenwärtigbleiben*) of God's already accomplished will to save all mankind. She is the permanent presence of Christ in this world, a sign of that Word by means of which God bestows himself on it and thus effects his own acceptance by mankind.[112] Besides, in her, as in Christ, human and divine natures, sign and signified reality are, though distinct and unmixed, inseparably one. Hence, in a certain way, in the Church the truth of Christ, his will, his ministry are 'incarnate'.[113]

Now, the *Handbook* does not draw the parallelism between the Incarnation and the coming-to-be of the Church. It prefers to underline her sacramental character. This implies that without the Church as proto-sacrament there are no sacraments at all. She is ontologically prior to, though not separate from, the seven sacraments. In the administering of these sacraments to individuals, the Church as a whole is fulfilled; in them she actualizes her own reality.[114] The seven are the 'performances' of the Church without which she would not be that which she has to be.

If, however, the Church is indeed a sacramental sign of God's presence, then it can be said that in experiencing the Church one can also experience in faith the reality she signifies. That which she signifies is the goal to which she points: God by his presence in Jesus the Christ has conquered this world and as such has been accepted by mankind. Thus, the Church points to the goal in such a way that she is already at the goal. This means that God's grace is already an inner principle of the Church's advance to final fulfilment. She does not proclaim that God is about to communicate himself, but that it has already happened and effected his own acceptance. And this is valid for the whole of mankind, even if the individual in the Church remains basically uncertain about his or her own salvation. But in the Church this salvation is already incarnate and those who deny it miss God's concrete presence in the world. To put it in 'Rahnerese': 'The Church is the categoriality necessary for salvation.'[115]

If, therefore, the Church is only a sacramental sign, it follows that she should never be identified with the actual presence of God. The Church is but the sign (*Realsymbol*) of it. Hence, she can never state that God's presence is only there where the Church is in her concrete historical manifestation: God's presence can be outside her visible framework. For the sign is never identical with what it points to: it points 'away from itself'. From this it follows that these properties of the Church's function on earth do not refer exclusively to the Roman Catholic communion. These properties do not constitute the Church as she *de facto* is: they do not distinguish one Christian denomination from the others – yet they are properties which can be counted for a real church-like engagement of individuals. Thus, if this engagement of an individual has taken place, even when someone does not belong to a certain (that is, Roman) Church in its sociologically distinguishable way, he or she is – in a sense – a member.[116] Any concrete engagement to a church-like fellowship functions as a sacramental sign of God's victorious presence to mankind.

(c) Under a separate heading, Rahner deals with a further characteristic of the Church's function in the world: in proclaiming God's presence the Church proclaims not a duty to be fulfilled as law, but the good news of the gospel. In other words, the Church is not just a pedagogue, but also a sign: she liberates man's freedom in granting him the acceptance of God's salvation.[117] She pronounces that God has already saved the world.

Nonetheless, the Church presents men and women with, what Rahner refers to as a 'radical' obligation – a kind of law the object of which is man's love for God on account of God's love for everyone. That is to say, the proclaimed gospel obliges men and women to do what has already been granted to them. In different words, Rahner repeats the maxim of St Thomas: the new law of the gospel not only prescribes a duty, but also grants us what it requires.[118] The individual who experiences the gospel only as an external law is caught in the tension between the insecurity of his or her own salvation and the security offered by the Church as a whole. This experience of insecurity can only be overcome by the person's abandoning him or herself to the ineffable love of God: for the obligation proclaimed by the gospel and the fulfilment of it are not separate realities. They are two aspects of God's victorious grace. There is always a law-like obligation imposed on the members of the Church, but this is a law of freedom and life.[119] Should the Church on the other hand, impose this law as a dire obligation, she would not be the Church but the synagogue of the Old Testament. This, in a transferred sense, is also valid for any legislation of the Church – including her Code of Canon Law. Her legislation is more of a call presupposing the ubiquitous presence of God's grace: it is more like an indicative formulated in the imperative giving us a task to be fulfilled, for which grace has been already granted.

(d) From the above there follows another property of the Church's action. If she is a pointer to grace and salvation already bestowed, she is an eschatological reality.

This means two things. First, that, at the end of time the Church will cease, as a sign, as a visible and social institution, to be the medium of God's self-communication. This is not to suggest, of course, that at the end in the 'immediate' vision of God everything will be absorbed in God's infinite reality. The humanity of Christ, the oneness of mankind in love, personal fellowship and created grace will always mediate the immediate vision of God. Even then his immediacy will be mediated. Of what this 'mediated' mediation will consist, we cannot know. The Church in the passage of time is and remains an eschatological sign of a reality, promised at the end of time.

Second, for even if the Church as a sign, as we know her now, will at the end cease, she will be close to that reality which she always signified. In our time she announces not only the eternal plans of God but also their categorial and concrete realization among us. She does not only point to the realized end, but also anticipates it. In this sense the Church remains for all eternity. This eternal permanence is grounded in the Church's origin – the 'once for allness' of Jesus the Christ; in Scripture, in the apostolic succession, in the permanence of the seven sacraments all through the ages and in the basic structures characterized by the primacy of Peter and the collegiality of her bishops. Briefly, in referring to the Church, Rahner can speak of an eschatological sign here and now, of a contingent reality signifying that which is going to be completed. And this contingent reality is the Church.

Hence, at present, the Church understandably has a 'traditional bent', even if, like every created reality, she looks forward to the ultimate judgement of God.[120] Nonetheless, she can legitimate everything that is 'new' in her life by referring it to her powerful tradition. For everything traditional reminds her that Jesus is the risen Christ and in him history, even in its as yet undisclosed secrets, has gained its ultimate meaning and is already at its eschatological dawn.

(e) As if to counterbalance the traditional bent of the previous property of the Church's action in the world, Rahner adds another one: God's presence mediated through the Church is a historical process.

The Church's being and function is the rendering of God's self-communication as his constantly renewed actual presence to the world. Mankind, to which her message is addressed, is through and through historical, just as the message that it receives in its ongoing history. Were the message of salvation ahistorical, it would only be a transcendental horizon in which we move, but which would be for ever unattainable. Hence, she renders God's self-communication in Christ neither as a past event nor as an unattainable goal, but rather as an ever new presence to the world. True, the Church is founded once for all, but as a historical entity she is in process. Her permanent elements, though once for all given, 'grow up' (*sie holen sich ein*) and this 'growing up' belongs to her very being. 'She is in becoming: she becomes, because she is, and she can only be insofar as she becomes.'[121]

(f) The last property of the Church in presenting God's self-communication follows closely from the previous. To put it more abstractly: the permanent and eschatological being of the Church (her 'once-for-allness') is proportionate to her renewed 'performance' in historical action.

In practice, this means that the Church in each new decision reflects her permanent being, yet what she decides is new and not deducible from her past. The historical moments of her ongoing progress are also formed by her legitimate alternatives in her present. Briefly, the temporal permanence and the change of the Church are not due to a theoretical, but to the concrete historical, action of her members. They result from a free and charismatic will active within the fellowship. The charisms of the Spirit uphold and mould the historical Church.

1.3.4 The Church as a 'pneumatic' institution

With this appeal to the Spirit of God, Rahner opens a new chapter of his ecclesiology.

Whereas, right from the beginning, the working of the Spirit was very much in evidence, now it will be specified. It is owing to the Spirit's effective presence that God's self-communication is committed to mankind. It is the Spirit who makes the believer realize that God's acceptance (*seine Selbstzusage*) of the human race in Jesus Christ is already basically reciprocated. It is again due to the Spirit that the fellowship of believers, in spite of their ongoing history, in spite of the changing expression of their way of life will never defect from their initial commitment.

The 'specific' work of the same Spirit with which Rahner rounds up, as it were with a corollary, his doctrinal ecclesiology refers to those individuals who are in the Church called to carry out her functions. He calls these the *Träger*, the 'carrier' of the Church's *Selbstvollzug*, her self-fulfilment, self-expression in concrete history. At the same time Rahner has to speak about the relationship of these persons who constitute the visible society of the Church. A visible society, however, is a kind of institution and as such in need of definite structures. And as a structured institution the Church is divided, at least in the sense that it needs leaders and persons to be led, organizers and persons whose action is to be coordinated. It is this need that creates the (ordained) ministry within the people of God.

Although I am going to return to this point (in Chapter 3), here I shall sum up briefly Rahner's argument in the *Handbook* for this inevitable structural division within the Church. He goes back to his starting point: the Church is the result of God's self-communication. The need for a hierarchical structure arises from the fact that the members of the Church must give witness to it, they must exteriorize their inner conviction about the Church. Otherwise the Church would not only be an anarchical, but also an ahistorical and an asocial conception. Now, if this structural division is not only the consequence of a socially transmitted salvation, but also was *de facto* so willed by the founder of the Church, then we have reached the notion of ordained ministry in the Church. Rahner speaks of this twofold division between the (ordained) ministry (*über das Amt*) and the laity as essential to the Roman Catholic concept of the Church.[122]

However, without at this point entering into a detailed discussion of the nature of the ministry, which belongs to another aspect of the Church (namely, the institutional), Rahner warns against two possible misunderstandings. First, the Church is not identical with the ordained ministry. The Church is and remains the fellowship, the communion of baptized Christians who, from the point of view of their societal organization, remain under the leadership of their, from Christ, legitimated pastors. To put it in more technical terms: formally, the members are those who constitute the Church and act on her behalf, but materially this action is performed in and through her hierarchical structure. Second, there is no opposition between ministry and laity. Both in their specific contributions to the life and function of the Church stand under the guidance of the Spirit's free charisms:

> Each Christian is baptized and lives according to his charismatic calling, as it were, embraced both by the sacrament and by the 'pneumatic' Institution' which is the Church, since the institution is the permanent sign of God's really efficient grace.[123]

Rahner resolves (as I shall discuss in Chapter 3) the opposition between institution and charism: the hierarchical structure of the Church, by remaining what it is, is superimposed through the charismatic. As Rahner asserts in the *Handbook*, the Church as a whole is a pneumatical institution.

§§§§§§

In this rather detailed presentation of the doctrinal ecclesiology of the *Handbook*, I have mentioned almost all the elements later to be elaborated in Rahner's writings on the Church. The last section has strayed into another field beyond the 'definition' and description of her existence: the 'institutional'. Does it formally belong to the essential or existential concept of the Church?

It is this aspect which Rahner's various interviewers held

against his unshaken churchmanship. Most of his questioners, whether or not they understood his vision of the Church, were ill at ease with this aspect. And so apparently was Rahner himself when, in the aftermath of the Council, he coined the expression: 'the Church in winter time'.

Winter comes always after the sunset of the summer. But Rahner was convinced that this wintry season carried within its womb the promise of a new spring.

Chapter 2

Comments and Questions: Communion of the Faithful

As far as doctrinal theology is concerned, ecclesiology is a relatively new discipline. Its history goes back in the form of Controverse Theology to the time of the Reformation and its classical shape as part of Fundamental Theology, intended as preparation for the study of Dogmatics or Systematic Theology. Its task was mainly apologetic: it tried to demonstrate the divine origins of the Roman Catholic Church, her hierarchical structure of authority, her teaching and disciplinary order.[1]

However, Rahner's approach to the Church does not fall into this category. The task he set himself was even more fundamental than that of 'Fundamental' Theology. He asked the question: How can we, leaving aside the basically defensive character of fundamental theology, propose and develop a theological reflection on the phenomenon of the Church?[2] His reflections are not preparatory to doctrines, but rather attempts at dealing with a single tenet of Christian faith: one 'believes the Church'. Believing the Church is rooted in an experience, reflection on which should lead to a systematic, doctrinal treatment of ecclesiology.

In this chapter, I have tried to gather the main insights that led Rahner to a more systematic presentation of his thought on the Church in the *Handbook*. So far, of course, it has only been possible to consider some preliminary aspects of his ideas about the Church. Therefore, before I go any further in this presentation, some comments and questions, (A) to (I), are called for and which I shall now briefly qualify.

(A) The methodological value of the diversity of Rahner's earlier references to the Church.
(B) If these are nothing more than the analysis of an experience,

I shall have to point out a dialectical tension in it.

(C) and (D) In these two points I shall, in accordance with my former reflections on Rahner's theology, propose my own understanding of this experience.

(E) This, then, will lead on to some critical remarks concerning Rahner's scheme of overcoming the basic tension within this experience.

(F) (G) and (H) As an extension, or even an alternative, to Rahner's definition of the Church in the *Handbook*, I shall introduce some insights of Dietrich Bonhoeffer's ecclesiology.

(I) This latter will lead to a reconsideration of Rahner's concept of the Church in the *Handbook*.

(A) *Rahner's method*

It is not easy to make a coherent summary of Rahner's insights which I have presented in some detail. Perhaps the best way is to think of him as a person deeply committed to his Church and personally engaged in her life; one who cannot help questioning his own existentially experienced *Lebensraum*, the phenomenon of the Church. Although Rahner's early articles point out his dilemmas in facing the experience of the Church, he tries to master his own difficulties by indicating an overall approach which comprises the whole reality of this experience. The Church is in line with God's Word becoming flesh (the incarnational approach); the Church is ruled by the dynamic presence of God's Pneuma (pneumatic approach). To express this in theological terms, sacramental theology lends its linguistic tools, according to which a sacred sign (a *Realsymbol*) reaches its irreversible fulfilment in the reality at which it points (symbolic or sacramental approach). The Church is like a sacrament deeply embedded in the history of salvation the eschatological victory of which she anticipates (eschatological approach). In these approaches the Church is a Mystery within God's mysterious self-communication. To come to a theological understanding of it, Rahner employs those suggestions of Vatican I concerning the understanding of faith: through the correlation of mysteries we gain a deeper insight into the Mystery of the Church.[3]

However, none of these approaches yield a 'definition' of the

Church. They may direct the believer's pious reflection on her, but do not confront the believer with the full reality which he or she daily encounters. The Church, unlike the Incarnate, is not a single personal reality, but a group of people, whose members can be counted. Yet, anyone reading Rahner must have noticed that the faithful as a group have a special relationship to the Church which is more than their rapport to any other human society. Rahner's early 'Membership' article (see 1.1.3) provides us with two traditional metaphors about the Church – the Mystical Body and the People of God. Both metaphors are used in Rahner's own theological interpretation[4] and as such leave us with two different aspects according to which Church membership can be understood. Indeed, we could characterize these two metaphors as two aspects of our experience and of the ensuing image of the Church. Yet neither these various approaches nor the two metaphors yield a straightforward concept. They belong to a different methodological category.

One could venture to describe the pattern of Rahner's early approach to the Church as a vision: it is a reflection from within the Church, which he 'believes' to be the same as viewing it, as it were, from outside the Church. It is a quasi-dialogue between a committed churchman and a man of our days, who happens to encounter the phenomenon of the Church.

In his writings Rahner fulfils both of these roles and thus projects a vision guiding him to a more technical, scientific 'definition' of the Church. In fact, it cannot be said that his reflections, which I have presented so far, constitute a genuine doctrinal ('scientific') theology of the Church. They are on the level of his 'indirect method' – a feature which I have referred to in previous volumes – a method sandwiched between the old-fashioned fundamental and dogmatic theology.[5]

What, however, Rahner states in these pre-scientific approaches is of paramount importance for a genuine doctrinal ecclesiology. As described earlier, I took (whether rightly or wrongly) Rahner's references to the Church in the *Handbook* for such a doctrinal summary. One could say that these preliminaries build up towards this work in which, within a pastoral theological project, Rahner had to give a succinct dogmatic foundation for living in the Church. In this chapter I shall reflect on this same work.

At the moment, however, I will remain with Rahner's (as I have ventured to put it) 'pre-scientific vision' of the Church. By vision I understand the description of an experience which already indicates its own interpretation.

(B) *A 'dialectical' experience*

Both the vision and, eventually, the notion of the Church arise out of a very complex experience. It is an experience in which two main lines of human convictions meet, so to speak, midway: the one is that of our belief in God and his self-communication which enables the Church to become and be known; the other is human will that goes beyond its individualistic confines towards the solidarity or objective unity with one's fellows. It is an experience that connects the believed 'downward' movement of God with the 'upward' motion of human endeavour to find salvation in fellowship with others.

Now, to evaluate this experience in order correctly to define the Church as she is in her 'essential being', one has to point out what comes from faith alone, what comes from a human experience, *and* what is the result of this encounter. I believe that this elemental tension (if not paradox) was, right from the beginning, at the heart of any thinking about the Church. In facing this experience the same tension is felt in various questions. We can ask: Is the Church simply given, as one finds a society in which we have been born? Or, is she rather a special kind of association which depends in being and form by the will of its members? In what way can we perceive the Church's dependence on God (or, as Rahner would say, on God's self-communication) *and* her dependence on associative human will?

It will be a recurring temptation to envisage the Church as the invisible bond of the elect and predestined faithful, as opposed to a very much visible society with all its virtues and shortcomings. Wickliff and Hus in the Middle Ages seem to have yielded to this temptation and later, in the sixteenth century, Catholics (though wrongly) suspected that the Reformers wanted to do the same. And, if we go right back to an important patristic source for the third century, Hermas's allegory of the Church, we meet this 'givenness' of an edifice from above to which selected stones are added for its completion. That the Church is at the same time a human association is a thought that never bothers the ancient visionary.

It is a later temptation – and one arising, I believe, with liberal theology – which, though paying lip-service to faith in the Church, refuses to speak of her in any other way than that of any ordinary human society depending on the will of its members. It is this tension which can become an either/or in our attitude to the Church. If either side is ignored or neglected one never comes to a viable notion of the Church. Nor is what can be seen in the practical strategy of our modern Roman Catholic Church a viable way of handling the two extremes of this tension: when sociologists apply their scientific observations to the Church, the excuse is that she is not a society in its secular sense and rules of sociology are not always valid for her. Or, on the contrary, against the claim of an entirely charismatic Church for which discipline and laws are secondary, it is argued that every society must have its institutions ruled by law and regulations. We cannot have it both ways without striving at least for a workable synthesis.

It belongs to the same basic tension when a static, for always established, Church is played out against a Church which is a historical process, or vice versa: the contemporary Church is entirely different from what she was before.[6] A similar tension emerges when the experience of the Church is seen only from within the confines of her fold. Her members speak their private language and their communication is not meant for a world outside. Her members forget or even refuse to see the Church with the eyes of those who only encounter her from outside, to whom she is only an association among others in the whole communion of mankind. The Church is, of course, also that which she seems to be in the eyes of outsiders; it is difficult to envisage her in her historical, therefore, developing permanence.

Now, in the first two sections of Chapter 1, I discussed Rahner's early approach to the Church. Here we can clearly discover this complex experience in the background and, what is more, Rahner's attempts at a synthesis. If not in strict chronological order, yet, according to our presentation, we can see the 'descending line'. In the words of the Church, God's word is 'given', she exists as God's movement towards mankind: 'She is God's eternal compassion and his Body, as it exists in space and time.'[7] In this latter sentence, Rahner indicates his incarnational or even pneumatic approach to ecclesiology (see 1.1.1) whereas his early essay 'The Church of Sinners' (see 1.1.2) deals with the very human side of a sinful Church. These different approaches are feelers towards a synthesis between the Church 'from above' and the Church 'from below'.

Even earlier, Rahner's 'Membership' could be regarded as a breakthrough towards this synthesis (see 1.1.3) and his later anthropological turn is anticipated by the experience of a Church, the people of God, which becomes the effective sign of the unity of mankind and the whole world. She has also in her visible reality members who, enabled by God, invisibly belong to her. In order to overcome the obvious oddity of this conclusion, Rahner, as far as I can see, integrates his thought on the Church in his transcendental method: 'the Church is the quasi-sacramental . . . redemptive liberation of the freedom of man'.[8] It is in this 'transcendental Church' that the diverse unity of Rahner's transcendental categorial *schema* will create a synthetic view. With this we are at the heart of Rahner's solution to that tension with which I have characterized all ecclesiological thought.

This then is at the back of his mind when in his later articles he analyses belief in the Church (see 1.2.2). Here it becomes quite clear that faith points to the 'Church of Christ . . . by reason of the fact that God's forgiving grace has taken hold of human beings . . . and has fashioned them into the Church'.[9] It is the Church 'from above' but at the same time 'from below', for 'the Christian of today . . . will see and experience the Church as the genuine representation of the nature of man as planned by God'.[10] On this foundation, I believe, he can construct what I have called his 'doctrinal theology of the Church' (see 1.3).

To this scheme of Rahner's pre-scientific ecclesiology I can only add some corrective remarks which may or may not distance me from his basic thought. I do share his vision of the Church, even if in detail I may disagree with him.

(C) *An experience of freedom*

In an earlier volume, I introduced readers to the basic experience of the Church.[11] There, in discussion with Rahner's experience of grace, I laid the emphasis on a collective 'we-experience' in which the redeeming grace of Jesus Christ could be felt. I even called it the 'privileged experience' to the exclusion of other legitimate religious experiences. I took it for an encounter between free human agents by making them one collective personality. In this encounter situation I have argued the emergence and/or transformation of the human person. Furthermore, I am in agreement with Rahner that the basis of this experience is human freedom already engaged in a responsible solidarity with the other(s). Thus it was welcomed when Rahner approached his 'transcendental Church' from human freedom. For him the Church was entailed in this freedom. It is this anthropological insight which can point to a synthetic view of the above-mentioned tensions.

Yet it is at this point that I have refused to go all the way with Rahner. First of all from the beginning of our dialogue, I held with the personalists[12] that the emergence and the definability of the person derives exclusively from this encounter – a tenet which in Rahner's whole work remains ambiguous. Person for him is man's reflective selfhood as well as a relationship to God and to the other.[13] Contrary to this I did not envisage this personalising free encounter necessarily as between man and God. We can become and are persons, because we live in communion (or refuse it) with other humans. It is free, because it presupposes a choice in some form, a decision the result of which is the permanence of the person. These three: choice, decision (or commitment), and the making of the person, belong together in order that our adjective 'free' can be correctly used.[14]

Whilst I agree with Rahner that the experience of the Church is somehow implied in freedom, I would go further and ask under which aspect of it this analysis yields this experience. An adult's conversion to the Church does presuppose a conscious choice (which is freedom's first aspect), yet in most cases at the age of reason one already finds oneself in the Church. The choice has been vicariously made on our behalf. At this point Rahner would say, freedom consists in freely consenting to a situation in which we were born. If by this consent not a passive acceptance is meant, but, at least implicitly, an active decision which results in a commitment to a community of other persons, then the foundations of this experience are given. It hinges on the second aspect of freedom where free decision becomes a commitment. It is what Hegel might have called a concrete freedom in which the objectives of a society are made actively one's own.[15] If then this community is gathered together on account of their belief in the story of Jesus the Christ, the by now committed individual may experience the Church.

This experience, however, discloses the Church as she is a human association depending on the will of her members. Contrary to Rahner, I cannot state that this experience at the same time implies the God-given character of an ecclesiology. Rahner was able to affirm this characteristic also, since for him a free decision as a human act implied God. I am afraid we are not in the same position; that the Church is the embodiment of God's will is, in my view, a matter of further interpretation. Though the objectives of the experienced association concern the story of Jesus, only one's commitment in faith can understand this experienced Church as God's creation and the embodiment of his will in human society. The Church as the 'Body of Christ' is not our human experience, it is faith's interpretation. Our own experience relates us only to the human side of the Church.

(D) *An experience interpreted by faith*

If my last statement is true, then it is worth reconsidering, first, the function of faith in interpreting a societal experience. In 'Piety' (as presented in 1.2.2), Rahner tried to show that faith in the Church is implied in our commitment to God; he speaks of the wider congregation of believers, who organize themselves as 'Church'. What he really affirms here, in my opinion, is the human side of the experience of the Church. Of course, with his transcendental method, he may read much more into this. Yet this reading something into the experience is nothing but an act of interpreting the same – from another point of view. For, in accepting the basic truths of Christian faith, we can reinterpret our communal experience of living together with our fellows who orient their lives according to the gospel and its tradition. A child is born into and taken up by a society governed by this belief. But this does not necessarily imply that the Church is God's redemptive will embodied in this world and for this mankind. It does not

imply the Trinitarian source of this society and its mysterious
unity with the Lord who permanently lives amongst us. Neither
does it imply the whole of salvation history which has reached its
eschatological peak in it. In one sentence, experiencing the concrete society or communion of believers does not yield by itself
faith's insight into the mystery of the Church. This is that dimension 'from above' which we have referred to, meeting the human
side of the Church. For it is from this point that we interpret our
very human experience of the community of believers and of
being one of its members.

My position (which is inspired by but not identical with that of
Rahner) presupposes a distinction between belief and faith. Born
as a member of a society we live within it and with its traditions.
Born as a Christian we take God's existence and his, by Jesus
Christ proclaimed, image for granted. We learn about the history
of the events of his life, death and resurrection. In brief: we
believe. Yet, at the same time, it is a challenge to see this with the
eyes of faith, to interpret it from the basics of our Christian convictions. The Creed we proclaim in our liturgy is a matter of
belief: 'We believe in . . . '; it holds that society together to which
we belong. But we have the right and duty to interpret the same
from the point of view of our most personal faith in Jesus the
Lord and his work in the Spirit. It is this mysterious trust (faith)
in him which enables us to hold onto the less palatable tenets of
our Creed, because our faith in the Church goes beyond the
former to her very source: the communion of the blessed Trinity.

This is why Vatican II grounds its doctrine on the Church in the
mystery of the triune God and not as something implied in man's
transcendental thrust. In Rahner's early articles founding his
ecclesiology, there are but desultory allusions to this mystery of
the existential being of the Church (see 1.3.2). It is in a way a gap
that ought to be worked out in ecclesiology.[16] At this point I shall
only state that the Trinitarian background of the Church is that
descending line which accompanies our experience. It is the
dimension 'from above' that meets our anthropological experience of the Church as a human society, as a communion of
believers. For if we accept in faith that there is an analogy
between the communion of the three divine Persons and the communion among the members of the Church, then from this aspect
we should take her for a 'collective personality' and not just as a

legal person. In this way she is 'given' before she is formed by human will. Rahner's distinction between 'believing in the Church' and 'we believe the Church' is only valid if with the first we refer to the Church 'from above' which is already faith's interpretation of our human experience. It is a faith in the Church which we cannot learn from the actual teaching of the Church, even if we formed our beliefs through being born into or being converted to her. It is God's gift of faith.

I am sure that Rahner would agree with this slightly altered approach to make room for the experience of the Church. All the more so in view of its practical consequences: it binds the faithful to an absolute respect for her mystery and at the same time liberates them for a critical yet creative membership of the historical Church. In short, it makes them men or women of the Church.

(E) *Some critical remarks*

As I have already discussed, too much emphasis on the mystery character of the Church runs into the danger of spiritualizing her. It could lead to a concept of the invisible Church, whose members are the elect to whom the grace of faith is granted. It may also lead to a generalization according to which the whole of mankind and every individual in it is, at least potentially, a member of the Church. I wonder, whether or not Rahner's generous 'Membership' is exposed to this danger. There he deals with the human, visible side of our ecclesial experience. Yet, starting from this human experience, Rahner comes very near to this generalization. In acknowledging the fact that there are people justified outside of the Church, he concludes that they belong 'invisibly' to the visible Church. The reason is man's transcendental thrust: 'When someone totally accepts his concrete human nature [later: his existential and societal situation] by his decision of free will'[17] and this becomes expressed, then one also gains a certain visibility in which God's saving will is realized. This will be the link that ties him or her to the visible Church. Presupposed is what I have called a 'transcendental' Church. Now, not to mistake this transcendental Church with the invisible one, Rahner connects it by necessity with its categorial counterpart which in its turn is its sacramental sign. As a *Realsymbol* the visible Church not only points to its transcendental counterpart, whose 'objectification' it is, but realizes, brings about the whole reality of the Church. With this transcendental-categorial scheme Rahner brings the two sides of our Church-experience in a kind of synthesis: the Church 'from above' and 'from below', the Church as man's transcendental experience and her concrete realization, her 'givenness' from the very beginning[18] and her historical shape throughout the centuries, are sighted in one and the same experience. She depends on God's self-communication as well as on the human will to finding one's salvation in communion with the other.

Apparently, a number of other theologians are uneasy concerning this solution. For instance, J. Dullaart and M. Kehl[19] expressed their doubt: if the Church is already grasped in man's transcendental experience then what is the need for her objectification in the concrete historical Church? Both Dullaart and Kehl feel ill at ease with Rahner's transcendental prelude to ecclesiology. Though in different terms, they see a gap between the transcendental and the concrete, categorial Church: Rahner has apparently not succeeded in bridging this gap.[20]

Indeed, the root of my own uneasiness has already been indicated in other fields of Rahner's theology.[21] For, in applying Rahner's transcendental-categorial scheme to the Church, one never knows whether the transcendental precedes the categorial or vice versa. If the transcendental precedes the categorial, then the palpable reality of the Church would indeed be the 'objectification' of our transcendental subjectivity. This would in practice mean that in encountering the Church in her visible shape, we could only accept her, because she matches our transcendental expectations. If, however, the categorial precedes the transcendental, then indeed the transcendental Church is a theoretical projection of the concrete historical Church: we tend to generalize our experience of the historical Church which is by its very nature limited and particular.[22]

Of course, Rahner could argue that between the transcendental and categorial aspects of our access to the Church we cannot speak of any precedence: But is it *de facto* the case? This is why I avoid Rahner's transcendental-categorial scheme and keep the two sides of the experience (the 'from above' and the 'from below') not in one act (as Rahner tries to do) but in two: first, the acceptance of the concrete and historical society and, second, its interpretation from the point of view of faith.

And this is why I am not happy with Rahner's theory of an over-wide membership of the Church – extended to those who 'invisibly belong to the visible Church'. For, if we maintain this view, then it is inevitable that we will eventually substitute something else for the Church. Indeed, Rahner seems to take belonging to mankind for belonging to the (transcendental) Church: in speaking of the necessity of the Church for salvation he distinguishes Church constituting (*Kirchenkonstituierede*) elements and elements which specify the Church (*kirchenunterscheidende*). To the former he reckons our belonging to a mankind which is already raised by the supernatural existential – that is, by Christ's saving presence in history.[23] It is not very likely that everybody consciously decides to become a member of mankind or with the same consciousness freely to accept this fact. Yet the decision to become a member of the Church or the free and conscious acceptance of Church membership is presupposed for Christian life. None of these decisions can be taken unawares and remain invisible. To become or to be a member of the Church comes about through the communal acceptance of the Christ-event and in joining the number of those companions who have done the same. Whether apart from this visible membership there are others who, without belonging to the Church, are justified by the Spirit, is similar to the question of salvation of the unbeliever. Just as I did not straightaway accept the theory of the anonymous Christian, I would not like to play with the idea of an anonymous membership of the Church.[24]

To become and to be a member of the Church is not possible without a preceding act of decision even if (as in the case of the newly-born) it is done on our behalf. This is why Rahner's access to ecclesiology was correctly built on an analysis of freedom. Yet, if the 'transcendental Church' is somehow implied in our human act of deciding, we doubt its freedom. At the most we can say that when this transcendental fact becomes conscious, in facing its necessary presence, we can freely accept or reject it. But either way it remains part of our transcendental experience. I remember in one of the interviews in Rahner's 'wintry season' he could not accept the fact that many are 'leaving' the Church; one cannot cease to be (though invisibly) a member of the Church, just as one cannot apostatize from being a member of mankind or living in this twenty-first century.[25] Would it follow from this that we could say to each and every Church leaver (the number of which, alas, is on the increase): 'You decided against the Church and left her officially, but in vain: no one can leave the Church [or at least the one transcendentally experienced one].'

One cannot honestly think or say this. Membership of the Church is not decided by the legal consequences of baptism (as Pius XII's *Mystici Corporis Christi* holds), but by one's own or by another's free decision. Granted, this free decision is not, in itself, a graspable fact – it can only be perceived, or rather guessed, in its outward manifestations. In one of the Eucharistic canons the dead are recommended to God's mercy 'Whose faith is known only to Him'.

(F) *Bonhoeffer's 'collective person'*

If faith in the Trinitarian mystery is one constituent which enables true belief in the Church, the society or communion of believers is its counterpart. This latter is an immediate experience of anyone born into the Church or of those who by a conscious decision opted for her membership. As we shall repeatedly see, this side of our Church experience is open to the analysis of anthropological sciences.

Dietrich Bonhoeffer, in his *Sanctorum Communio*,[26] provided an outstanding anthropo-sociological analysis of an otherwise theological insight. Within this, Bonhoeffer, the later martyred theologian, tried to develop the concept of the Church. His access to the Church starts from the criticism of German idealism[27] and develops his ideas about man and his society in dialogue with the anthropological sociology of M. Scheler, M. Weber, and E. Troeltsch.[28]

Bonhoeffer's ecclesiology is vaguely akin to that of Rahner's later writings: theirs is a person-centred anthropology. The relationship of 'I and Thou' is for Bonhoeffer a basic characteristic of the human spirit. It is with this relationship that one can grasp man's personal being, which is not only open to society and communion with others, but this communion is constitutive of the human person. Personal being is not an additional quality of the self-conscious human being who, by an act of the will, may or may not join in communion with others, but rather the other way round: it is human sociality which enables personal being to be.[29] This implies that the person's will is essentially open to another's will.[30] However, the openness of the human person to others is at the same time closed in on itself, because the will for the other does not strive for a union in which the willing subject would be absorbed, but for a bond, a communion: it is distanced from this alien will. If now society is grounded on this open yet closed will, then society should be of a similar structure as the human person. In other words, I am myself, because I will society to be;[31] but once it really is, then it is a collective person with its own acts of knowing and willing (*ein Aktzentrum* on its own). Bonhoeffer insists that the collective person is not the sum total of individual persons; it is not before the coming-to-be of the individual person nor does it come about like the individual person does. Theirs is a correlationship: in their realization the one originates from the other and vice versa.[32]

To conclude Bonhoeffer's heavy-going argument, a biblical reflection:

> God created man and woman directed to one another. God does not desire a history of individual human beings, but the history of the human *community*. However, God does not want a community that absorbs the individual into itself but a community of *human beings*. In God's eyes, community and individual exist in the same moment and the rest in one another. The collective unit and the individual unit have the same structure in God's eyes. On these basic relations rest the concepts of the religious community and the Church.[33]

Although Rahner's philosophical background is similar to that of Bonhoeffer, I do not think that he has ever gone so far as to take the Church for a collective person. As I have indicated above, I am ready to follow Bonhoeffer by thinking of the Church in the basic category of a collective person. I do that, however, with a restriction: the Church is a 'collective person' insofar as we regard her from the perspective of that mystery which enables her being. This mystery is the blessed Trinity of our faith. Looking at the Church from the everyday experience of a historical society she is, like any other human association, only a legal person.

With this, I have come a step nearer to a more exact definition of my concept – the Church. In order further to explain and specify this approach I shall again refer to Bonhoeffer.

(G) *The double-faced reality*

The difficulty which can be raised against my position here is that in viewing the Church from these two aspects I divide her and introduce a certain schizophrenia into man's relationship to her. At one minute one can treat the mystery of the Church with awe and reverence, but at the next one can behave only as a citizen in the society of the contemporary Church. 'Contemporary' means that this society in its structures and its members in their relationship to it are in accordance with the prevailing idea of societal living. In the Middle Ages both structures and relationship of members were of a feudal pattern; nowadays, the tendency to democratize the Church is obvious. Rahner too was aware of a similar danger when he spoke of an ecclesiological monophysitism versus ecclesiological Nestorianism.[34]

Bonhoeffer, as I see it, overcomes this difficulty with an appeal to a theory which must have been in Rahner's mind also: that of the distinction between *Gemeinschaft* and *Gesellschaft*, between communion and society, as proposed by F. Tönnies.[35] Bonhoeffer presupposes that, in any human association, we have to do with the reciprocal will of humans for being together. In the society type of association it is always the objective that brings its members together, while in the communion type it is the very togetherness that is binding. In practical terms, a chess club is a kind of society – the purpose of which is the practice and perfecting of that game. On the other hand, an association of families or of friends living together is a kind of communion.[36] It does not mean, of course, that such a group may not have a reason for their togetherness (for example, financial benefits) or even a purpose for a common undertaking. That these are not the ultimate grounds of their communion (*Gemeinschaft*) is what is decisive. Their experience of a common life is immediate, whereas in the society type of human groupings it is mediated by the common purpose. A communion could be regarded as a bond of persons, whereas in society free individuals aiming at the same objective associate with one another. The membership of children in a communion is, on account of their parents' will, not only possible but almost expected. On the contrary, a mere society could not regard children below the age of free decision as full members. There is another distinguishing mark between these two types: a society being a free association of adults, exists at the actual will of its members. Hence, it does not need to fall back on long-standing traditions in choosing the means for the actualization of its aim. In other words, societies are in principle traditionless and open to constant change. Almost the contrary qualifications could be affirmed of a communion.[37]

It would be a mistake to assume that these two types can exist in their pure form. There is always a mixture and in a concrete human association, it would be almost impossible to draw a line between the two distinct types. Hence it is valid to say that there is no communion without the elements of society's characteristics within it and there is no society without the elements of communion. Our experience of a community or a fellowship comprises both without, however, denying the validity of their distinction. Because the two are diverse, in a concrete community the one type may dominate or even absorb or practically ignore the other. Therefore, in any community living the correct integration of the two types of human associations is always a challenge. We can see it best in its application to the Church.

Since Vatican II there has been the tendency towards a so-called 'communion-ecclesiology'. It is also shared by Rahner. Very often, however, one feels that the notion of communion as against society[38] is not clearly determined. This is true especially as regards the power and temporality which, though in different ways, are implied in both types. In a society, power is deposited in appointed or elected representatives whose hierarchical order is inevitable. This is why a society as such cannot be 'addressed'; the individual within it cannot enter into a dialogue with it, unless with some of its representatives. Were the Church to be a society in its purest form, any hypostatization of it would be a mistake. On the other hand, there is also a certain power in a communion but this is not necessarily invested in any of its representatives. In a communion power is shared, because it is built on reciprocal responsibility – that is, on the solidarity of its members.

So also is the relationship of these two types to time. A society should be dedicated to its present objectives. This of course does not exclude a constant reference to its past, however, always in order to manage its future. Yet with the cessation of its objective, which held its members together, a society has reached its end. A communion type of human grouping in a certain sense transcends the limits of temporality. Bonhoeffer calls it *grenzzeitlich* against society's *Zeitbegrenztheit*.[39] For instance: if the sole purpose of a marital union is the generation and education of the offspring, it will cease to be as soon as the children are grown up. If, however, a marriage is (or tries to be) a true communion, its duration is through a common history (the shape of which is moulded by significant events) until the death of one partner: past is integrated, and future anticipated, in the present. The difference lies in the very nature of these two types of association: a communion reaches out from its past and present to its fulfilment, without aiming at it. Yet this future fulfilment is constitutive of its present shape. A theological communion is eschatological: it is now, yet it is still on the way.

In working our way towards an adequate definition of the Church we are obviously inclined to regard her as a communion, or a kind of association, where the characteristics of a communion prevail. Yet we are not at this definition. Our experience of the Church, as briefly mentioned above, is a mixture of these two types with their own characteristics. Indeed, a mixture in which these elements are not as yet harmonized. This, to put it strongly, confusion could be illustrated by recent events both in the universal regiment of and through the local crises of the one Church. In her over-centralization under the reign of Pope John Paul II, the Church appears to be a world-wide society which for the sake of her present objectives (for example, the re-evangelization of a thoroughly secularised humanity) is ruled like an army trying to conquer the world in a battle already lost. At the same time within the Church, ideals like the celibacy of priests, which obviously belong to her communion character, are regulated by Canon Law – a means to the ends of a society. The same could be said about the *praxis* of *ipso facto* excommunication: a society can exclude some of her members if they do not conform to her purposes, yet it is questionable whether a communion, like a family, could do the same. We must therefore look further into the reasons of this confusion.

(H) *Church: a redeemed communion*

The reason for this disharmony can again be found in Bohoeffer's approach to the concept of the Church. Rahner's two articles about the sinfulness within the Church (see 1.1.2) was in its time a daring attempt to explain the shortcomings which we inevitably experience within her. These are not to be ascribed to individual sinners but, as Rahner's second article puts it – to the Church herself. It was of 'a Sinful Church' that he wrote. To my mind, Bonhoeffer radicalizes the same insight: we could not correctly define the historical Church without reference to original sin. It is only in faith, from which it is supposed that we interpret our experience of the visible community, that we can describe her with Paul's words (Eph 5:25f):

> Christ loved the Church . . . that he might present her to himself in splendour, without spot or wrinkle or any such thing, that she might be holy and without blemish.

Only on account of this aspect of our experience, in which we acknowledge the mystery of the Church, can we speak of her as being beyond the effects of universal sinfulness.

Although I do not entirely agree with Bonhoeffer's apparent excursus on original sin,[40] it is true that if God had not intended mankind to be a communion we could not speak of the universal spread of sinfulness and therefore everybody's need of redemption. For communion, and not society, is built on an all embracing solidarity where the sin of one member is to the detriment of the others and the victory of one can raise the whole race to the fruits of redemption. The mystery character of the Church assures us of the possibility of a human communion which can fulfil God's intention, which can restore what may have gone wrong in the history of mankind. In the Genesis myth of original sin, one of the consequences of the fall is exactly a kind of social confusion pronounced on the woman: ' . . . yet your desire shall be for your husband, and he shall rule over you' (Gen 3:16b).

As a result of the fall, the common responsibility of husband and wife is lost. Adam blames the trespass on Eve, and Eve, washing her hands in innocence, attributes the sin to the serpent. Their communion is lost. It is Christianity's faith that this original communion cannot be recovered unless through the second Adam and his Church. This recovery is not complete, it is only a real possibility offered to man's freedom for realization. With our freedom alone we only muddle towards it in the vain hope that in building a society the lost, or never achieved, communion of mankind can be won. It is this hope which dwells in the historical Church. In her belief she regards herself as a communion of persons, but often has acted and still acts as a society of regimented individuals to be on their way to a common objective.

In what follows I shall, inspired by Rahner, attempt a definition. In this, the above mentioned aspects will have to be named or presupposed by a workable concept of the Church.

(I) *A 'definition' of the Church*

In his critical survey on the use of metaphors in ecclesiology and the various attempts made by post-Vatican theologians at defining the Church, H. Rikhof does not mention[41] Karl Rahner. Nonetheless, this painstaking study introduces Rikhof's criteria for a doctrinal, 'scientific' definition of the Church which is applicable to Rahner's early forays into ecclesiology up to the *Handbook*.

For a doctrinal ecclesiology, Rikhof maintains the need of finding, beyond the various possible meanings of the word 'Church', a strict terminology apt for a scientific discourse. Now, in speaking of and describing the Church, use is made of a variety of metaphors (Mystical Body; People of God; Bride of Christ, and so on), of models or thought patterns leading toward the understanding of the Church in various contexts (as a Mystery in the line of the Incarnation or of the sending of the Spirit) and of analogies (like Church as a sacrament), all of which may yield an adequate description of the Church.

Are these, however, capable of developing a precise terminology with which a basic statement about the Church, a real definition can be compiled?

Such a statement

> . . . should be open enough to elicit and reveal the myriad of connections . . . and precise enough to determine which of the possible interpretations and explanations about the Church is coherent and thus possibly correct or not.[42]

Thus, in defining the Church, one is after a real definition which is not only concerned with words in order to settle or state the meaning of a concept within a certain context, but with the reality to which it points. In order to arrive at such a definition one has to find a terminology which can be understood, even to a certain extent independently of the context within which it is used. If I say, the Church is the Mystical Body of Christ, the meaning of my statement can be understood in the special context of a Pauline theology. Or, if I am speaking of the Church in the context of a small community, where it is said: 'We are the Church', my statement refers to one of her properties and not directly to what the Church is independently of the immediate context. Furthermore, a real definition requires a *genus proximum* and a *differentia specifica*. Thus, the classical definition of man points to the class of animals and specifies the same with the most characteristic quality of being human: *homo est animal rationale*. In other words, a real definition points to the very essence or to the quintessential quality of the reality of which we are speaking.

This is why, as already mentioned, many ecclesiologists refuse to give a real definition of the Church. A mystery cannot be defined and, if you try to come up with a definition, you will reduce the Church to something which she is not. Instead of definitions, one should be satisfied with the description of the vision we have of her. For indeed, none of the aspects of our experience and none of the 'visions' trying to synthesize these aspects could stand for a real definition.

Now, do the 'definitions' at which Rahner arrives, especially in the *Handbook*, conform to Rikhof's requirements? If we turn back to the earlier part of of this book (see 1.3) and re-read Rahner's 'definition', our answer will be both Yes and No. He states there:

The Church is the socially legitimated fellowship (or communion) of people in which through faith, hope and love the eschatologically fulfilled revelation of God (understood as his self-communication) in Christ becomes real and true and as such present to the world'.[43]

Rahner starts with what we can take for a *genus proximum*: the Church is a communion (*Gemeinschaft*). Here he obviously prefers the aspect of communion, yet he immediately adds that the reality of the phenomenon, Church, belongs to the genre of human groupings which may be a club, a reunion of people, a team, an association. She is like many others within the confines of human society, 'socially legitimated'. If I understand him rightly, Rahner states that the immediately experienced communion can be taken as a society with its visible structures (*legitim verfasste Gemeinschaft*). The two aspects go together as a human fellowship.

So far so good. However, the specification of this fellowship, the *differentia specifica* is much more complex. Rahner seems to state of this fellowship:

(i) a common conviction ('through faith hope and love', where the subject is the fellowship);

(ii) an act of God (revelation, self-communication) which, in and through Christ, has reached its fulfilment (the subject of the statement is 'God through Christ'); here, apparently, he refers to that dimension of our experience according to which the Church is a mystery and yet this mystery is already named and known in Rahner's own theological background;

(iii) this is real and true: this may qualify God's action through Christ or imply that God's mysterious will for the Church is realised in the form of a society;

(iv) it is permanently present or to be presented to the world. This seems to be a further qualification (still a *differentia specifica*?) either of God's action through Christ or the fellowship itself without saying under which aspect: communion or society.[44]

The trouble with this complex specification is that it contains too much and requires an all-too-long explanation (see 3.1). Rahner had to extend and even interpret his own 'definition'.

Almost immediately he adds to this 'definition' that the Church is both a fruit and a medium of salvation (*Heilsfruncht* and *Heilsmittel*). Does this precision belong to the quintessential statement about the Church? Furthermore, does the suggested action of 'making present' (attributed either to God or to the fellowship) belong to this basic statement? Then, in assigning what is to be presented, Rahner refers to the mystery of God's self-communication; for this he uses the analogy of the sacraments.

One could ask whether or not these further explanations belong to the real definition of the Church? Can such a definition specify its subject by naming its task or its function, however permanent these are. This would be the case, if the function of the fellowship is the 'making present' of God's self-communication. If this is so, then Rahner's definition of Church society is functional – an objection which may be raised against him. For if the fellowship (subject) does not visibly make present to the world the fact of God's self-communication, will it cease to be the Church? On the other hand, by taking the mystery of God's self-communication into the definition, we may ask: Can a 'mystery' be used in a real definition? Surely, if we 'define' the Church as the mystery of God's self-communication, we have already interpreted something which in itself has not been and cannot have been part of our original experience. If Rahner takes in or explains his definition with the sacramental character of the Church, then he defines it with an analogy. But can an analogy be taken for a real definition?[45]

My remarks are not intended as a challenge to Rahner's own 'definition' of the Church. Provided that his differentiating term (*differentia specifica*) can be simplified, he has, in my estimation, given a real definition. Rikhof in his study proposes such a simple statement about the very essence of the Church: 'The Church is the communion of the faithful.'[46] This statement is indeed an abbreviated formula which is intended to be sufficient for a theological discourse about the Church. Although its parsimony (contrary to Rahner) is praiseworthy, I do not believe that it is sufficient. The subject of the definition is, as in Rahner's, the experienced communion. As long as Rikhof's statement does not exclude at least a minimal societal organization (regarding which, see Chapter 3), we can accept it. It is, however, not said that this communion belongs to the family of societies (*genus proximum*). Furthermore, Rikhof's statement in specifying this communion as Church is too wide. The tag 'faithful' should be extended by stating what the faith of the faithful is about.

It is here that I apply my above distinction between belief and faith. *The Church is a community (society) of those who believe in the event of Jesus Christ and its permanent significance for the whole of human history, and in faith understand themselves as a communion on the pattern of the triune God.*

The second half of this statement does not strictly belong to the definition of the Church, yet it qualifies the mystery character of the fellowship without which the Church would not be the Church of Christ.

With this extension I have not defined the Church through her task (though in qualifying belief by 'active' I have indicated it without assigning its task), nor by naming her in my definition a mystery (though I indicated that this fellowship is to be interpreted from its angle), neither did I explain her nature by means of a metaphor ('Body of Christ', 'people of God', etc.), or as an analogy (the sacraments).

In fact, I have tried to find an adequate statement which corresponds to the phenomenon of our experience. With this, I believe, all the elements of Rahner's further explanations and interpretations can be accommodated without, however, tying me down to his understanding alone. Other definitions too, provided that they conform to my basic statement, can fairly be discussed in a theological dialogue. It is an open statement.

Rahner's various attempts at defining the Church were often criticised as being abstract and theoretical.[47] If one means by 'abstract' that, from the point of view of systematic theology, his basic statement is too general, too wide for any practical use, I would not agree. On the contrary: his 'definitions' of the Church invite us to accept it, however, without Rahner's own theoretical *praesupposita*. And this is exactly what I have tried to avoid. By upholding my basic statement on the Church, I am much nearer to the original experience in which the followers of Jesus were engaged and with which outsiders were confronted. It was a visible group of people, gathered together by a remarkable event, the believed significance of which for themselves and for the whole world was to be made known. Their function of witnessing (or as I have put it 'making present') can, but not of necessity, follow from my basic ecclesiological statement. Thus the various functions, the 'how' of their subsequent actions is left open to history.

It is on this insight that in the Bible metaphorical or analogical interpretations are built towards a pre-scientific vision of the Church. And this is taken over, developed by the everyday language of the faithful. If, in a strict theological discourse, what is said of the Church on this level is coherent with my statement, we are not only allowed, but encouraged, to retain the hallowed language of our vision of the Church. I believe this was Rahner's task in writing his *Handbook*. His 'definition' was preparatory to the *praxis* of pastoral theologians and, at the same time, consonant to his personal attitude towards the Church.

§§§§§§

The question with which I concluded my Introduction can now, in the light of Rahner's fundamental insights, be better answered. These and his *obiter dicta* in the 'wintry season' can now reveal his personal attitude to the Church. It is a synthesis of a traditional-orthodox and a 'liberal' relationship to the Church. Rahner's attitude is orthodox in the sense of a necessary commitment to the Church, as disclosed in the ecclesial horizon of human experience and as quoted in my Introduction: 'If one loves God in Jesus Christ, one also loves the Church.'

It is 'liberal', and to a certain extent free, as regards the concrete historical Church in which, however, Rahner is deeply engaged – precisely this free engagement in the historical shape of the Church which, I believe, prompts him to find an aspect of the Church which is a necessity for the salvation of every man and woman. This aspect is, what I have called the 'transcendental Church', as a counterpart of man's silent and anonymous option for the self-communicating God of salvation history, whose presence is felt not only in solitary reflection but much more in the communion with one's fellows. The Church under this aspect is an inevitable historical *a priori*.

On the other hand, as regards the historical Church in her present shape, Rahner can couple an unshaken commitment with the freedom of the children of God. When Rahner, in his 'wintry season', was asked about some positions disturbing contemporary mentality, he could qualify them as 'secondary' statements. These secondary statements, or even decisions pronounced by the authority of the Church, do not arise from the transcendental Church (which is *his* option), but from the visible and historical Church: they are a challenge to freedom within our indomitable commitment. This attitude, I believe, describes and characterizes Rahner's genuine churchmanship.

Chapter 3

The Two-Faceted Church

The concept of freedom plays a central role in Rahner's theology of the Church. It was the analysis of freedom which underpinned his early attempts at disclosing her notion – a Church wide enough to embrace the whole of mankind. Those who knew Rahner personally and followed his writings, must have had the impression that all through his life he was a valiant fighter for freedom, both within and without the Church. This freedom, as I have suggested, refers also to the visible, historical aspect of the Church, to the institutionally structured one which depends on the will of her members. Even though Rahner always maintained the basic unity of these two aspects, we can still speak of a two-dimensional, of a *two-faceted Church*.

It would be tedious to refer the reader to a list of publications in which this freedom within the Church is explicitly treated, touched upon or just presupposed. Their *leitmotiv* can be summed up by Rahner's much repeated, reprinted and translated address at the opening of the Austrian *Katholikentag* in 1962: 'Do not stifle the Spirit!'[1]

It was, then, the beginning of Vatican II and Rahner's main preoccupation seems to have been for courage to change, for charismatic freedom, both in the ordinary members and in the official ministry, to obey the 'imperatives of the time'. It was an appeal for freedom to prepare the way for a global Church (*die echte Weltkirche*). It is obvious that this call for courage was directed in the first place to the visible and institutional Church.

In this chapter I shall try to present Rahner's thought on the relationship of the individual to the institutional Church, his approach to the actual structures of the Roman Catholic Church and her organs. After presenting in detail his, mainly post-Vatican, ideas of how the Church should be, some points for comments and questions will undoubtedly emerge, which I shall deal with in the next chapter.

3.1 Church and Institution

It is not Rahner's job in dealing with the visible Church to define what in contemporary sociology institutions and structures are. He never explicitly borrows from the social sciences whose task it is to describe the meaning of these terms. In the *obiter dicta* of his 'wintry season' he takes it for granted that his interviewers know what they are after when they express their misgivings concerning the structures and institutions of the visible Church. He assures his young questioners that any association will sooner or later find its own rules and thereby become 'institutionalized', according to the structures which emerged in its life.[2] One wonders if this *ad hominem* answer can also explain the structures and institutions of the Church, even if it is inevitable within human associations (*Vergesellschaftung*). Many Christians still believe that the social organization of the Church is unchangeable, supposedly being of divine origin. To tease out Rahner's view, we have to see his treatment of various topics concerning the visible Church in his developing thought.

3.1.1 The individual and the institution

An early article in *Stimmen der Zeit* deals in more generic terms with the relationship between the individual and society.[3] There is, as Rahner explains, a tension between the protest of extreme individualism (a heritage of the *Aufklärung*) and the attitude of Church members who blindly rely on ecclesiastical directives and neglect their obligation to decide for themselves (*Entscheidungspflicht*).

Rahner introduces his essay with a philosophical-theological discourse on the individual and he, too, like Bonhoeffer, considers the Church in two ways: as a communion (*Gemeinschaft*) and as a society (*Gesellschaft*). 'Communion' corresponds to an association of man as a spiritual person and 'society' to man as material-biological individuum.[4]

Approached from the side of her institutions, the Church can be seen as a society[5] with her legal system that rules and helps (*unterstützt*) the individual's free decision. Already in this early article, Rahner leaves room for the individual to follow his or her conscience even within the Church as a society. Individual conscience is not directly under the rules and regulations of her institutions, since they are 'only' secondary helps for the individual on the way to salvation.[6] In face of an ecclesiastical 'collectivism', as Rahner puts it, the individual is not only free, but has the duty to follow his or her own 'imperatives' and charisms.

Rahner's *Meditations on Freedom and the Spirit* (1977) includes an essay of some significance in which he again tackles the concept of the 'institutional'.[7] It is here that he attempts to bring his notion of freedom face-to-face with social and ecclesiastical institutions. His sentence, 'Institution somehow refers to truth' (*Institution hat etwas mit Wahrheit zu tun*)[8], was often to be repeated. It presupposes the ambivalence of all institutions: on the one hand divine revelation reaches us through the institutions of our society, the Church, but on the other hand, institutions are prone to manipulate the freedom of the individual. Institutions, however, are inevitable since they can extend freedom's realm of alternatives (*Freiheitsraum*); yet they can be restrictive since in them one is confronted with the exercise of an alien freedom. If this latter is imposed against the consent of the individual, one can speak of '*sinful*' manipulation. This applies also to the Church which, as a society (and *not* as man's inevitable transcendental experience!) can extend or restrict the range of individual freedom.[9] In Rahner's opinion, however, the Church is more obliged than all other societies to maintain and increase the range of the individual's freedom.[10] The Church's institutions should be at the service of man's salvation.[11]

In 1970, with publication of his essay, 'Institution and Freedom', Rahner addresses himself more extensively to the above problem of Church as institution, even trying to describe these two notions in their coherence:

> . . . all institutional factors constitute, in a social sense, the outer periphery and the utterly secondary (although not inessential) realisation and concretisation of that which is called structure and

order in the world. The more so, since these institutional factors are to a large extent dependent, in their concrete forms, on the free will of man himself, and so are much more liable to change than those which pertain to the structures investigated by the natural sciences and intellectual disciplines inasmuch as these are concerned with what is permanent and enduring.[12]

In this complex description of institutions Rahner assumes some permanency to structures and orders and relegates institutions as a secondary (although not inessential) concretization of the same. He also asserts that while their becoming is due to freedom (which also explains their liability to change) there is no freedom without corresponding institutions and their structural order. If, however, freedom is the condition of institutions, then already established institutions can also be subject to freedom. Would it not follow from this that even structures, whose permanency Rahner admits, can also be affected by freedom?[13]

Rahner dwells repeatedly on the ambiguity of freedom. It consists in the fact that freedom can enable institutions and, at the same time, institutions can restrict the exercise of freedom. In certain situations Rahner reckons with the reaction of an 'aggressive demand for a greater freedom': that is, if 'freedom were to be a condition in which it is possible to get rid of a situation which is regarded as undesirable and capable of being abolished,'[14] then freedom is challenged to further action, the result of which is again ambivalent. The mere abolition[15] of a restrictive situation without foreseeing its consequences could lead, on the one hand, to further institutions and to a fresh curtailment of freedom: ' . . . freedom creates its own compulsion within itself[16] or, on the other hand, freedom can live with its own objectifications.'[17]

Thus, Rahner concludes this essay with, so to speak, wishful thinking, valid both for theology and the social sciences: one should strive to create counter-institutions 'more effective in their functioning, if they were consciously interpreted . . . as institutions for safeguarding freedom against restrictive effects of other institutions.'[18]

It is obvious that in these considerations Rahner assumes an analogy between religious and secular freedom, religious and secular society, in order to explain the coming-to-be and function of the organization of the visible Church. If not explicitly, he enters into a dialogue with the social sciences: from the findings of sociology as a theologian he can understand, interpret and correct his view on the visible Church, and from the nature of a religious society he is ready to suggest changes in a secular society.

Only later (that is, after 1972, when he published his rather challenging book *The Shape of the Church to Come*[19]) does Rahner concentrate his interest more and more on *social* change within the Church. Does this change affect only the institutions, or does it change also the very structures of Church society? At first sight he reaffirms that structures are permanent: instead of changing they regulate the change of institutions.

> Leaving aside any subtle politological and juridical definitions of terms, by 'structures' here is meant simply everything that exists in fact in the Church . . . permanently and universally as a reality determining the action and decisions of the office holders and church members or as a norm for this action and these decisions.[20]

This quasi-definition, though it does not mention institutions, corresponds more or less to the present view of sociologists.[21] Although structures tend to be permanent, nothing hinders Rahner from pointing out structural changes in the present and in a future Church. Though they remain, they can take another form in the future and their change can shape the future history of institutions.

This seems to be Rahner's preoccupation in his later writings. In an essay published in 1976 he gives a theological justification of the Church's engagement in development work[22] and in another essay he assesses the individual's freedom in secular society. In a way, both essays attempt to underline the relevance of the visible Church in modern society. However, the main question of the second essay comes nearer to our matter in hand. He asks: If the Church – which is of course also a society – has from its very nature a mandate to promote greater freedom within itself, what is the Church's task in regard to all the aspirations and struggles of nations for more freedom, emancipation, and the abolition of illegitimate power structures in the world?[23] With this question, we seem to be back at the topic with which we began this chapter: man's freedom in facing institutions and structures of visible societies.

The gist of this latter essay, however, goes beyond Rahner's earlier articles. Whereas in his 'Toleration in the Church', published in 1977,[24] he restricts himself to concrete problems within the Church, here in 1979 he suggests that the Church should influence secular society *by way of changing her own structures* for the greater freedom of the individual. The promotion of freedom in the world should be the task of the Church, it is her responsibility. Now this task, Rahner thinks, can only be fulfilled if modern society shares similar convictions and faces similar problems in her situation as the visible Church does. For in civil society, too, the freedom of the individual seems to be out of balance with authority; it has to live with a similar plurality of views and interests as does the Church at present. Why could she not through her *structural changes* develop new models as an example for secular society? Why could not the Church, which has lost her political and sociological power, show 'that relations between base and ministry will and must be given a form very different from that to which we have been accustomed'?[25]

It is immaterial now what kind of changes Rahner suggested for secular society. At the moment it is enough to register Rahner's almost utopian dream that not only institutions but also 'permanent' structures can indeed be changed and that these changes are bound to influence secular society. He dreams of more freedom for the individual within the Church and, through this, extended freedom for men and women in the world.

However, the analogy and the implied mutuality between secular and Church societies do not equate these two. Rahner does not reduce the visible Church to secular society. On the contrary, he is about to deal with structures and institutions proper to the Church in order to establish within these the freedom of the individual. He speaks of the *charismatic freedom* within the Church.

3.1.2 Charisma and freedom

Like any other society the Church is based on her more or less permanent structures and institutions. This statement, built on the analogy of secular and religious societies, needs to be extended.

The Church is existentially *more* than any human association. In order to work out in what this *more* consists there are two directions from which her nature can be approached.

Older ecclesiologies which developed in the wake of Trent and Vatican I tended to describe the nature of the Church as a 'perfect society'.[26] Her perfection was due to the divine origin of her structures and institutions. The main stress here was on the structural or institutional factors, by means of which the Church is the depository of indefectible divine truth to be proclaimed to the world and on the sacraments through which she dispenses the goods of salvation to her individual members. To fulfil this function the Church is provided with a stable organization (structures and institutions) of divine origin: she is a hierarchical body, indeed, the 'mystical body of Christ' which is at work through the organs of her institutions, equally of divine origin. She is the so-called *Amtskirche*, the Church of her ordained ministers.

Whereas this older approach still prevails in the first *half* of the twentieth century, Vatican II's doctrine seems to be a watershed introducing an alternative. Already, the newly-emphasized image of the *people of God* on the way to salvation suggests that the nature of the Church will not be described as starting from her hierarchical organization – so to speak – *from above*, but from her basis, the ordinary Church members. Their association, being *more* than merely human, is a process built up by the work of God's Holy Spirit through his gifts, the *charismata* distributed to individual members.

Rahner's writings about the nature of the Church are on this second line of approach. For him the Church is, as we have already seen, not only the means leading to salvation, but also the fruit of God's self-communication. As a human association, called communion or *Gemeinde*, she is 'sustained in being by the victory of God's grace . . . and in virtue of the love of God and neighbour practised by her members.'[27] This 'sustaining power' is the Spirit present through his charismata. Although never discussing the biblical notion of the charisms,[28] Rahner speaks of them in two ways. First, he regards the charismata as elements of a divine unrest of freedom and, secondly, as an element constitutive of her visible organization (structures and institutions). Following the first notion, the Church is developing as a unity in tension – even in facing 'opposition and hostility' *(feindlicher Gegensatz)* to anything stable within her organization. Yet at the same time by means of the same charismata, the Church contributes to the coming-to-be of more or less stable structures and organs. Both, apparently contrary, notions were overlooked by older ecclesiologies.[29]

Thus, in Rahner's view, the charismata seem to be the common denominator of the more dynamic and free aspects of the Church *and* of her more or less permanent organization. Their unity in tension is analysed at three stages of Rahner's writings and whilst the emphases of his argumentation may be divergent, the conclusion points to the same concept of a charismatic Church. These three I briefly qualify here.

(A) *The dynamic element*

Rahner discusses this topic in the context of his 'existential ethics'.[30] He is about to find a middle way between the morality of obedience, as based on fulfilling the demands of the Church, and the ethics of a situation in which the concrete circumstances of the individual serve as a norm for moral action.[31] His distinction between objective duty fulfilled and the concrete imperatives of the individual's conscience already points to the role of the charisms of the Spirit. From this he develops the 'logic of concrete individual knowledge', exemplified in the exercises of Ignatius of Loyola.[32]

Nonetheless, the Church retains her ultimate and absolute authority in matters of faith and morals. The head of the Church, the Pope, has the fullness of juridical power – a subject to which I shall presently turn.

Now, in a secular state, where there is always the danger of abuse, under certain circumstances the rights of individuals or groups can be defended by recourse to a higher court of appeal or, in extreme cases, to revolt. Since neither of these ways are open in the Church, there must be an inbuilt control beyond the hierarchy and the Pope. From this, Rahner argues that authority and power within the Church are under the control of the charisms of the Spirit, meaning that

> . . . such an office held by a human being, if it is not to be an
> absolute tyranny, must itself ascend to a sphere to which no juridi-
> cal criteria can be applied. It must necessarily itself be
> charismatic.[33]

If it is so, then the supreme authority within the Church is also
constituted by the dynamic and charismatic element. With this
postulatory argument Rahner presupposes, on the one hand, that
the charismatic is beyond the juridical sphere; it is irreducible to
juridical terms (*unverrechtbar*) and, on the other, that for the
Church there is one, and only one, source of ultimate authority.
Even the institutional ministry in all its manifestations must be
charismatic: it owes its existence to the abiding Spirit and his
work in the Church.

It would, however, be a misunderstanding to assume that
only the institutional side of the Church is the vehicle of the
charismatic. For, in order to avoid an ecclesiastical totalitari-
anism, 'there are charismata, that is, the impulsion and
guidance of God's Spirit for the Church in addition to and outside of the official ministry.'[34] And this is not merely a
sporadic, intermittent phenomenon in the Church, it belongs
essentially to her. A long quotation from Pius XII's *Mystici
Corporis*[35] (to the effect that both the official institutions and
their ministry enjoy this direct influence) seems to substantiate
Rahner's thesis. In the two-faceted Church there is, then, a
two-fold structure, the institutional and the dynamic, whose
harmony and oneness cannot be juridically controlled – it is of
its nature charismatic.[36]

We should note here that Rahner, in arguing the relationship
of the institutional and charismatic, calls them both 'structures'.[37]
Rahner seems to use 'structures' not in the same sense, univo-
cally, but in an analogous way. He is almost apologetic in
pointing out the misunderstanding of the sixteenth-century
reformers: had the Church been (as in her history she has often
appeared) merely a human institution and not under the power of
the Spirit (as she always was), her rulings, her interference with
charismatic phenomena would indeed have been a tyranny.[38]

Nevertheless, Rahner deals with the 'structures' of the non-
institutional only in generic terms while emphasizing that the

charismatic element is not exclusively confined to members of the Church. And this will be his later *leitmotiv*. The work of the Spirit does not know frontiers – it is all-embracing[39]; it is a motive force, an interior call to everyone drawn to the Church. Yet, despite its basic unity, 'the institution is always the same and develops . . . from the palpable, unambiguous principles it embodies from the outset. . . . *But the charismatic is essentially new and always surprising.*'[40] Indeed, this surprising charismatic quality was soon to be manifested in the event of Vatican II.

(B) *The 'self-accomplishment' of the Church*

For the ecclesiological foundation in the *Handbook*, which had already been written before the first phase of the Council,[41] Rahner's basic thesis is the *Selbtsvollzug*, the self-accomplishment of the Church both in the official administration of the sacraments and in the free charismatic action of her members. We saw that both are constitutive elements. Whereas in *Dynamic* Rahner's intention was to find an appropriate place for the charismatic alongside the institutional, here the free charisms of individuals (or groups) are affirmed to build up the Church both as a communion and a society. Although in themselves they are not subject to institutionalization (*nicht verwaltbar*), without charismatic people there is no Church distinct from the synagogue of the old dispensation. For they are those who according to their individual talents are at the service of the community. Even the objective efficacy of the sacraments, the *opus operatum* of Trent, presupposes the charismata both in the ministers and recipients: in one way or another the correct disposition, the *opus operantis*, the moving force of the Spirit can be presupposed in both spender and receiver.[42]

From these premises follows not only that the objective efficacy of sanctification is basically charismatic, but also that the institutionally not manageable (*nicht verwaltbar*) charisms have something to do with the Church as a society. They are 'ecclesial': they have – or rather they create their own – structures different from the institutional. Neither the institutional nor the dynamic element of the Church can exist on its own. Only if both, the ordered and free, the not manageable, are realized in the action of the Church, can she be what she is: Christ's irrevocable and eschatological presence in the world.[43]

(C) *The charismatic in the Church*

Later, in 1989, in an essay on the same subject,[44] Rahner already presupposes that the Church is the victorious and eschatological presence of Christ in the world. The institutions and the official ministry of the sacraments represent one side of the Church, while the free and charismatic is now spoken of as the extra sacramental gift of all who are called to her. Only their interplay overcomes the rigidity of a *closed* social system. The distinction between a closed and open system[45] explains more coherently the two-faceted Church. By a closed system Rahner understands a society in which the ultimate and determining factor of its operation is *within* the system itself, whereas an open system is

> such that the definitive condition in which it actually stands and should stand neither can nor should be defined in any adequate sense in terms of any point immanent within the system.[46]

This 'point outside of the system' is God, and the Church which God enables to be is not institutional in character, but truly charismatic.

> The charismatic element does exist in the Church, and it does not merely stand in a dialectical relationship to the institutional factor as its opposite pole, existing on the same plane. Rather it is the first and the ultimate among the formal characteristics inherent in the very nature of the Church as such.[47]

The relationship between the institutional and the charismatic seems to have been inverted: it is not only that the former tolerates and controls the latter, but that the 'operation', the 'action' of the whole Church '*are charismatic rather than institutional in character*'.[48]

Without denying the institutional side of the Church, Rahner clearly opts for the predominance of the charismatic. In the interplay between the two, he repeatedly asserts the all-pervading presence of the charismatic: it is not only an intermittent and particular phenomenon, its 'operation' is not confined to a limited sphere in the Church's action, her effort of discovering and teaching the truth, to the developing of her dogmas, to her response to contemporary problems. Indeed, *all* these suggest the true all-embracing presence of the charismatic. It can be conceived as the creative freedom of the present in facing an incalculable future. In brief, Rahner seems to regard the relationship of the institutional to the charismatic in the way in which the categorial is referred to the transcendental:

> . . . the charismatic is, if we may so express it, transcendental in its character, not one element in the system of the Church but a special characteristic of the system as a whole.[49]

Rahner is led to this conclusion having buttressed it with the tenor implicit in Vatican II's decree on the Church.[50] His more systematic argument for this is based on a revised notion of the Church, which is a *process* moulded by history. The Church of Christ is a developing organism; she is the *historical* self-communication of God but realizes herself as a society for the progressive sanctification of mankind. Although God reveals himself once for all through Jesus Christ, the gradual perception of his action makes it appear to us as an ongoing process – perhaps even beyond its eschatological fulfilment. If the Church depends on God's historical revelation and mankind's sanctification, which is in history, then the Church is, as an open system, an historical process.[51] That is to say: the life of this organism is given once for all, but its development is dependent on its interior and exterior circumstances. The Church is a process which integrates in herself, by means of the charismatic freedom of her members, the structures and some of the institutions of secular societies. On this ground, Rahner will be able to speak of the 'structures of the people of the Church'.[52] Although the Church by her nature is institutionally organized (*hierarchy*), ' . . . the personal history of the individual as uniquely vested with freedom belongs intrinsically to her existence'.[53] The various groupings in their own social manifestation contribute their charisms to her concrete being. This means that not only the official ministry but every member of the Church is consecrated to the service of the Church.[54] Beside being an institution, planned and devised under God's permanent presence amongst us, the Church's whole reality is also the free association of charismatic individuals or groups moulded by the free gifts of the Spirit.

From this image of the Church as an open system, Rahner will be able to answer many of the contemporary questions. Such an image can envisage the Church's hierarchical organization without thinking of it as a rule of ministerial aristocracy; the primacy of the Pope and his infallible rulings without mistaking the Church for a monolith governed by an autocratic monarch; the ultimate teaching authority without taking it for a 'thought-police'; the present-day proliferation of basic communities in their coherence with the centre of the Church, and so on.

The quest for a 'more democratic' Church, which Rahner at various instances of his writing tried to face,[55] can be answered by the Church as an 'open system'. She is indeed an organic process and, as such, beyond the secular categories of ecclesiastical absolutism or democracies ruled by different party political interests. She is what she was always meant to be and, by the assistance of the Spirit's charisms, she is becoming what she is to be to the end of history.

Having in the first instance characterized the one, charismatic and free side of the Church, the question remains whether Rahner is able to define adequately its counterpart: her institutional side.

3.2 The Catholic Claims of Rome

The structures and institutions of the visible Church are claimed to have originated from her founder, Jesus the Christ. They exist not by the will of its leaders or members, but by divine right, *ex iure divino*.

3.2.1. The Founder by divine right

Now, in Rahner's many references to the Church there is only one attempt to prove this claim of divine right and it is to be found in the seventh chapter of *Foundations*.[56]

(A) *The notion and the evidence*

In accordance with the whole method of *Foundations*, Rahner argues not so much from scriptural evidence for this claim but rather from the whole religious situation in which a Roman Catholic believer can be convinced of his own legitimate belonging to the fold. The believer will try to answer

> . . . why he believes and is convinced that he really encounters Jesus Christ in his Church, and that he has no reason to abandon or to cast doubt upon the membership in his Church which has been handed down to him as his own existential situation.[57]

In other words, Rahner moves on the 'first level of reflection' and tries to avoid exegetical and historical details in proving his claim. First, he shows (along with some other non-Catholic Christians) that the historical Jesus had founded a Church and then proceeds to argue that this Church corresponds to her Roman Catholic shape.

Rahner's argumentation is based a on a 'minimalist' requirement – the historical Christ had the *intention* of founding a community which, after his death, will stand for Christ's message of the eschatological Kingdom of God. This can be seen from the fact that Jesus had gathered a community around himself, first of Israelites awaiting salvation and then of everybody who will believe in the permanence of his message. Within this community, entailed in this belief, Jesus and his followers also presupposed that their belief in the Kingdom is at the same time an irreversible offer of salvation which not only accepts Jesus as the Lord, but within it God's acceptance of the whole of mankind. This faith is no more a merely human choice among many alternative possibilities, but a gratuitous gift of God and his Holy Spirit.

If we understand this faith as a public profession within the ongoing identity of a believing community then we ought to conclude, first, that the foundation of such a community was – at least implicitly – the *intention* of the founder, Jesus Christ, and, secondly, that this faith in an earlier epoch forms an irreversible norm for future generations. Historical continuity rests both on the intention of the founder and on the early *constitution* of the believing community. It is this constitution which should imply the distinctive structures and institutions to be developed in the Church of Jesus the Christ.

Presupposed by this requirement is that there is 'a legitimacy of a process of becoming in the church from out of her origins into her full essence.'[58]

To prove this we do not have to go back to any explicit saying of Jesus. It will be enough to interpret those deeds and actions which betray his intentions. The fact that Jesus gathered disciples around him proves that he intended to form the circle of twelve symbolically representing Israel's twelve tribes in their eschatological fulfilment. This circle was about to share his own mission, his own power 'which was a sign for him that the eschatological kingdom as a present and pressing reality was operative here and now in him.'[59] Furthermore, the intention of Jesus is expressed in the institution of the Last Supper as directed to the new order of salvation, the new covenant. One can likewise find the same intentionality in the words of the risen Christ, who seems to bestow his powers upon the twelve for the continuation of his work in the world (Mt 28:16–20; Jn 20:22f). It is also an established fact that in this mission of the twelve, Jesus meant to convey an important role to Kephas who has been named Peter, the Rock, on which Jesus intended to build his Church to last to the end of time (Mt 16:16f). It was the same Peter who was told to stand by the others in times of temptation (Lk 22:31) and to whom the power of the keys to bind and loose and the role of a shepherd (Jn 21:15–17) were committed. If it is true that in these deeds and words the intention of Jesus to found a Church can be traced, then we have a basic constitution for the Church to come. To this Rahner adds:

> . . . beyond these basic provisions Jesus left everything else to the Spirit who was promised, and to the history of the Church which was guided by the Spirit, and especially of course to the history of the original Church.[60]

As for the history of this early Church, Rahner attributes to her members a 'creative theology', which must have been grounded in their knowledge of the intentions of Jesus. This is why, in the various books of the New Testament, there are several primitive ecclesiologies which already bear a strong *institutional* stamp and thereby create an ecclesiological tradition. It has bishops, deacons and presbyters, and is organized according to particular offices and powers having a definite rank and place in the early community. In this rudimentary constitution – apart from other sociological aspects – we can find its main, yet developing, lines as intended by the founder. This intention will constitute the right on which Catholic ecclesiology will be built.[61]

So much for the direct biblical evidence with which Rahner tries to underscore his thesis: the historical Jesus did intend to found a Church. Rahner relies on the exegesis of selected Catholic scholars[62] without, however, entering in detail into the difficulties of others who cast doubt on the authenticity of precisely those sayings of Jesus which Rahner quotes. According to him, the burden of proof is on his adversaries: they have to show that Jesus could not have made these statements – for example, because of the expectation of an imminent parousia – or he could not have behaved as he did. The contrary opinion of the adversaries can be 'neglected', especially on the grounds of what I have called Rahner's anthropological and transcendental considerations.

That Christ must have been the founder of a Church is also argued by means of a transcendental deduction as the presupposition of the Christian faith in Jesus. The argument by now is well known: Christianity as Church belongs to the religious existence of man as such, 'quite independently of the question of how it must be constituted more precisely in the concrete'.[63] Man, in his existential self, is an ecclesial being who anticipates a socially structured and – in a way – authoritative Church claiming his free decision. The requirement of a Church follows from the concretization of God's salvific deed in Christ and the question as to which of the existing Christian denominations best corresponds to this is to be decided on the criterion of 'continuity with the origin', of 'preserving the basic substance of Christianity'. In order to establish these criteria, subjective experience must coincide with 'objective authority'; and if they are applicable to the

Church, then the Catholic claim of Rome becomes evident as against its revision by Protestant Christianity.

(B) *Jus divinum*

The key to Rahner's argumentation is his theory about divine right. It is derived neither from natural law nor from a positive ordinance of any human legislation, but a fact which should be traced back to Christ 'as a permanent feature of the Church and an ordinance which even the highest authority of the Church cannot repeal.'[64]

To this category of *Jus divinum* belong also certain structures and institutions of the Church with which the Catholic faithful are daily confronted. Such, in dogmatic parlance, are the papacy, the episcopal and monarchical constitution of the Church, the fact that the sacraments are seven in number, the obligation incumbent on the baptized to submit their mortal sins to the Church's power of the keys, and so on.

Hence, not only the question about the founding of the Church, but also that of her basic organization ought to be traced back to the intention of her founder. This is why the Councils of Trent and Vatican I,[65] opposing contemporary challenge, wanted to root these institutions in the divine will impervious to human interference. However, in the light of modern historical criticism it is almost impossible to trace their origins back to definite sayings, to explicit ordinance of Christ, or even to a positive legislation of the primitive Church which was meant to be permanent. Thus it can be presupposed that, owing to the intention of the founder, some features of the present Church are basically of divine origin yet, as Rahner argues, the divine law can never be just 'imagined', it must have historical roots.[66]

Thus, the real problem about divine right is its historical nature. Truths and laws, for which by the Church divine right is claimed, are bound to historical circumstances in which the primitive Church had to take a decision concerning her way of life from among several alternatives. Since then these circumstances have been, at least according to their form, changed in the course of history.

The question concerning divine right is now very similar to the development of dogmatic statements out of their presupposed source of divine revelation:

> How are we to conceive a change of form [*Gestaltwandel*] which, while leaving the nature untouched, yet can really be conceived in the way in which according to the testimony of history, it obviously took place?[67]

Theories, however, about the development of doctrine have an additional difficulty: an ordinance, the existence of a structural element within an institution, both have their history, so how can we take them as divine right in their present shape? For it is hard to prove that a decision at an early stage of Church history was indeed intended to be so absolutely permanent that a later generation could not pronounce it in a different way.

Although Rahner's answer presupposes the main lines of his theory of revelation and doctrinal development, his central argument is based on a *human decision* in facing the divine will. Such decisions are historical and time-bound. There are, however, 'one way historical processes which are no longer reversible.'[68] They are *historical*, since they have come to being at some point in time and yet even in a changing form they can become formative of future behaviour. These decisions should not be necessarily implied in the very nature of a process of choice (*wesensnotwendig*); if, however, they are congruous to this latter (*wesensgemäss*) they can become irreversible. It is, hence, possible to say that a free moral person and corporate personalities are capable of, and do indeed take, decisions which will be irreversible for their later history. But once they are taken, they determine the 'physiognomy', that is, the basic structure of the life of the individual or community. If this is possible, then we can speak of them as irreversible decisions.

From this follows Rahner's thesis:

> An irreversible, law-establishing decision of the Church which is in conformity with her nature [*wesensgemäss*] can be regarded as *Jus divinum*, when it took place at the time of the primitive Church.[69]

By appealing to the 'primitive Church', Rahner presupposes

two things. First, that revelation was not closed – at least until the demise of the last member of the apostolic generation. A statement which I have discussed in a previous volume,[70] is used here to buttress his view. And, secondly, Rahner emphazises the fact that to a revelatory event there is always a corresponding human decision which can be part and parcel of the revealed word. He refers to the decision to take Mattheas into the college of the apostles, to Peter's decision to go to Rome, and so on. The divine right emerging from these decisions can have the character of revelation. It is, therefore, a law divine as well as human and in it God's will is revealed:

> Free events . . . can certainly have the character of revelation in the age of the primitive Church. They are human decisions, and in them precisely is accomplished God's will to reveal, a will which desires, brings about . . . this event in all its characteristic nature in and through this freedom of decision pre-defined by this will.[71]

Of course, this presupposes not only the very nature of divine revelation but also the quality and form of the revelatory event. In formulating these qualities the primitive Church can take a legitimate decision, which becomes an irreversible process of juridical concretization: a permanent law is established as an actualization of the Church's juridical nature. This decision can then become a permanently binding precept for all later generations – 'notwithstanding the fact that this decision originated out of a multivalent situation . . . of the primitive Church.'[72]

Rahner's approach to divine right is thoroughly historical even in an evolutionary sense. Therefore, the question is not altogether inappropriate whether or not a post-apostolic decision of the Church can be regarded as of divine right, *jure divino*. One could presuppose that some facts being of divine right could have been (at least seminally) decided by the primitive Church, as seems to be the case in the development of the monarchical episcopate as distinct from the collegial government of the individual congregations already in the primitive Church.[73] However, it is almost impossible to verify this claim in historical research. Thus, no historian of theology can assert with certainty that, for example, the jurisdictionary primacy of Peter and his successors was unequivocally developed out of the primitive Church.

Nonetheless, the question is not *a priori* superfluous: though it may have undergone some remarkable changes already in the post-apostolic time yet it has remained compatible with the nature (*wesensgemäss*) of a previous decision in the primitive Church. If there is some evidence, or even suspicion, of this, then this fact and its consequences can be regarded as of divine right.

There are, however, important ordinances, obviously introduced later in the post-apostolic Church, which by no means could be reduced, or even connected, with divine revelation. For instance that 'Eugenio Pacelli was rightful Pope' is a statement which is evidently not revealed, and yet on this depends the 'binding power of any infallible definition given by him.'[74] Would this not mean that Pacelli was head of the Church *by divine right*? To accept this fact is not only by 'ecclesiastical faith', as maintained by some theologians, but an answer to divine ordinance (that is, 'divine faith'). To argue this possible position Rahner refers to infallible definitions of the Church, as being revealed by God, yet pronounced in a much later time than the death of the last apostle. Something similar could be asserted of later decisions of the highest Roman authority: they are latecomers in the history of divine right.

Thus, the burden of Rahner's argument is basically anthropological: there can be irrevocable decisions in which the individual or the community freely opt for one of many alternative ways of communal behaviour, and these are binding for subsequent generations. So it seems to be for the structures and some institutions of the Church – but it is also valid for the very constitution of the Church which, in the same way, traces her origins back to the revealed will of Jesus Christ, the founder. The visible Church is the concrete realization of divine revelation.

3.2.2 The structures of an open Church

In the years following Vatican II, Rahner was more aware of this historical and changing character of the Church's constitution. Although he never gave up his interpretation of divine right, as the basis of the visible Church, its concrete application was to be considerably muted. Thus, he could still write in 1971 that, on the one hand, this juridical constitution with the central office of

Peter (the primacy of the Pope) and the episcopal organization, is something 'already predetermined . . . and not subject to [further] decisions'– because they are of divine law.[75] On the other hand, what the Catholic believer immediately experiences in contact with his or her Church is a 'process of change'. In this, however, an unchangeable factor is concealed. The Catholic is on the way to a goal, on a pilgrimage in which he or she should find among the changeable factors a continuity which is changeless. Rahner speaks of an open Church whose members, in all faithfulness to the Church's dogmatic, moral and constitutional teaching, will have to learn to distinguish between divine and human (merely ecclesiastical) law.

Rather than considering now the details of this situation of change, we should first concentrate on those whose task it is to grasp the unchangeable factors amongst the changeable. In 'Changeable' Rahner speaks of the 'open-minded willing and well-instructed Christian' who should recognize in believing the Church – even though this Church undergoes changes – a way of life and laws of the ancient Church in its abiding nature.[76] His question about the sociological structures of the people of the Church could provide an apt framework for our contemporary situation.

(**A**) *The laity*

In his later writings, Rahner's more sociological consideration of the Church comes to the fore. It is, according to him, a constant temptation for the Church to concentrate merely on her own God-given nature *ex jure divino*. The Church, being a visible reality, must take into account the actual 'structures of the people of the Church'– and these people are the laity.[77] The theologian not only may, but must, examine trends in the groupings within the Church which 'emerge from below' and discover a concrete structure within the people of God. As already mentioned, Rahner speaks of a 'process of individualization' within the Church in contrast to the 'uniform and homogeneous people . . . of former ages, to which the hierarchy could adopt a fatherly and paternalistic attitude.'[78] The Church does not consist merely of the hierarchy, but also of these groupings of laymen and laywomen within the visible Church. Now, these groupings belong to the body of the Church in different ways: among them are 'borderline Catholics', 'still half-Catholics and Christians' and 'Catholics on the way', and so on, who apparently do not follow in every detail the Church's ordinances. Their belonging to and their participation in the life of the Church should not be judged by the fulfilment of singular commands (think, for example, of the Sunday Obligation). Rahner would even go one step further: Catholics who are in a sociological sense 'non-conformists', can be or are still members of the Church. Whilst they may be in the wrong, their reactions could be signs of their groping journey towards the fullness of faith: 'Hence the effects of sinfulness and assaults on the faith in the individual are also to be numbered among the structures of the people of the Church.'[79]

There are, then, a variety of structures emerging from sociological factors affecting the people of the Church. To disregard these would be to disregard nature on which grace builds.

In this, relatively late, article Rahner speaks explicitly of laymen and laywomen and presupposes his earlier essays in defining the people of the Church. Already in 1955 he tries to discuss the, not altogether obvious, notion of the layman within the lay apostolate.[80] As in the old Code of Canon Law he starts with a negative definition.[81] Laymen are those who do not share either in the sacramental or juridical power granted them by the Church. It should, however, be added that jurisdiction does not require a sacramental ordination: it is an appointment, depending on commissioning by the sovereign act of the highest Church-authority, of a person to an habitual possession of a right to perform actions on behalf of the Church. Therefore not the *manner* of transferring this right (for example, ordination) but the *content* of what is transmitted can raise the person to the level of the clergy. Thus, a woman who is a 'lay catechist', or a 'parochial helper' can officially participate in the power of jurisdiction and thus belong to the clergy.

This negative approach, however, does not define what it really means to be a layperson within the Church; what determines the layman and laywomen is his or her position in the world. Rahner speaks of a position which is the laity's right on account of their birth: 'The layman is originally in the world in virtue of the pre-Christian (but not "godless") position in his existence' and, as such, a person fulfils his or her mission in the world as a baptized Christian.[82] For the layman, just as the clergy, is called by God and (on account of his baptism and confirmation) is supposed to realize within the Church God's grace in a historical and tangible way; he becomes, whilst remaining in the world, part of the manifestation of the Church to the world and necessarily shares in the Church's inward and outward mission and responsibility.

In a way, this essay anticipates Rahner's later concentration on the charismatic element. For, just as the charisma, so is the participation of the laity in the mission of the Church a free act – the choice of an individual which, however, gives him or her not only duties but sovereign rights within the Church. For this responsibility and duty freely taken upon himself, the layman's state should be protected by law – hitherto neglected by the Church. And this legal status enables the laity to partake in the apostolate of the hierarchy. Clergy and laity are advancing towards the same goal, the one with the existential commitment of his or her whole life and the other intermittently while remaining in the world.

When we, however, consider these two roles within the Church, the dividing line between them becomes blurred. In a very early essay (1936), Rahner speaks of the *consecration* of the Christian in generic terms: it includes the receiving of a power by the receiving of a commission.[83] This second aspect applies to the laity which, on account of baptism and confirmation as well as marriage, is commissioned to 'care for the soul' of his or her human neighbour. For these three are the sacraments of the laity which entail the duty and power to perform a pastoral task.[84] And these three 'lay-sacraments' also play their respective roles in this human intercommunication.

The consecrated life of the individual is a topic which Rahner reassumes after forty years, considering it now from the pragmatic point of view of the present situation in the visible Church. Whereas the 'commission' transferred to every Christian through the three 'lay-sacraments' in the 1936 essay speaks of a spiritual duty, Rahner now regards it on the lines of his, well-known, supernatural existential: ' . . . a consecratedness, a sacrality, of man, present in advance as the condition of possibility of any ecclesial-cultic consecration', is already presupposed when a person is located 'in the public-sociological area of the Church',[85] in other words: when that person is ordained or officially commissioned by Church authority.

Owing to baptism there is, therefore, a 'consecratedness' previous to this commissioning. Whilst baptism 'locates' the person in the social context of the Church, the interior power of the sacrament means the free acceptance of the objective sanctification in the world and mankind. The three lay-sacraments, as mentioned above, give a status to their recipient in the sociological dimension of the Church, even if that person is subjectively not sanctified. And in this analogous sense they can be called sacraments of consecration.

> What really happens in such a sacrament of consecration is the historical manifestation and the sociologically concretizing specification in the dimension of the visible Church of holiness and consecratedness which has always existed inescapably in that person in the form of an offer in virtue of God's salvific will.[86]

The priestly ordination or the commissioning of a person by the authority of the Church means not a higher grade of holiness, but solely his or her allocation 'in the dimension of the sacramental sociological reality of the Church.' The priestly ministry is not an additional task undertaken as supplementary to one's being a Christian, but a *specific* way of being a Christian.

From this – to my mind, revolutionary – approach, there arise a number of contemporary problems as regards the ministry of laymen and laywomen as well as of the ordained clergy. In the pastoral care of the faithful there have emerged new forms of apostolate and, corresponding to these, new forms of participation in the Church's mission in the world. The first, Rahner touches only by the way. If the ministerial priesthood is only the way a person lives out his basic 'consecratedness', then priesthood *for a time* seems not altogether out of the question.[87] Furthermore, apart from the priesthood and the renewed form of diaconate in the Church (to which I shall presently turn), there are pastoral ministries which do not presuppose any sacramental consecration but rely 'solely' on the commissioning of the Church. There are laymen and laywomen who, by the appointment or tacit agreement of the Church, undertake essential functions and thereby participate in her work. Rahner thinks first and foremost of lay pastoral assistants who, given the shortage of ordained ministry, are serving the faithful: they can hold community leadership, they administer, with the exception of Eucharist and penance, the sacraments, they preach the word of God, and so on – yet they are sacramentally not ordained. What is their position in the Church? Should they be ordained and thus sacramentally recognized for what they actually accomplish?

Rahner leaves this question open, but reverts to it within a year. First, he turns to the function of ordained deacons who are not merely auxiliary workers alongside the priest in the parish, but 'have their task and function *a priori* different from the ordained priest' in the apostolate of the Church. More difficult is attempting to define the function of pastoral assistants who, according to a statement of the German hierarchy, are not to be confused with the priest. Most of them are – at least in the case of the German-speaking world – academically well trained, are commissioned sometime even to the leadership of an (often priestless) community, and *de facto* fulfil the function of a priest (apart from administering some of the sacraments). Their 'different' existence from the priesthood and diaconate poses a difficult dilemma within the organization of the Church. Either we regard the ordained priest as merely a 'cultic functionary' (that is, restricted to the administration of the main sacraments), which is unacceptable in view of Vatican II, or we acknowledge, as regards the permanent commission, the service of pastoral assistants as a sacramental reality.[88] One cannot argue here that the permanent nature of priestly celibacy is the only mark that distinguishes the priesthood from the office of pastoral assistants. The insistence on this distinction alone would be – to quote Rahner – a 'schizophrenia' through which the Church would be 'involved in a tacit Protestantization . . . merely because of the desire to link priesthood with . . . celibacy.'[89]

Rahner, however, does not seem to suggest a formal or implicit sacramental ordination for lay leaders of Christian communities. He is satisfied to say that there is wider scope for sharing in the one sacramental office of sanctification within the Church. The forms of participation in this one and only office in the Church could have much more variety than textbook theology has ever recognized.[90] The question is how we define the relationship of sacramental ordination and the tasks entrusted to the ministry, in which laymen and laywomen take part. If the tasks are defined from the sacramental ordination alone then we have to restrict these to the power to preside over the Eucharist and administer penance. If we proceed the other way round, by defining the office from the various tasks, as the trend is today, then the mentioned sacramental powers could be extended to a lay leadership of a Christian community with all the functions it involves. Since these tasks 'cannot really belong exclusively to any single individual',[91] could they not be divided within a group of pastors? In this group, laymen as well as laywomen could share part of the sacramental power of a formally ordained priest.

This approach, therefore, is not exclusive to the male sex. In fact, Rahner in 1964 seems to have anticipated a problem about the position of women in the Church which became cogent in the 1980s. In a rather long-winded paper he raises his voice against the exclusive supremacy of men in the moulding of the Church's life:

> When the Church speaks of the position and the task of the layman in the Church . . . she must apply equal standards to men and women in real fact and not simply by paying lip-service to the principle of equality between them.[92]

This is necessary when, on account of the changing situation of the Church in the contemporary world and its social order, unexpected possibilities for the lay apostolate emerge. Considered as tasks of Christian existence, the differences of sex are irrelevant. All the more is this requirement suggested by the dearth of ordained priests. And if men can be called to share the apostolate which, as a rule, previously belonged to the hierarchy, then women cannot be excluded. In which form this female participation is to be shaped, is not to be decreed by the clergy or by the lay half of the Church, including women.[93] In 1964, when facing a female audience, Rahner avoids the crucial question of ordination of women and advises patience.[94] This call for patience is still maintained in 1977 when he criticises the arguments put forward by Paul VI against the possible ordination of women to the priesthood. None of the officially proposed arguments seem to set the seal on the (presumably only human) tradition excluding women from the priesthood.[95] The discussion must go on.

Rahner's preoccupation with the layman and laywoman in the Church leads him to a reassessment of the structures of the Church to come. Already in the *Handbook* he opts for a Church whose members are Christians by choice and not by custom. With this he plays down the importance of a popular Catholicism (*die Volkskirche*) which, in predominantly Catholic countries of Western Europe, has played an important role. In a rather long contribution about the position of religion and the Church in modern society in the second volume of the *Handbook*, produced with N. Greinacher, the authors define this concept:

> [By *Volkskirche*] we mean the reality in which a nation [*Volk*] and Church, Imperium and ecclesia, were to all practical purposes one and the same. Whoever was born in a certain nation was automatically a member of the Church. . . . One cannot seriously doubt that the end of this 'Volkskirche' is at hand.[96]

This statement does not in any sense invalidate the basic role of the Church in society. On the contrary, she can be much more the sacramental sign in the world when her congregations are made up of members who have joined her out of personal conviction.[97] The opposition of *Volkskirche* and *Glaubens*, or *Gemeindekirche*, is a topic to which Rahner frequently returns. It is indeed a theme with which he introduces his 'Position of Woman' in 1964: in contrast to the Church of ordinary people (*Volkskirche*), in which some strive to maintain her past form at any costs, she will become the Church of 'those who believe as a matter of individual and personal responsibility.'[98] It is from this stance that the later Rahner manifests a growing interest in basic communities as new structures emerging from the present situation of the Church.

In the last years of his life, Rahner published a number of short articles in the —in a way avant-garde – periodical *Entschluss* in Vienna. Most of its readers are young Christian laymen and laywomen in search of new forms of ecclesial identity. Their fascination with the South American Church and its small communities prompted Rahner to face the problem: is the South American experiment, if not in its social programme, then in its inner organization, a viable pattern for the European Churches? In a 1981 article[99] Rahner tries to reflect upon this phenomenon and agrees to the necessity for basic communities within the traditional framework of the parish. These associations have always existed in a certain form in the European Churches, however much they assimilated themselves to the rather bureaucratic shape of the established Church.

The proliferation of South American basic communities is regarded by Rahner much more as a challenge for Europe than a paradigm to be copied: one cannot import them as they are, but their example can inspire similar experiments. In this article, however, Rahner is more cautious than encouraging. One can feel a certain fear of sectarianism 'which severs its links with the sacramental and priestly Church with episcopal supervision and administration.' Although he sympathizes with the present-day yearning for a more intensive communion among Christians exceeding that of the old-style parishes, he cannot give a positive answer to the dilemma: Should European basic communities be started for specific activities, as in South America, or are they to become just a personal fellowship of praying and believing Christians without any determined task? In the first case these communities will soon fall back to a parish-like organization and in the second they might be exposed to sectarianism. Nonetheless, Rahner appreciates the aim for such communities which, according to another similar contribution, can form the future shape of the Church.

Again, writing in *Entschluss*, Rahner tries to underline the necessity for basic communities from the diaspora situation of the modern Church. A brief statistical survey of the European Churches today leads him to the conclusion:

> We are going to have communities made up from a small minority of people, since it is by no way foreseeable that European secularisation would be in foreseeable time converted to a practising Christianity. In other words we are going to have small congregations with few priests.[100]

Nevertheless, he can envisage these small communities as oases in a non-Christian world, to which they bear witness of salvation already granted to the world. In this sense they should be missionary communities representing the message of the basic sacrament, which is the Church. Their missionary witness should be the communication of their joy and happiness within the world and their presence within the Church should prepare the necessary development of ecclesiastical structures. In these, the role of a priest will certainly be different and so, too, the relationship of laymen and laywomen to the priesthood. It is important that in these basic communities everybody should have his or her own task according to the charisma of the individuals themselves. Their leaders will not necessarily be the priest, or the best-living Christians – apart from the ordained ministry, they can be led by 'priests for a time', by a deacon or other persons appointed to this task (where, of course, women are not to be exceptions!).

This future shape of new communities should not militate against the permanent hierarchical principle within the Church: the threefold division of deacons, priests and bishops – although in a different sense – can remain, even if their function in relation to other ministries should be redefined. These tasks towards the world and towards the inner structure of the Church are the responsibility of basic communities as well as their individual members. In short, we have anticipated Rahner's dream of a future Church in which her divinely founded hierarchical structure will have to come to its own.

(B) *The sense and meaning of the hierarchy*

These last references were taken from the occasional writings of the ageing theologian. In them Rahner, while maintaining the hierarchical structure of the Church founded by Jesus Christ, builds it up as it were from below: from the individual lay member and communities to the official functionaries. This view of the Church is not due to a more recent insight: it was basically operative from the 1960s, during and after Vatican II. There is, however, another approach to the structures of the Church which could be termed 'from above'. It starts from the general idea of the Church.

In a rather rambling paper, given in Freiburg-im-Breisgau on the occasion of the sixtieth anniversary of the Bishop of Freiburg, Rahner does exactly this.[101] He tries to sum up his whole concept of the Church which allegedly implies her hierarchical structure. In doing so he avoids entering into discussion about the pre-Easter founding of the Church with her hierarchical basic constitution (*Verfassung*): it is simply presupposed that the present Church is in continuity with the Church of apostolic times. His choice is more fundamental and he begins, so to speak, with Adam and Eve: with the mystery of creation itself. For it is in creation that the immediacy of man's relationship to God is manifest with no need for a hierarchical mediation. It starts from a state in which there was no necessity for priesthood.[102] Without trying to translate Rahner's hymnal rendering of the mystery of creation, his argument is otherwise well known: the created world is God's daring self-communication, his ecstatic love for the creature different from himself. It aims at the free history of man's created spirit to the point where, in Jesus Christ, God's irrevocable acceptance (*Zusage*) of the world will be manifest and received by his creature. This can happen anywhere and in any individual in the world – without the mediation of the Church. Grace and salvation are free and not bound to ecclesiastical structures.

Nonetheless, within this dynamic unity of the world with its creative source, there arises a community whose task is to witness to the eschatological victory of Jesus Christ, the salvation of the world which has already taken place. This is the purpose and meaning of this community that is the Church. Now, in order to fulfil this task, the Church should be one and live in a coherent order; the community should learn to know her own testimony to Christ in depths, should proclaim it to the whole world whose salvation is the object of her witness. It is in this context that one can meaningfully speak of a hierarchy, of the ministry of the Church. Also, regarded as an earthly society, the hierarchical ministers are the authoritative guards (*Träger*) of this common witness and warrants of its unity.[103] Otherwise this society is not a workable unit and the Church is not viable. Speaking of the hierarchy in this sociological context, Rahner seems to regard it as a natural and human consequence of the Church's societal constitution. That it is so willed by its founder is presupposed. There is a mutual need for complementarity between the ordinary members and their ministry. On their own they have no meaning.

This almost naturalistic approach to the need for a hierarchy is further illustrated by a later remark in the paper. Speaking of the limits of the ministry, Rahner compares the Church to a chess club in which not always the best chess player is its chairman. His functions are defined by the members: thus the sense and meaning of the hierarchy depends on the societal organization and structures of the Church. So far the analogy of the club is correct. The difference comes from the sense and meaning of the task itself which the Church has to perform. He distinguishes between the meaning of a hierarchical structure (as regards the purpose of a society) and the hierarchical organization of the same.[104] When this difference is ignored the ground is laid for an anti-clerical feeling in the faithful and its contrary, an anti-lay sentiment in the ministry. Therefore, in order to assert this sense and meaning of the hierarchy as essentially different from a merely human grouping, Rahner has to redefine the task of the Church. It is the message which the Church has to proclaim to the world.

In doing this Rahner goes back to its first condition of possibility: the mystery of the Trinity, the essential and ecumenical ground of salvation history.[105] I shall first try to render his systematic approach by the sketch below of the notions used and their connections.

GOD					hierarchy
Father *generation*	communicated	FAITH	teaching office, i.e. Magisterium		
Son *spiration*	accepted	HOPE	leadership: pastoral 'power'		
Holy Ghost	witnessed to world	LOVE	sanctification: sacramental power		
(1)	(2)	(3)	(4)		

The two Trinitarian processions (1) retain their distinctiveness in God's self-communication to the world (2). The first corresponds to the manifestation of divine truth through the Logos made flesh, whereas the second is the power of grace by means of which this latter is received by the world. This acceptance is existentially embodied in the 'divine virtues' of faith, hope and charity (3) and practised in its communitarian aspect under the guidance of the threefold power of the hierarchy (4).

It describes the historical process of a victory initiated by a divine offer made in Jesus Christ and its acceptance by the world in the power of the Spirit. It is aimed at faith, hope and charity, of which the community is a free witness. This threefoldness of the witness at the same time defines the functions of hierarchical powers. The Magisterium is the depository of revealed faith and its truth; the pastoral power is the guidance of putting this faith into action (*das Tun des Glaubens*); in hope within the still ongoing history of salvation and through the ministry of sacramental grace, the individual member is drawn into a love-union with God who has once for all communicated himself to human history.

Thus, though the hierarchy corresponds to the natural need of a human association, at the same time it is to be regarded as a living instrument in God's self-communication in grace to the world. That there is a hierarchy in the Church follows not only from below but, being assumed into God's design for man's history, also as it were, from above.

To avoid, however, any appearance of sacralizing a certain class within the Church, Rahner hastens to point out the limitations of its power. These limits apply not only to the Church as a human society: they are theological (*theologische Wesensgrenzen*[106]) and built into her historical nature, subject to change and development. We have already seen these essential limitations of hierarchical powers: they are today not necessarily bound to social prestige as in the times of the *Volkskirche*; they function as service and assistance (*dienende Funktion*); they 'manage' the Church alongside the charismatic groups and individuals and should be aware that their ministerial power is by no means proportionate to their personal nearness to God's grace. In other words, the hierarchy is not identical with the free and charismatic Church. Hence, the ministry should beware of the danger of institutionalism, of a practice performed by routine, of ambition for power, of legalism – in short, of the evils of human religiosity. The function of the hierarchy is *de facto* only regulative and not creative as regards the community in which God's grace works. The task of the ministry is, rather, to draw the boundaries and assure room for charismatic freedom. For they are not representatives of Christ in such a way that the work of the Holy Ghost only operates according to their devices; in following God's will in their conscience, Church members can act even when no starting signal is given by the hierarchy – and their action is not always furthered by the ministry. Certainly, there is a necessary obedience in the Church. It is, however, only genuine when the charismatic freedom of the individual is respected. Where there is freedom in the Church, there is room for justifiable criticism.

The genuine practice of freedom, however, is only legitimate when it has learned to obey and is at the same time self-critical. Briefly: it is more in the action of individual Church members, where God's grace is continually operating, than in obedience to the leadership of the ministry. It is on the level of the individual Church member that salvation is directly received (*Heilsvollzug* or *Heilsprozess*) whereas obedience to hierarchy is salvation through mediation, through word and sacrament (*Heilsvermittlung*).[107]

These two aspects are central in Rahner's writings on the Church. On the one hand, *Heilsvollzug* is due to God's immediate presence to the soul in the shape of the Holy Ghost, whilst *Heilsvermittlung* happens in the historical concreteness of the Church. Though really distinct, one is implied by the other: salvation works 'ministerially' or 'instrumentally' – or to put it another way, through an 'exhibitive' word or sign by the ministers of the Church.[108] The sense and meaning of the hierarchy is thus defined by the concreteness of the historical Church and her structures.

Reading 'Hierarchy' gives the impression that a Church without a hierarchical ministry is not viable. However, examination of the role of the hierarchy reveals that it is marginal in its historical contingency. The statement that the hierarchical structure is inseparable from salvation can be the primary experience of those actively engaged in the Church. Its marginality, on the other hand, might appeal to those whom Rahner called 'marginal' Christians, or to men and women outside the fold of Christian communities. Indeed, Rahner's concern about the various sorts of ministries could underscore the first aspect: the experience of the

Church is bound to her hierarchical structure irrevocably willed by her founder, Jesus the Christ.

3.3 The Organs of the Church

The Church is not only a communion (*Gemeinschaft*) of those who believe in the event of Jesus Christus and its historical permanence, but also a visible society (*Gesellschaft*). It is also believed that the whole Church (at least as a society) is 'hierarchical' in her visible structures. In the common usage, however, *hierarchy* itself refers to the top of the pyramid – that is, to the *sacred ministry*. To remain with the same image: the top as well as the *bottom* are composed of various institutional units of which we have already seen the laity in its stratification. In order to avoid the 'privileged' use of the hierarchy, I shall term institutions on the top of the pyramid *organs of the Church*.

I shall look first at the institutional units which can be subsumed under the term of 'sacred ministry' (or 'office') within the Church. It is sacred insofar as persons belonging to it are sacramentally ordained; it is a ministry, a *Dienst* with its tasks and duties, an office, an *Amt*, with inalienable rights and powers. The diaconate, the priesthood and the office of a bishop should be the basic articulation of leadership within the Church, whereas the office of the Pope, as I shall discuss, is not the fourth 'unit' in this organization – it should be seen in collegial unity with the bishops, however much is attributed to his leadership. Granted, the office of the Pope is surrounded by further administrative organs, but these, strictly speaking, do not belong to the sacred ministry even if their exponents happen to be ordained. They assist the Pope in the exercise of his tasks. Of these, I shall discuss the teaching office. The Church under this aspect will be referred to as the Magisterium.

3.3.1 The sacred Ministry

In the late 1960s, Rahner was to become preoccupied with the 'identity crisis' of the ordained clergy arising, apparently, from the new image of the Church in Vatican II. This is why he repeatedly tackled the question of the nature of the priesthood and revised his former view about the diaconate, as revived by the Council itself.

(A) *The priesthood and the diaconate*

The root of this crisis is the waning awareness amongst sacramentally ordained individuals of the specific character of their office and the proper field of their ministry. It is not clear what deacons and priests are in themselves and how their status and their function differ from that of the laity and other functionaries of the Church. No doubt the enormous social changes of our modern age can explain a great deal: with the loss of the *Volkskirche* in largely secularized national states, deacons and priests have difficulty deciding to which level of society they belong and what in the circumstances is demanded from them. The Council, too, with its emphasis on the general priesthood of all baptized, with its encouraging practices similar to contemporary democracies, was not exactly buttressing the old image of the clergy. They find themselves in search of a new image or even challenged to re-define their own identity as ordained ministers.

Thus, it is no wonder that Karl Rahner gives no less than five lectures in 1968 and 1969 (and later publishes them) on the same topic.[109] In view of his approach to the laity, which we have just seen, it is no wonder that in these lectures he finds it hard to put deacons and priests in their proper place. Nor should one assume that this uncertainty in Rahner's thought is recently induced by the Council alone. Its seeds lie in his initial concept of the Church as, already in 1942, explicitly applied to priestly existence.[110]

However, in 'Priestly Existence' (1942), Rahner was not much interested in the priesthood as an institution belonging to the visible structures of the Church and addressed himself to the problems of individual ministers as to the nature of their own priesthood. He certainly excludes the view that the priesthood is just another profession within the framework of society. As he will later say:

> For at least fifteen hundred years, and since the much criticised Constantine era, the institution and function of the priest in the

church have also come to be regarded as a profession . . . like any other profession . . . [and it] had been fitted almost without any friction into the structure of secular society by the *corpus christianorum*. . . . The priest has had a function in human society which has been recognized and valued by that society itself. It has been taken for granted that the divine calling to the priesthood is at the same time an earthly profession.[111]

But once this social status had been duly lost (for 'there is nothing in the nature of the priesthood itself which makes this necessary') priests could appeal to the cultic powers communicated to them in the *character indelebilis* by their ordination. Furthermore, they could point out that they are the official emissaries to whom preaching the authoritative word of the gospel, the administration of the Eucharist and penance are exclusively entrusted. They could regard themselves as unique mediators between God and man, and authorized leaders of Christian communities. They could have recourse to the word of revelation which seems to suggest a hierarchical order within the Church, consisting of deacons, presbyters and bishops. They could emphasize the sacral and spiritual manner of their life (as for instance, celibacy) which separates them from ordinary Christians. There are apparently many grounds on which the priest should not waver about his self-identity.

But Rahner wants none of these as the point of departure in defining the nature of the priesthood. Although his position in his 1942 article is still couched in traditional terminology, some basic options in approaching the nature of Christianity and hence that of the priesthood are already specifically 'Rahnerian'. One of these is his approach to the Church, which we know from his 'Membership'. In order to define ministerial priesthood he presupposes that which I called 'transcendental' Church: for 'every man lives necessarily in an order of existence which includes the reality of Christ'; the order of human history to which Christ belongs is already 'Church' – in inverted commas as Rahner puts it here.[112] With this idea of the 'Church' in the background he points to the essential change in the conception of the priesthood in the New Testament as distinct from other religions.

Priesthood in general used to comprise two functions: first, the cultic-priestly one which by sacrifice and prayer establishes a relationship between man, his society and God and, secondly, the prophetic announcing and making visible the word of God to man.

These two functions are fundamentally changed in the dispensation of the New Testament. Indeed, the basis of the Christian faith is the fact that it is not man who tries to get into contact with the Divine but rather vice versa: God in Jesus Christ 'has offered the absolute and final sacrifice which fundamentally redeemed mankind'.[113]

In order to point out the characteristic of ministerial (or official) priesthood, Rahner starts his rather complex argument with this changed situation. It is due to the 'eschatological' nature of the Christian message which enables every believer to become a sacramental *sign* of this already achieved salvation.[114] As in the sacraments, however, to be a 'sign' of salvation is only then efficacious if it is accompanied by the supervening word of a message to be announced. In the new dispensation it is God who posits the sign in the incarnate Christ and it is Christ's words and message which, heard by mankind, let the hearers share in salvation.[115] Now, to be the sign and to announce salvation sums up the general *notion* of the priesthood in Christianity. Primarily it is realized in Christ himself in whom salvation is once-for-all (that is, eschatologically) fulfilled and subsequently in the 'Church' (in inverted commas!) whose every member shares the priesthood of Christ. Their participation, however, in Christ's priestly power is only 'subservient' (that is, secondary) on two counts: it is dependent on Christ's priestly function *and* on the priesthood of the Church and her members:

> The priesthood of the official priest is . . . purely a ministerial one both in relation to the active existential priesthood of Christ, and to the passive existential priesthood of the faithful, insofar as it makes a permanent sacramental presence possible.[116]

Thus, in 1942, Rahner anticipates the teaching of Vatican II about the universal priesthood of all the faithful.

From this follows that priests are not 'mediators' in the sense of initiating an action as 'middle persons' between God and man 'as though previously there had been a chasm which they are now for the first time bridging.'[117] Their priestly function is of that class of effective signs which primarily belongs to the whole Church. Later, in 1969, writing now on the official priesthood, Rahner puts the same point more lucidly: the function of the priest is but a manifestation of an already existing grace-given relationship of man to God which is granted 'without any mediation on the part of official priesthood.'[118]

Thus, the nature of the universal priesthood of all the faithful can be regarded as *cultic* (insofar as every believer *is* a potential sign of salvation) and *prophetic* (because they have the duty of proclaiming salvation). The 'official' priest is no exception. This statement stands even as regards the teaching of the Council of Trent, according to which the priest's proper function has something to do with the sacrifice of Christ in the Eucharistic celebration.[119] Rahner does not seem to be satisfied with this exclusive characteristic for ministerial priesthood: although 'the official priest makes [Christ's once fulfilled sacrifice] present . . . as the sacrifice of the *Church*, he dispenses [however] the grace which *belongs from the first not to him but to them*.'[120] From this it is also understandable 'that the universal priesthood of all the faithful [as a sign] is *anterior* to the official priesthood and not merely its reflection.'[121] Something similar can be said about the prophetic function associated with the cultic nature of the priesthood. Because in the message of Jesus the prophecy of the Old Testament is fulfilled, the prophetic function in the New Testament consists in pronouncing the good news of salvation 'ministerially', that is, on behalf of Christ and the Church. Rahner borrows here the biblical usage distinguishing between the genuine prophet and the 'son of the prophet' who repeats, continues, the preaching of his predecessor. Christ the true and last prophet does not speak *about* the word of God, but in his words the saving word of God makes contact with mankind. The words of the priest (that is, the prophet's son) do not materially contain anything not said by his predecessor (it is its continuation), and the audience to which he speaks 'already inhabits that order of reality which is announced by the message' of *the* prophet. What he effects is not the divine word's first intervention in the human order, but rather a *growth* aimed at supernatural faith.[122]

Therefore, the two functions, the cultic and the prophetic, cannot define the nature of ministerial priesthood: invested in the same person both are derivative from the unique deed of Christ and from the universal priesthood of the members of the 'Church'.

Nor can the specific nature of the ministerial priesthood be explained by an appeal to its *character indelebilis*, the firm teaching of the Council of Trent reasserting an ancient tradition.[123] By means of this quasi-ontological mark of the ordained, one has tried to sustain the exclusive self-identity of ministerial priesthood.

For Rahner, however, this appeal to the 'indelible spiritual mark' is nothing but a 'formal generalisation [which] will yield nothing useful for the answering of our question' about the priest's identity.[124] Thus, in this early article, he tries to reinterpret what is for him a much over-valued proposition.[125] Rahner's aim is rather to demonstrate the specific nature of the ministerial priesthood from the existential significance of the priest's total involvement in the activities for which he was ordained. As I mentioned above, these activities are partaking in Christ's primary priesthood, as both cultic and prophetic. Rahner's question now becomes: Which of these can yield the *existential meaning* he is to stress in place of the *character indelebilis*?[126]

Contrary to the traditional view, Rahner does not try to deduce this deeper existential meaning from the priest's cultic power and function (that is, from the administration of the sacraments). Although this power and function is received through the sacrament of ordination, it is only partly an official authorization. That same sacrament also confers grace, a 'disposition of the person in his innermost existential kernel towards God and his own salvation.' Although the authorization and grace conferred involve two different qualities, both are conferred in an 'inseparable union'. The power and official authorization connote the formal possibility of a man as 'a public person exercising a specific activity directed to the community'; grace, on the contrary, is 'the disposition of a person in his innermost kernel towards God and salvation.'[127] Both qualities, Rahner affirms, affect, although differently, the 'existential kernel of the person concerned'. Grace conferred by the sacrament (in unity with the official authorization) supports the 'vocation' of the ordained as a 'sign', that of acting as a priest, just as the the so-called other 'vocational' sacraments do. The cultic power, therefore, is no different from that of the other 'vocational sacraments', like baptism, confirmation and marriage. There are, in all of these 'lay sacraments', cultic actions which 'signify' the increase of sanctifying grace. If the official priesthood is to have its own particular grace, it will be basically of the same kind as the grace signified by these same 'lay sacraments'. However,

> . . . if a priest enters into the meaning of his cultic activity, then he assumes in fact that existential attitude which is proper to the *universal* existential priesthood [of the faithful]. [Hence:] The cultic power of the priest . . . is a new obligation to bring to development the old 'vocation' given by baptism and confirmation; not a new obligation to a new vocation of existential import previously possessed.[128]

In other words, we cannot deduce from the cultic power of ordination alone that exclusively specific involvement proper to the priest. Rahner illustrates this fact by comparing the existential presence of Christ's sacrifice in both lay and ordained members at one and the same Mass: the result of the priest's positing this sacramental sign is exactly the same as that of 'ordinary' Christians entering into the grace-giving celebration of the Eucharist.

Concerning, however, the prophetic function of the priest, Rahner is now in a position to propose an existential attitude specific to priestly existence. He asks, firstly: Can the preaching of the Word of God really involve the whole person? His answer is affirmative: the Word announced in public requires an inner commitment of faith not only by the priest, but also by any Christian who ought to live by of this Word. This kind of preaching is not yet exclusive to the ordained minister: it can be regarded as the 'existential significance of the apostolic element'[129] shared by all the faithful. In the case of the priest, however, it is a sacramental activity derived from the grace of ordination, a supernatural power capable of efficiently communicating the message that the word contains.[130] The ordained preacher announces the word in a new way: he is not only addressed by the word of God, but also 'authorised', is 'sent' through the apostolic succession to utter God's word. He, the priest, unlike persons in lay-apostolate, does not bear witness to his own Christian life as such 'but he speaks the word of Christ itself'. Whereas the preaching of lay people is determined by their own situation in the world, the official priestly emissary witnesses immediately to Christ. And this is the new existential significance of his priesthood.[131] This conviction remains Rahner's own in 1969, when he sums up the very essence of the priesthood:

> . . . proclaiming of the word and dispensing of the sacrament . . . spring from a single common root and are ultimately one in nature. [Thus:] The priest is the proclaimer of the word of God, officially commissioned and appointed as such by the Church as a whole in such a way that this word is entrusted to him in the supreme degree of sacramental intensity inherent in it.[132]

Whether this rather tortuous argument for the specific nature of the priesthood in Rahner's early (1942) essay is an apt reinterpretation of the *character indelebilis* or rather a skilful substitution for it, is anybody's judgement. I do not believe, indeed, that it can help the waning self-identity of some of the ordained clergy at which it was aimed. It tends to serve, in fact, the later development of a priestly image, the outcome of which we begin to sense among committed lay people. Distinguishing the specific nature of the priesthood from its cultic activity opens new possibilities in the interpretation of priestly office, something that Rahner himself was to point out in later considerations about the priesthood.

The exclusive right to celebrate the Eucharist (along with penance and the anointing of the sick) was based on the connection between the priestly character and cultic activity. If, however, and according to Rahner, the sacramental grace conferred by the so-called 'lay-sacraments' is on the same level as the priest's cultic power, is it conceivable that a baptised Christian could celebrate a Mass? To my knowledge, he never puts this question in so many words, but insists, nonetheless, that this exclusivity is not implied in the priest's cultic activity. We can argue from the New Testament only for the specific nature of the official priesthood as the 'function of official *leadership* of a Christian Community', whereas the exclusive power to celebrate 'has, *at least in normal cases*, been reserved to the priesthood'.[133] The apostolic Church so initiated it and as such it is *jure divino* which, as we have previously noted, can be modified in concrete practice, owing to changing historical circumstances.

There is an advance certainly in 'Priestly Ministry' beyond that of the 1942 article. After Vatican II, leadership is emphasized as the main effect of ordination instead of the prophetic power of preaching. What is more, Rahner's essays of 1968/69 acknowledge that, although the biblical triad of deacons, presbyters and bishops lays the foundations of a hierarchical structure in the Church as a society, the concrete division of these offices are blurred, or at least uncertain. This is why the medieval Church could extend these grades, as it were, downwards: it recognizes other ministries apart from the biblical triad. Trent, even, speaks of, subdeacons, doorkeepers and exorcists who belong to the organs of the Church, while Vatican II does not even mention them. This shows that the single 'office' of the Church allows for a far greater variation and modification among the official posts than we are accustomed to nowadays. This single 'office' in its inner division is 'far more elastic, flexible and fluid' than has been realized in the last few centuries.[134]

Priestly office, therefore, may assume ever-changing variations in the social structure of the Church. Indeed, Rahner suggests in 'Priestly Ministry', 'Priesthood' and especially in 'Priestly Image' a number of variants always, however, keeping in sight the permanent nature of this office. Against those who still stick desperately to traditional forms he points to the sociological changes which now affect and once did affect this institution in the course of history. The changing image of the Church necessarily modifies this institution, and assigns new tasks to the priest beyond his cultic and prophetic function.[135] Therefore,

> . . . we only safeguard the abiding essence of the priesthood when we maintain an attitude of freedom and openness towards change in the external forms and when this is demanded by the situation of the Church today and in the future.[136]

Rahner's *desiderata* for the present and future priestly office comprise a scale of suggestions, which are dispersed in his writings of 1988/89. I shall only mention a few without giving exact references to them: they are more than repetitive in these essays.

Whereas in 1942 he required total commitment concerning the preaching of the word of God, he advocates, more recently, the case of highly-specialized priests working even outside the traditional parish, for instance for a smaller portion of the people of God, as schoolmasters and social workers do. There could be priests who exercise their ministry 'part time' or alongside other secular occupations. Though he insists on the commissioning of priests by higher authority, he can envisage priests selected from within the community. At some future time there can be married *viri probati*, or even ordained permanent deacons raised to the priesthood. There will be a need to reintegrate laicised, married priests and so on. Rahner seems to regard these newly institutionalised forms as compatible with the very essence of the priesthood, and he holds that these possible changes need not be imposed on the Church through a shortage of priests, but as 'something that has positive opportunities and advantages' for the Church. The condition is that the priest who finds his 'new' office outside the customary image should not regard his position as a hobby, 'either in the concrete existence of the individual, or in a theological sense'.[137] The self-identity of future priests is still, as in 'Priestly Existence', the existential commitment to his activities. Rahner is now ready to settle the matter of *character indelebilis* with a short sentence: ' . . . for this doctrine [of Trent], on a precise view, is concerned merely with the impossibility of ordination being repeated.'[138]

It will be one of my tasks in 'Comments and Questions' to assess the practical consequences of these Rahnerian suggestions and point out the reasons for an apparently changed theological attitude to the priesthood. My attempt to sum up may leave a feeling of uncertainty, not so much concerning the nature of this institution but rather as regards the viability of its anticipated shape.

An element of uncertainty is also noticeable in Rahner's cherished project of revitalizing the institution of the *diaconate*. Together with H. Vorgrimler, he advocated the case of the diaconate before the Council and was involved in its implementation. This office in the recent history of the Western Church was *de facto* regarded as a step of an ordinand approaching the priesthood. Now Vatican II argues in three instances for the restoration of the office in its own right.[139]

In 1965 Rahner added some theological reflections to commentaries already existing on these Council texts.[140] The essential point in these decrees is the firm reaffirmation of the institution of the permanent diaconate and its sacramental character. According to Rahner, the reason why this topic gained special attention in the Council is the simple fact that it comprises functions already performed within the Church, and especially in missionary lands, which belong to the essential tasks of the Church:

> It seems to me to be necessary on theological grounds that grace should be conferred upon [persons] which does exist in the Church for these official functions.[141]

With these words Rahner underlines the sacramentality of the diaconate.

In 1968 he slightly alters his argument. His starting point is in viewing the different offices and functions, as listed by Vatican II and already performed by laymen (or even laywomen). These are such that they deserve to be raised to the sacramentality of the permanent diaconate. Taken in isolation, they can be conferred upon one who is not an ordained deacon.[142] How, then, can he show in the *present* situation of the Church the necessity of this permanent diaconate within the universal *diakonia* obligatory for every Christian?

To start with, there are only three essential points clearly established by tradition and taken over by Vatican II:

(i) in the laying on of hands the deacon receives his office together with powers and duties appropriate to it;
(ii) the conferring of this office has a sacramental nature; and
(iii) it should be performed in the civic publicity of the Church.[143]

With these essentials no proper functions are defined. This means that the tasks of a future diaconate can be – in accordance with the concrete demands of the local church – freely assigned.[144]

The specific function of the diaconate cannot be the formal leadership of Christian communities, except in the case when this *de facto* leadership is temporarily taken over by an ordained deacon in a community without a priest. Neither is the deacon a

mediator between clergy and layfolk. His official function cannot
be deduced from specific cultic powers, even though he baptizes,
performs Christian burial, gives communion, and so on. Nor can
the deacon, Rahner continues, preside at the Eucharistic liturgy
which is, after all, proper to the priestly office (although a deacon
actively taking part in the Eucharistic celebration can witness to
the unity of a community).[145] After these negative demarcations,
Rahner's positive suggestions are surprising. According to him,
from the religious and social point of view, mankind is today in a
state of disintegration. Hence the central task of Christian ministry is the 'building up' of communion 'by integrating man into
the civic and ecclesiastical community.'

The contemporary deacon's assignment is needed within this
task. It cannot be fulfilled

> unless those charged with it have specialized formation of the
> most varied kind at their command, such as bishops and priests
> cannot possess. It is this position, therefore, that makes it neces-
> sary to have the diaconate as a special official institution.[146]

What Rahner really understands by this task is not quite clear. At
first sight, he expects future deacons to be social workers of a
special kind – something which he already envisaged in 1967.[147]
Though he is right that this integration is a human need, it is hard
to show why it requires an ordained ministry. As subsequent
practice up to date reveals, laymen and laywomen, and not
recently ordained deacons, are more apt to fulfil this requirement.
Nevertheless, he is right that future deacons can neither be mini-
priests nor all-rounders in their ministry, but ought to be
specialists who are ready permanently to engage themselves in
and put into practice the spirit of fraternity within the Church.
The ordained deacon's work should symbolize the much desired
unity of mankind.

Many of Rahner's suggestions are concerned with the priesthood and diaconate, such as their collaboration among
themselves and with the 'ordinary' faithful. Their assistance as a
hierarchical body to the bishops belong to Rahner's dream of a
future Church regarding which, as we shall see, his predictions
have only partially been fulfilled. For the oneness of pastoral and

sacramental office in the Church cannot be conceived without their unity, without the bishops and their collegiality. This symbolic function indeed must have been envisaged for the future situation of the Church, as it seems the number of ordained priests can further diminish and the remaining ministers will be engaged in the leaderships of several Christian communities. In each local or professional gathering there should be a focal point where sacramentally ordained persons (even without a special task) can sum up the unity of the faithful. This symbolic centre is the deacon or eventually the deaconess.

(B) *The bishops and their college*

It is Rahner's firm conviction that the Church as founded by Jesus Christ is a hierarchical institution. The communion of the faithful is hierarchically organized: there is an ascending line of officials from the ordained deacons up to the local bishops, while bishops all over the world constitute a college under their head who happens to be the Bishop of Rome.

As we have seen with the priestly office, this hierarchical organ does not imply an ascendance in dignity or in the value of the individual's faith. It stands, rather, for the service of the divine word, it is a ministry, a *Dienstamt*, with the task of making present in the world the event of mankind's salvation in Jesus the Christ. Their ministry is to teach, to lead and to sanctify or, from another point of view, to help people to realize what they already are.

Although twenty centuries of episcopal tradition in the Roman Church have hitherto been successful in fulfilling this task, there are all the same at the present time some theological questions which ought to be clarified. These can be summed up:

(i) Is the office of bishops sacramentally different from that of priests? In other words, is the consecration of bishops somehow a sacrament in its own right, distinct from priestly ordination, conferring on its candidates the grace of office?

(ii) What is the relationship of individual bishops to their fellow bishops all over the world?

(iii) Is their mission and task only for their own territory or is it related to the worldwide Church; and

(iv) Is their mission and task also related to the Roman Pontiff?

First, (i): it has not for a long time been clear whether the consecration of bishops resulted in a more intensive (or even ontological) reality different from that of sacramentally ordained priests. Medieval theology which, as is known, worked out the theory of the seven sacraments, did not, on this level see a difference between bishops and priests. Their difference came from the legal power vested in their respective offices. Technically speaking, their *potestas ordinis* was the same, yet the *potestas jurisdictionis* raised the bishops above the 'simple' priests. They were regarded as helpers of the bishops in exercising their legal powers.

In the second place, (ii): the concrete history of the Church is unimaginable without the 20 or 21 ecumenical synods or councils at which the bishops acted as a body in defining the details of Christian truth, in regulating the organs of the Church and in ruling the ethical conduct of the faithful. Yet their convening was limited to extraordinary situations, indeed mostly to times when error threatened the very essence of faith and/or to occasions when reform was needed. After a council each bishop was supposed to return to his own territory. One could hardly speak of a *permanent* institution comprising the whole body of world episcopacy outside their synodal conventions. Although the college and collegiality of bishops existed in principle, in fact it was restricted to these extraordinary situations.

Hence, (iii): it was not clear whether or not the individual bishops after a synod or council had a task and a mission to fulfil beyond the confines of their own dioceses.

Lastly, (iv): the government of the universal Church seems to have been left to the Pope and to his officials in Rome entrusted with certain aspects of her life. The gradually emerging Roman Curia under the universal power of the Pope has received a considerable share in the decision-making in the whole organization of the Church. Its officials, unless they were raised to the dignity of a cardinal along with regional heads of different dioceses, have not elected the new Pope. Yet their influence has been felt more and more. This centralization accounted for the impression that the local bishops seem to have been only executive organs of the Pope working with or through his Roman curia.

This state of affairs was, of course, not the original constitution of the visible Church. It has developed in a history which, in the early Middle Ages, acknowledged the feudal supremacy of the Roman Pontiff, and just before the dawn of the age of Columbus, asserted the Pope's universal power even over and above the assembly of bishops in an ecumenical council. The so-called *anti-conciliarism* triumphed against tendencies of regional supremacies in Europe about to divide itself into national states. This, in every respect necessary, development reached its peak at the First Vatican Council in 1870 when the traditional primacy of the Roman Pontiff and his infallible teaching authority in faith and morals became a defined doctrine of the Catholic Church. The abrupt ending of Vatican I left the Church with these doctrinal tenets, but without any further definition of the Pope's relationship to the world episcopate and to the College of Bishops. Unfinished, and in a certain sense lopsided, this arrangement lasted almost a century before it had to be revised. Among others, Rahner's theology of the Church was to be a contribution on the way towards a solution to be achieved at Vatican II. One can hardly present his approach to the episcopal office without *Lumen Gentium*. Rahner's writings on the episcopacy are either leading to the main ideas as expressly taught by the Council[148] or explaining, interpreting, the texts laboriously formulated on it. His later essays concerning the same topic are, to put it crudely, further elucidations drawing the consequences that actually (or, according to his mind, should) follow from the text of the Constitution on the Church.[149]

Since these early writings on the episcopate are mainly concerned with the relationship of bishops to the Pope's primacy, I shall discuss the details in the next section. However, the premises to this relationship is Rahner's stand on the genuinely sacramental character of the episcopal office. It is a view developed parallel to and after the Council.[150] Whether it has influenced the text of *Lumen Gentium* or was 'in the air' among theologians at the Council is an open question. The fact is that, within a couple of years, *Lumen Gentium* formulated roughly the same doctrine as that held by Rahner before the Council.

The question concerning the essence of the episcopacy was

first faced by Rahner's 'Episcopate'. He tried to approach it, on the one hand, from what seems to have been the basic constitution of the visible Church and, on the other, from the divine right (the *Jus divinum*) of the bishops on the grounds of which they are related both to 'simple' priests and to the Roman Pontiff. As to the 'constitution' of the Church, Rahner's argumentation is based on her structure, which is neither monarchic nor democratic. If the Church were a monarchy she should, as a rule, be a hereditary one – but the Pope is elected. If she was indeed a monarchy then the bishops could be regarded as subaltern officials of the Pope and the diocese an administrative district of the universal Church. In fact, none of these conclusions are true.

There is, however, a second line of argument which is more important:

> In an absolute monarchy there are no constitutional authorities beside the monarch existing independently of the monarch's will. [In the case of the elected Pope, even though he is invested with highest authority, he is all the same not an absolute ruler.] The will of the pope . . . is limited by a reality which, according to the very will of God, belongs to the constitution of the Church, namely, the Episcopate.[151]

From this it follows that the Pope cannot abolish ('at least legally', as Rahner puts it) the episcopate as such, since it is of *divine right*. Granted, it is the Pope who, in a way, empowers the bishops, but their power, by the will of Christ 'is distinct from that of the Pope (even though subject to it).' Can this state of affairs – namely, 'the universal and direct primacy of jurisdiction of the Pope,' – on the one hand, and the divine institution and indissolubility of the episcopate, on the other, be reconciled? This is the main question of present-day ecclesiology.

The solution which Rahner outlines is the already mentioned 'event' character of the Church which lives on and realizes herself again and again in an ongoing history. This characteristic of the whole Church ever renewing herself comes not only from her essentially charismatic nature, but also from her actualization in smaller units. Although the universal Church, as a society, can be regarded as one and whole, its constituents, the territorial bishoprics, the local parishes down to a Christian community celebrating the Eucharist, are not merely tiny parts of the one and universal Church, but the Church herself in her entirety. 'The Church which Christ redeemed . . . is the universal Church; but the individual community at a certain place is also the Church.'[152]

It would be odd to say this of a secular society (London is not the United Kingdom!), but it holds true of the Church, since 'in the local Church, the whole Church becomes tangible.'[153] The Old Testament idea of the 'faithful remnant' of Israel through whom divine redemption has worked, up to and after the coming of Christ, is the biblical insight buttressing his view. Rahner concludes:

> Therefore a local Church is not brought about by an atomising division of the world territory of the universal Church, but by the concentration of the Church into her own nature as an 'event'.[154]

Thus, the problematic relationship of episcopacy and primacy, between the universal and local Churches, cannot be worked out along the lines of secular societies. It is the sacramental nature of the Church which characterizes this extraordinary relationship. Just as the local Church is a concretization and actualization of the universal Church, so is the episcopate a concretization of the redeeming power entrusted to the Apostles and their successors, the bishops. Hence, one can speak of the social constitution of the Church only in a very restricted way: 'And this shows why the Church cannot have an adequate constitution.'[155] She is neither an absolute monarchy nor a representational democracy.

This sacramental approach to the problem in the background helps Rahner in pointing out, on the one hand, a certain equality between the Pope and his bishops (he is after all, the Bishop of Rome) and, on the other, the difference between consecrated bishops and ordained priests. For there is no such thing as an 'office of the Pope' sacramentally different from the bishops' consecration, but there seems to be a difference between the episcopate and the priesthood. How can this view be substantiated?

Rahner's answer is prior in time to *Lumen Gentium* and as such its argument is an *ad hoc* counterposition of the medieval view. It is, up to a point, true to say that the difference between bishops and priests cannot rely *alone* on the sacramental power (*potestas ordinis*). It is obvious that the juridical status of a bishop is other than that of a priest,[156] nonetheless it does not mean that, primarily, priests differ only by their legal power (*potestas jurisdictionis*). On the contrary, the greater legal power, as granted to the bishops *inheres* in the *potestas ordinis* conferred to them in their consecration.[157]

Now, if this 'greater' power came to the bishops at the will of the Pope alone, it would only be a human law (*jus ecclesiasticum*) which could be withdrawn at any given time. Theoretically, the Pope would then be able to withdraw from each and every bishop the power which he had granted to them and thus abolish the College of Bishops. This latter would be an untenable conclusion. Whilst Rahner admits that the Pope can depose an *individual* bishop, he could not withdraw the power of the episcopate as a *college*:

> Therefore the papal rights over the individual bishop must be exercised in such a way that the divine right of the universal episcopate as a college is not, in effect, abolished or its nature threatened.[158]

With this, Rahner has reached the notion of a collective subject of episcopal power: it is not the single bishop who acquires this right at his consecration (he can in principle be deposed by the Pope),[159] but the episcopacy as a whole. The bishop has his legal powers as member of a collective subject. This power (which is legal as well as sacramental) is granted to the college of world episcopate and as such it exists of divine right.

In arguing his case, Rahner *de facto* anticipates the doctrine of *Lumen Gentium*. Both powers are based on the analogy of the college of the apostles and their successors, the bishops. The analysis of the apostles' power in relation to the power granted to Peter will enable Rahner to draw an important conclusion as regards the Pope and the episcopacy as a whole. Here, however, it is enough to register the trend of his argument; what Christ intended to found from the outset was the college of the apostles, whose successor is the collegiate unity of bishops.[160] Now, this collective subject means a prior and primordial fact: the individual bishop has his power because he belongs to a body which is supposed to continue the task and to fulfil the scope of the apostles' college.

This laborious deduction of Rahner ending with the collegiality of bishops gained a clearer formulation at the Council. In a lengthy commentary on the third chapter of *Lumen Gentium*,[161] Rahner appreciates the significance especially of three main statements, explicitly proposed by this official document of the Church:

(i) the formulation about the existence of the College of Bishops in continuity with Vatican I's decrees on the Church;
(ii) the quasi-definition of the sacramentality of episcopal consecration as different from the ordination of priests; and
(iii) the intrinsic connection of the bishops' various offices.

Although none of these statements is new in the theology of the Church, Rahner sees in this document the ratification of his own view on the episcopate.

The Council's approach to the episcopate lends Rahner an easier way of explaining his position about the sacramentality of the episcopal office. For, as we have seen, Rahner tried to find a solution, in spite of the medieval view (the difference from priestly ordination being in the full legal power of the bishops which was granted to them through the *missio canonica* by the Pope) according to which this power is rooted in their sacramental consecration. Now, Rahner hinges his understanding on the threefold office of Jesus Christ, the high priest; namely, the power to sanctify, to teach and to govern in the sacred ministry. The Council sums it up in the words *sacra potestas*.[162] This 'sacred power', as Rahner understands it, is not due to the ministers on account of their commissioning by a higher authority, but is given in the sacramental nature of their ordination. Now, this 'sacred power', though common to the whole of the ministry, is first and foremost realized in episcopal consecration. Thus, the episcopate

> is not regarded in the light of the (simple) priesthood, but envisaged in itself as the full priesthood in all regards, while the ordinary priesthood is to be explained as a limited share of the full priesthood: episcopal consecration is the primary and comprehensive instance of sacramental ordination to office.[163]

This means that the sacrament of the episcopacy is not the 'highest degree' of the priesthood, but *the* priesthood *tout court* from which the same 'sacred power' of 'ordinary' priesthood derives its efficacy. Whilst the medieval view regarded the bishop as a priest entrusted by the Pope with full legal power, Rahner understands the Council in the reverse: priesthood in its full sense is the office of bishops by means of which they are enabled to represent Christ in a special and historically tangible manner 'according to his threefold office' (*munus*) which is bestowed on them through their consecration. This change of approach, Rahner believes, 'represents an advance on the ordinary theology of the schools.'

At first sight it is hard to see the significance of this alleged 'advance'. Yet, this slight change which, as Rahner states right at the beginning of *Commentary*, leads to 'a changed mentality which takes a critical attitude towards a certain type of Roman centralism and curial administration earlier in vogue.'[164] He explains why the traditional distinction between *potestas ordinis* and *jurisdictionis* flows from the same sacramental source rather than only being conceded by a higher authority. It shows, in spite of their difference, 'very clearly the intrinsic unity of the two powers and hence the ultimate oneness of their nature.' The practical consequence is that bishops can be ordained (as they indeed were) without previous ordination to the priesthood; that bishops who are not entrusted with the government of a diocese are bearers of the same 'sacred power' of episcopacy apart from their commissioning by the Pope: a 'titular' bishop can equally be a member of the college as local ordinaries are; that (and I believe this is Rahner's foremost interest) the wording of the decree is seen as emphasizing the basic unity of all official authority in the Church,

> . . . its sacramental basis and its pneumatic nature, which extends to legal powers. Doctrine and law are also 'spiritual', and in the Church are rooted in the grace which is sacramentally manifest.[165]

Of course, the text does not answer further questions of practical legislation, one of which is the role of the traditional *missio canonica* or the legal power conceded for actual application (*potestas actu expedito*). Yet, certainly it speaks of this 'sacred power' not on the level of its juridical, but sacramental significance.[166] And this indeed is presupposed when Article 22 states the existence and nature of the College of Bishops. Their collegiality is not a juridical concession from a higher authority, but a *communio* based on the bishops' sacramental consecration.

From the sacramentality of the episcopal office there follows another important conclusion. If the episcopate as a 'sacred power' is rooted in the consecration then the task of the bishops, whether diocesan or titular, is not limited to a defined territory. They have rights and duties as regards the whole Church. This, of course, does not mean that they can legally exercise their power outside their own realm. Nonetheless, there must be an intermediary forum where this right can be put into practice.

Rahner had already envisaged the theological nature of bishops' conferences and, before the final promulgation of *Lumen Gentium*, wrote in more detail about their importance for the future functioning of the Church, venturing beyond the field of a dogmatic theologian into that of Canon Law. For Rahner, it is theologically evident that

> this universal responsibility of the individual bishop . . . cannot be allowed to remain a merely abstract and formal requirement but must be embodied in a concrete and visible way.[167]

This 'embodied' expression is that of *bishops' conferences*. As a 'newcomer' in the history of the Church, their existence cannot be a requirement by divine right as, for example, the difference between bishops and ordinary priests is. However, their concrete function seems to be a 'must' at the present time: ' . . . the bishops' conference is a possible and today perhaps even an absolutely necessary expression of an essential element of the Church.'[168]

Hence, this comparatively new form of common duty of bishops in a larger territory is, as it were, in search of its own legal powers. Rahner mentions the already functioning conventions of regional bishops which, however, according to the then existing Canon Law, had only a consultative and not a legally binding character. The new Code of Canon Law 'soon to be drawn up' should in Rahner's thought recognize their sovereign power and their right to make their own independent decisions without being subject to Rome's approval and ultimate decision. No doubt, he would have preferred to see the centralism of Rome curtailed and, if his theological premiss is correct, his suggestion of a juridical nature is justified.[169]

Another of Rahner's forays into the field of Canon Law and practical theology, namely 'Office', was published in the same year (1963), soon after his article on bishops' conferences.[170]

'Office', this rather rumbling and repetitious article, had been written in the time between the acceptance of Vatican II's decree on the Church (*Lumen Gentium*) and its solemn promulgation. In that time, it was not yet clear what were the theological implications of collegiality and how this idea will be applied to the organizational life of the Church. As for the first, Rahner's essay is speculative and already proposed in other publications; as for the juridical and practical consequences it is – as he himself admits it – highly experimental. Nonetheless, the main ideas which govern Rahner's 'Office' have a special twist in making it significant for his future attitude to the implementation of collegiality.

First of all, there is a tendency which I would call 'sacramentalisation'. This means that the powers inevitably conferred to an institution or to a person derive from the Church as a proto-sacrament. Wherever the Church is present and active there is an effective communication of grace. Grace is not only transferred by the seven sacraments, but is also given in the various tasks with which these institutions or persons are entrusted. This is based on the original intention of Christ in founding the college of the apostle and his will to transmit the same to the college of bishops up to our time. It is therefore of divine right, *jus divinum*, that collegiality is invested with this 'sacred power' (*sacra potestas*).

Secondly, this power in its entirety is entrusted to the College of Bishops all over the world. This 'supreme power', however, invested in a collective unit is in a reciprocal relationship with the individual ordination of each member. This means that the power of a single bishop to sanctify (*potestas ordinis*) and to govern (*potestas jurisdictionis*), even if this latter for practical purposes can be separated from the former, derive from their 'inner unity and ultimately indissoluble connection'[171] and is intimately connected with his membership of the college.

Thus, it is immaterial from which side the appointment of an individual bishop can be seen: either from his ordination granting him the above 'two' powers or from his adoption by the College of Bishops. In this way, the elected candidate to the papacy can be seen from his appointment as the Bishop of Rome or, conversely, because he is now the supreme pastor of the Church he is the Bishop of Rome.[172] The same analogy is valid for bishops appointed for a certain territory or for individual cardinals co-opted by the college of cardinals.[173] For the future implementation of collegiality Rahner prefers the second approach: a bishop *is* bishop, because he is a member of the College and not *vice versa*; because he is appointed and ordained, therefore, he becomes a member of the *collegium*. This approach, which I would call the 'principle of collectivity', is applied to various legal and practical cases within the present and future organization of the Church. Rahner explains this in 'Office' and in his later writings.

In the third place, the practical and juridical suggestions of 'Office' is guided by a principle which I would call the 'collective democracy' within the Church. This means that the permanent hierarchical structure of the Church (which is *de jure divino*) does not exclude a certain autonomy of the different collective units. Each institution is subordinate to the one standing on the higher hierarchical scale as a social unit, has some power of decision, even if it has to be approved by a higher instance. Thus, in the relationship of Pope and College of Bishops, of a territorial conference of bishops to the world-wide *collegium*, of the body of priests, the *presbyterium*, to the bishop of the diocese the same autonomy should be implemented. From this also follows that a higher instance, at least morally (if not in a juridical sense), is bound to the decision of a lower one. This is illustrated (among others) in the relationship of the bishop and his priests:

> . . . the fundamental theological structure of the Church . . . demands a bipolar unity of monarchical and a collegial element inseparably related to one another . . . [Thus] if the principle of collegiality is applied to this relationship at least as a guide . . . , then . . . the priest enters by his priestly ordination into a college,

> the *presbyterium*, which is . . . a college at the disposal of the bishop.[174]

Within this relationship, priest and bishop are mutually responsible in performing their pastoral task. The same principle applies to other hierarchical relationships within the Church.[175] This was, incidentally, the point which was misunderstood by D. T. Strottmann's article – published explicitly against Rahner's suggestions – in 'Office'.[176] Strottmann believes that Rahner's insistence on the unity of the one office in its various applications to different social units reinforces the centralization of power, comparable to the *céphalisation* which the (then, not yet promulgated) decree on the Church was supposed to overcome. Strottmann did not notice that Rahner's account attempts to balance a merely hierarchical government by a kind of democracy attributed to collective units and their relative autonomy. To what extent, on account of this principle, the centralization of the Church can be avoided will have to be seen in the events of the year following the publication of 'Office'.

In these years, Rahner repeats his earlier comments and acknowledges the practical weakness of the decree on the bishops: it gives the impression that, in speaking of the bishops, the Council addresses itself to the *theoretical* and not to the *real* structures of the Church.[177] For it is often the case that the bishop remains a higher administrative official in the Church, whereas the real life of the Church of the communities, where the Eucharist is celebrated and the Word of God announced, is in fact the parish under the leadership of 'simple' parish priests.

Rahner's tendency to draw practical conclusions from the Council's doctrine reinforces itself in the decade after the Council. One wonders if in these years the foretaste of that 'wintry season' of the Church, as in the last years of Rahner's life, could be felt. For in the wake of the Council he had to face questions of practical significance in the concrete application of the Council's theology. In these, Rahner must have felt a certain paternalism on the part of Rome and of some of the bishops or even a resistance, as he politely says, stemming

> . . . not so much from an undeclared and ultimately unChristian desire for power, or from some naive attitude of self-assertion, but

rather from the fear that . . . as a result of [a certain kind of] 'democratisation' in the Church . . . the purity of faith, the truth of the gospel and the abiding nature of the Church would be exposed to danger.

This above point was made concerning a suggestion regarding the possibility of bishops being chosen by the people rather than appointed by the Pope.[178]

In fact, in these decades there were some events which needed a theologically prudent and yet hitherto unwonted realization of Vatican II's doctrine. Such were, for instance: the General Pastoral Synod of German Catholics, convoked for the year 1969/70; in 1969, the rather short-lived International Papal Commission of Theologians whose membership Rahner then enjoyed;[179] the emergence of new organs within the framework of the Church and their corresponding office bearers, as the pastoral assistants without priestly ordination; and the new types of Christian communities apart from the traditional parishes. These new aspects of the Church had to be explained from the Council's doctrine, their legal status defined and their pastoral tasks outlined from the point of view of the dogmatic theologian. It was indeed a period of experiments in which the Council's still theoretical constitution on the Church had to be adapted to structures or institutions already existing or emerging in her life.

Apart from repeating the Council's doctrine on the episcopate, there are some new emphases in Rahner's ecclesiology. In view of the Pastoral Synod in Germany, he defends the right of pluralism within the Church, 'despite the tendency towards uniformity in the world.'[180] There must be a certain autonomy of regional Churches, even if their particular character has to be defended 'against attacks from Rome.' It is not enough theoretically to defend the rights of particular Churches which 'do not run counter to the unity of the Church but rather represent a blessing for the whole Church.'[181] Now, just as in the case of episcopal conferences, Rahner expects theological reflections from a *pastoral synod* which, though it has no doctrinal authority, should envisage themes of investigation concerning the whole Church. Hence, some legal power should be granted to such an assembly. Though he accepts Rome's directives according to which the synod has only a consultative power, he sees no difficulty in claiming more concrete competence in its decisions which can bind bishops and their conference. Admittedly, the bishops' power of decision is of divine right, yet as he here qualifies his own theory of *Jus divinum*, there is a human right which 'constitutes – at least in many cases – the concretization of the *Jus divinum* such that without it this would have no reality at all.'[182] This concretization of divine right would, on the one hand, be the 'expression of an indestructible continuity of law in the Church', and, on the other, it would be morally binding not only for the bishops but also for the Pope.[183] Thus, the conclusion is at hand:

> We are declaring then without reserve at the level of dogmatic theology that the statute [in convoking the synod] should be formulated in such a way as to give the synod as such the right to take part in the decision making, and not merely to have an advisory function.[184]

As is well known, Rahner's standpoint was to remain an empty dream.

Accepting that, among the members of a national synod, laymen and laywomen with their priests constituted a body alongside the bishops,[185] Rahner devotes a good number of pages in 'Aspects' to another organ of the Church's constitution: to the college of priests. It is in fact a further explanation of his doctrine on the presbyterium. Rahner argues from the analogy of the Pope's relationship to the College of Bishops that a similar structure holds true in the leadership of a diocese. He sees no difficulty in a collegiate leadership for a local Church. Just as the Pope was advised by the Commission of Theologians in Rome in 1970 to subject himself to rules in working together with the episcopal college, so should the bishop be morally bound to the rulings of his own presbyterium, including for instance, 'the setting up of a court of appeal such that even a bishop, at least in normal cases, would be bound to its decisions.'[186] The contrary of this principle would certainly favour that paternalism which engenders frustration instead of 'setting freedom itself free' against a kind of regimentation. This, of course, holds true also for the election of bishops by the college of priests or by some other organ, just as the Pope is elected by the college of cardinals.

The principle which underpins Rahner's suggestions for pastoral theology is the multiform oneness of ecclesiastical ministry. Though it is of divine right that the Church's hierarchical edifice is thought of in the division of three offices (deacons, priests and bishops) the practical application of this *Jus divinum* does not exclude further differentiation.

The criterion on which this is possible seems to be sociological. It is to be

> deduced from the encounter at the empirical level which this official ministry makes with the concrete general social conditions, and, on this basis, the ecclesiastical conditions too affecting the preaching of the gospel.[187]

For the application of a divine right is not a mere application of prior general principles, but

> rather it is an event of freedom, and thereby of a future which is unique in each particular case and as such has an autonomy of its own, being something more than merely a handmaid of a theory.[188]

In these remarks, one can witness Rahner's sociological turn in the interpretation of the Church's organization. As a dogmatic theologian he leaves the door open to pastoral theology for a kind of conformity with concrete social situations and, with regard to these, he envisages the Church to come as built up also from below. And this conformity should not overlook socially marginal groups of Christians hitherto not organized according to the old parish principle and not even integrated into existing social divisions. These communities of Christians under the leadership of their priests, should belong to the core of the future Church.[189]

Indeed, Rahner goes well beyond the framework envisaged by the Council's theology of the episcopate. As later events in the organization of the Church have proved, his view goes also beyond the actual *praxis* of Rome and that of the present Pope. Rahner, perhaps fortunately, was not alive to see appointments to the episcopal office as governed by the principle of blind obedience to the Pope and his officials: although the collegial government of the Church is maintained, bishops are selected to say 'Aye' to an even more centralized Church.

And this is exactly what Rahner had tried to avoid by his understanding of the relationship of bishops and the Roman Pontiff.

(**C**) *The Pope: symbol of unity*

In the various writings of Rahner's ecclesiology the 'office' of the Roman Pontiff seems to have been dealt with by way of *obiter dicta*. To start with, the Pope has, properly speaking, no 'office' of his own other than that of the Bishop of Rome, one among the members of a world-wide *collegium* whose head he is. Whilst there is a difference on the sacramental level between bishops and priests, one cannot affirm the same between the Pope and the bishops. From this it seems to follow that the papacy can only be treated in relation to the College of Bishops and to the whole Church.

This apparent neglect can be explained by two main factors. First, Rahner's historical circumstances made him concentrate on the role of bishops in the Church. Hence, the authority and power implied in the primacy of the Pope always appears *in relation to* the authority of bishops or to the whole Church. Secondly, right from the beginning, Rahner's desire for the decentralization of the Church is there in the background. We have seen it in his writings about the basic constitution of the Church which, at times, amount to a de-mythologization of the papal power. In *The Shape of the Church to Come*, Rahner writes:

> The style of papal devotion as it developed particularly in the nineteenth century may rightly seem to many to belong to a vanished age . . . we have the right to reject the claim of *Civiltà Cattolica* that our own faith and our own religious life flow from the Pope.[190]

Rahner's reserve about this kind of piety, which belongs to a past 'Pian' Church, does not deny the universal function of the Pope in regard to the whole Church, for the

> papacy belongs to the abiding content of our faith itself, in its place within the hierarchy of truths and in our own Christian life. This holds absolutely.[191]

Thus, in the wake of Vatican I and during the reign of the Pius Popes, Rahner has presupposed as a matter of fact the all embracing primacy of the Roman See. His practical problem arose during the debates of Vatican II: after having defended the summary power of the College of Bishops he had to find a meaning for the primacy of the Pope. Shortly before the Council, he had already dealt with the crucial question of the relationship of the two powers within the Church.[192] However, after the Council he had to face the same problem again.

It is a well-known fact that, in the formulation of the third chapter of *Lumen Gentium* concerning the different powers within the Church, Pope Paul VI personally intervened. The crucial question was not so much about the doctrine on the collegiality of bishops but rather on its relationship to the supreme power of the Pope. It seems to have been a problem which was raised by the various *modi* of the participants in the Council to the extent

> that the doctrine of the primacy, which no one doubted, was inculcated too often in articles 22 and 26 in repetitions inspired by over anxiety, even in contexts where it was not called for by the subject matter.[193]

This is why a *nota explicativa* was added at the wish of the Pope in order to qualify this relationship. In it, it is emphasized that the plenary power of the world episcopate is only valid if it is headed by the Pope, 'who in the college fully retains his function as the vicar of Christ and pastor of the universal Church.'[194] The Pope can therefore exercise his power at a given time on his own – *seorsim* – whereas the College can act only with the consent of the Roman Pontiff.[195]

It has already been mentioned that in ordinary human society such an arrangement could become the source of conflicts. In the Church it can even lead to schism, as it indeed did in the fourteenth to sixteenth centuries. In that situation, the Western Church was divided between Popes and anti-Popes each claiming the right of supremacy; to many the view which subordinated the papal power to the ecumenical council of the universal episcopacy seemed preferable. At the Council of

Constance, the primacy of the Pope was reaffirmed against the so called 'conciliarism'.

Now, during the preparation of the articles of *Lumen Gentium* about the collegiality of the bishops, it seemed to many that a tendency (as proposed by Cardinal Frings of Cologne), which was similar to that of fifteenth-century conciliarism, was gaining the upper hand: the desire for a permanent synodal presence of the world episcopate in Rome in order to express the parallel powers to be exercised by the college.[196] Rahner is correct in stating that the problem of Vatican II was similar to, but not the same as, that of conciliarism. He affirms that the question about the power of the Pope and that of the college has now been 'presented in a better and more realistic form, as the question of the precise relationship between Pope and the united episcopate.'[197]

At Constance the reassertion of the supremacy of the Pope's power over and above the Council was not intended to abolish the supreme power of the episcopate. Anti-conciliarism does not seek to install the Pope as an absolute monarch. Hence, between Constance and Vatican II the dilemma concerning the relationship between the two remained unsolved in the ecclesiology of the schools and was inherited, now in the context of episcopal collegiality *versus* the Pope. One assumed either an inadequate distinction between these two, or one asserted the absolute unity in the power of the Church as possessed by the Roman Pontiff. Rahner does not agree with either of these solutions. If we assume this distinction, however 'inadequate' it is, we involve ourselves in a contradiction which, according to Rahner, could endanger not only the unity of the Church but also the very primacy of the Pope. If the power of the episcopate is maintained, then the supreme and plenary power of the Roman Pontiff would be derivative of the power of the united episcopate. If, however, we maintain the absolute unity of these two powers as vested in one person, we could not reasonably speak of the supreme power of the bishops. Rahner states:

> This consideration is enough of itself to show what a dangerous presupposition precisely for the *papacy* itself underlies the opinion that the supreme power of the united episcopate or Council can be derived from the power of the Pope.[198]

Thus, either the distinction between the two powers or the absolute unity of the two would make these interdependent: either could be derived from the other. Consequently, neither of these two could reasonably be called 'supreme' powers.

Rahner does not adopt one of these opinions. It is not an either-or, a distinction or absolute unity, but both together, albeit on different levels. This other level was already indicated by Rahner well before the conciliar debate: although there are two different powers within the Church, the eventual conflict of these could be checked by a third, namely, that of the Spirit:

> . . . the unity of the Church is sufficiently guaranteed by the power of the Spirit in spite of power in her being vested in two completely distinct subjects.[199]

He is well aware that this solution in itself, on the juridical level on which the conciliar debate moved, is inadequate. Yet he tries to formulate it in such a way that it may become applicable in practice:

> There is only one subject endowed with supreme power in the Church: the college of bishops assembled under the pope as its head. But there are two modes in which this supreme college may act: a 'collegiate act' properly so called, and the act of the Pope as head of the college.[200]

In establishing this thesis, Rahner follows the words of the 'preliminary note' attached to *Lumen Gentium* – however, with a twist of his own. The 'preliminary note' reads:

> Because the Roman Pontiff is the *head* of the college, he alone can perform certain acts which are in no way within the competence of the bishops, for example, to call together and direct the college, to approve the rules of procedure etc. . . . [201]

This, indeed, is the sense in which post-conciliar popes have used the power due to them alone. Rahner, however, adds that this power is not given to the Pope alone, nor is it derived from the College of Bishops, but from the divine will which intends to have the one power exercised in two ways: either the Pope uses his power in virtue of being the head of the united episcopate, or the College acts upon its power in union with its head the Pope. It is true of both these facts that

> . . . the one implies the other in the *same* sense, and with *equal* validity: the fact that the office of the pope relates to the universal Church implies that it relates in the same sense to the united episcopate and vice versa.[202]

But, even this formulation, Rahner feels, can be misunderstood: the reciprocal relationship of the 'two' powers does not mean that the Pope acting on his own (*seorsim*) does so by being commissioned by the bishops, or in the reverse sense – the College of Bishops acts only in the name of the Pope. Neither of these understandings is correct, so for further precision he adds that the Pope acts 'in virtue of the commission given to him directly by Christ,' but acting so his act is

> *ipso facto and in itself* an act of the college [*not* a collegiate act], because this power conferred upon him 'in person' and not on 'him alone' by Christ of itself makes him the 'mandatory' of the college.[203]

Behind this laborious reasoning and quizzical solution, Rahner intended to establish the 'ontological nature' (as he wants it) of the Pope's act in exercising his power, as the image of Christ originally founding the college of his twelve apostles and *then* appointing Peter as its head. The suggestion is that it is from this sequence of events that Peter 'obtains his primatial authority precisely as *head* of this college.'[204]

The theological significance of this concept corresponds to the basic constitution of the Church in which unity and diversity are implied along with the harmonious oneness of a supreme power.[205] But this can only be affirmed beyond the juridical level: the sacramental power (*potestas ordinis*) of the whole episcopate, including that of the Pope, is the source of the juridical power (*potestas jurisdictionis*) belonging to the hierarchically structured Church. Indeed, the Pope in his 'office' is the visible and sacramental sign of the unity in the diversity of 'powers' belonging both to the College of Bishops and its head. The papacy 'represents the unity of sacramental power in the Church.' The act of the Pope is ultimately the sacramental sign of effective unity within the hierarchical structure of the Church. The primacy is the ground which allows the Pope to act on his own, but his is a symbolic action which effectively represents the power of the Spirit who is the ultimate unity of the Church. The Pope's power, though exercised in legal terms, is in itself para-canonical. Its significance is basically sacramental.

With this position Rahner returns to his preconciliar opinion, already hinted at earlier: the highest instance of jurisdical power as possessed by the Pope ultimately relies on the charisma of the Spirit and is not measured by the principles of an objective jurisprudence. Even when the Pope invokes his highest authority, it is not possible

> to oppose his decision with the claim that he has exceeded his power . . . and that his judgement is not binding on that account. For it is not possible to verify that he has kept within the scope of his competence by applying a criterion to him, as though by a juridical process to test his conduct.[206]

The only guarantee that he acted within his competence is the promised assistance of the Holy Spirit. The ultimate power is not that of the Pope but of a spiritual reality in which we believe and to which we freely consent. 'Here,' Rahner concludes, 'is an office which is to be what it is, passes into the charismatic sphere.'[207] The primatial power of the Pope is a matter to be believed.

This does not mean that we cannot rationally argue for this view. Rahner is convinced that we can deduce the authority and effective power of the Pope from the nature of Christianity. In the second edition of *Dictionary of Theology*, published with H. Vorgrimler (in which the authors already presuppose and refer to *Lumen Gentium*), after having summed up the positive doctrine on the primacy as taught by the schools, they argue from the nature of religion for the probability that it implies a Church-like organization and that this latter cannot be without a visible head. A religion

> which comes from God and must therefore be authoritative, a religion which is eschatological and therefore always obligatory, a

> religion that is catholic . . . is meant to be personal despite and even in its social structure.[208]

In other words, Catholicism cannot be a religion built merely on the objective authority of a book (with which obviously an extreme Protestant view of *sola scriptura* is meant). It requires a personal head.

This line of argument prevails up to *Foundations* and will be later reasserted in terms of social philosophy. In a rather long-winded article from as late as 1982, Rahner tries to define the intrinsic nature of authority and its relationship to power.[209] The first half of this essay is sociological and refrains from applying his considerations to the authority of God or that of the Church. Its aim is to show the necessity of authority invested in a person or group of persons within a concrete society. In general, authority is 'a relationship between the person holding the authority and the person determined by the authority.'[210] With this, of course, the nature of dependence ('determined') is not yet decided, but it is clearly indicated that authority is or should be something personal presupposing freedom on each side.

Why authority becomes necessary is deduced from the fact of inevitable frictions within a concrete society. In order to prevent or regulate frictions, freedom itself requires social regulations which are not given *a priori* in human associations. They, as a rule, arise from human decisions in concrete situations where the ensuing regulation is not dictated by objective norms. There is, as Rahner says, some 'arbitrariness' in the mandatory power implied in the exercise of authority. It can be good or wrong, more or less correct, and as such it demands acceptance from those under authority. Both the decision and its acceptance exist in a historical process and can be 'considerably modified according to the concrete nature of the society in question.'[211] Nonetheless, in varying circumstances authority can be defined as

> the morally justified capacity of a human being to regulate and determine social relations among members of society in a way that is binding on these members.[212]

It is to be noted that the above definition does not envisage the possibility of a collective bearer of authority identical with the society in question. Although in a secular democracy the theoretical bearer of authority is the people itself ' . . . in the ordinary case . . . the bearer of authority is the individual human being.'[213]

If this is so, then the question arises about the manner of appointment by delegation or designation. While delegation presupposes that the social group commits its own authority already possessed to an individual of the group, designation claims that the authority of the person comes from elsewhere (for example, from objective social norms or from God). In whatever way a person is appointed, he or she will have the right of exercising a mandatory power within the society. Hence, a certain coercive power in exercising his or her authority may accrue to that person. Power understood as (sometimes physical) force is not necessarily connected with authority. The two 'entities' are by no means identical: 'Authority can be quite real even if it is not linked with coercive power,' yet the efficient functioning of a society may make the use of force inevitable; hence, 'authority does not necessarily exclude in its bearer every capacity for the application of physical force.'[214] Of course, the use of force by someone in authority is strictly within the limits of the concrete requirements of the society and may not abolish the personal dignity of those who are subject to authority, otherwise the use of force (including punitive justice) is immoral.

Having thus outlined the nature of authority, Rahner tries to apply it to ecclesiology. His argument, unlike that in the *Dictionary*, does not suggest a necessary connection between religion and social authority, since a 'Christian conviction and mentality may even exist in an individual instance without there being a real socialization.'[215] But wherever Christianity *de facto* emerged as a common mentality, a common faith, it has in various degrees manifested a socialization and with it a claim to making binding regulations proper to a society. It is the degree of this socialization which is the basis of authority in various Christian denominations.

This merely sociological induction which, in itself, does not explain the Church as a society or the degree of authority within it, is immediately extended with a theological reasoning. For Christian socialization presupposes, albeit in very different ways, that authority has another origin. Hence the 'nature of authority in the Church is conditioned by its origination.' This view, common to all Christian denominations, theoretically leaves it open whether the appointment of those in authority comes from below, from the mandate given by the Church's people, or from an even 'higher' authority. In fact, in the self-understanding of Christianity from its historical beginning it was understood that authority in the Church originates directly from Jesus Christ who founded her. The traditional Catholic argument has upheld this foundation

> by explicit and formally expressed words of institution, that through Peter and the Twelve he appointed in an unambiguously juridical sense a college of officeholders for this Church whose task it is to continue and to propagate her mission even in a distant future.[216]

According to this conviction, the designation of bearers of authority must be bound to a visible handing over of power ('apostolic succession') beginning with Jesus through the first officeholders up to the present day.

This conception about the source of authority in the Church has been questioned from the time of the Reformation and, even more, since the Enlightenment. The objection, which may be valid in its merely exegetical content, has, according to Rahner, overlooked the imminent expectation of the eschatological end. In his view, without even referring to a verbal institution, such an authority can be upheld by an appeal to the eschatological character of Christian faith:

> If Jesus crucified and risen is to be God's unsurpassable, historical self-promise for the whole world, there must exist for all times a community of faith that accepts this self-promise of God in faith and bears witness to it before the world.[217]

I believe the most important word in the above sentence – which, according to Rahner is equivalent to a (missing) verbal institution and handing over of authority – is 'witness'. The *raison d'être* of the Church as a society, and of the authority it implies, is the witness of the Church to this eschatological self-promise of God. The way this witnessing is to be performed and the concrete modalities governing the exercise of Church-authority can be ascribed to a development of the post-Easter Church. The concrete structures of this Church-authority, the specific requirements for its bearers, the mode of handing on authority have emerged from the irreversible decisions of the apostolic Church and, because of that, they are liable to change in their historical form.[218] In other words, although the Church and authority therein originate from Jesus, in their concrete shape they are historically flexible. This means, on the one hand, that particular structures and the authority contained in them are permanently normative and, on the other hand, that these (being also products of human decisions of a historical Church society) are unavoidably bound to those concrete conceptual models of the time in which they were decided. These time-bound modalities of authority cannot be regarded as its abiding essence. Thus, it is possible in a dogmatically binding way to define the primacy of the Pope, but it is by no means of its essence that his authority be exercised according to the model conceived at certain points of history. Briefly, the Church as a society originating in the teaching of Jesus Christ, must claim an authority on the ground of her very nature. But, from this, one cannot speculatively deduce 'that it would have to be a Peter,' – nor the way the primacy of the Pope was exercised at various times.[219]

Thus, if I correctly understand Rahner's bold statement, whereas the authority claimed by the Church is deducible from her essence, the exercise of papal primacy is grounded on the historical decision of the post-Easter Church. Provided that Rahner's theory, according to which the post-Easter decisions of the Church are of *divine right*, is correct, then the existence of the primacy is a dogmatically *not* reversible fact, even if its concrete exercise is historically changeable. So also is his further conclusion which, for the present time, practically denies any coercive power due to the primacy of the Pope. To be precise: the authority of the Church may include a coercive power, however, only as far as her authority reaches.[220] In historical times, when the Church and secular society were in symbiosis this kind of coercive power, even beyond the extent of Church-authority, was legitimately claimed by Canon Law. It is, however, not applicable in our pluralistic situation:

If we take into consideration the Church's understanding of itself
as a free community of like-minded persons in contrast to societies existing from natural necessity, we will be permitted to say
that the Church . . . does not have to be conceived as of being
equipped with a power of social coercion.[221]

Is then the authority of the Pope without effective power?

A more literary attitude to the primacy is in the form of a med-
itation on the perennial actuality of the papacy. In a contribution
containing a fictitious letter of a future Pope, Paul VII, Rahner, as
it were, sums up a charter of conduct for a Roman Pontiff. In this,
speaking on behalf of 'Paul VII' he repeatedly underlines his
unconditional belief in the primacy:

I will live and act with the conviction which we have learned and
made our own . . . that my office possesses the fullness of power.
Vatican I remains, of course, fully valid for me.[222]

Or:

Undoubtedly the pope must lay claim to the teaching authority
that Christ and the Church have given him; he must speak like one
who has power and not like the scribes . . . I believe in the papacy
and accept my task.[223]

This unconditional conviction is grounded on belief in the
Church, one of whose doctrines is the primacy. Yet he hastens to
admit: 'The papacy, although objectively binding, is not the
highest or most fundamental truth in the hierarchy of truths.'[224] Its
existence can be inferred, however, only for those 'who have
already found God in Jesus Christ,': it belongs to the mystery of
faith and as such, even a Pope 'recently elected' finds it hard
entirely to grasp the meaning of his own primacy. He can and
should honestly state:

I know that the doctrine of the papacy, like all other truths of our
faith, is surrounded by all the obscurities that, despite the greatest
conceptual precision, lead into the mystery of God. I know that the
doctrine of the papacy is valid throughout time . . . although we

express them with concepts and images that are . . . historically conditioned.[225]

His governing the Church, his duties, are described with concepts derived from our Western culture and are to be applied to the whole world. The imaginary Paul VII is aware of his primacy of jurisdiction, but he can honestly ask what it exactly means. His *plena potestas* is hedged in by limits which are never clearly defined by *canonists*. It is understandable that he should ask the question: 'What then is the true nature of the papacy, as it operates in word and sacrament for the Whole Church?'[226]

In answer to this question about the meaning of papacy, Rahner does not appeal to divine institution or to 'apostolic succession,' but to the end of time which contains the eschatological promise:

> The true and happy outcome of world history is irrevocable. By dying on the cross and rising from the dead Jesus has made it irrevocable. That is the reason for the papacy; to this is it the basic and definitive witness, from this it derives its task and its fullness of power. Because this message can never die . . . and never be surpassed, this message about the end of time is also the promise that the gates of death will not prevail against the papacy during this endtime until the Lord comes, who will also put an end to the papacy.[227]

This 'essence' of the papacy is everywhere presupposed in Rahner's theology. Its heart is that witness for which the Pope as head of the College of Bishops stands. All the rest is subject to historical change. This is why the best characterization for the primacy of the Pope is beyond the terms of legality. It is rather to be seen in its sacramental powerfulness.

In an essay, 1981, discussing the absolute claim of Christianity, we can find another *obiter dictum* concerning the function of papacy in our changed times. In earlier days, Rahner says, the papacy 'was conceived more or less as an absolute and universal monarchy.' In this changed social order one has to have recourse to different concepts derived from our present-day experience – for instance, the Pope's function is that of the guarantor and guardian of unity.[228] The Pope with his primacy is the effective symbol of the one universal and Catholic Church.

Is this view also valid concerning his infallible teaching office?

3.3.2 The Magisterium

Whatever has been said of the authority of the Church, of the bishops and the Pope can be qualified by one of the Church's main functions: it is a teaching authority, the Magisterium.

Rahner takes for granted that the Church as a society is not only derived from the common faith of its members but is also responsible for the content of what they believe. Truth, as mentioned elsewhere, has something to do with institution;[229] it is the guarantor of the objectivity of the believer's subjective conviction and the guardian of the unity of the manifold variety of human words in which faith is confessed. Thus, it follows *a priori* from the self-understanding of the Church and from the Church's hierarchical structure as based on the Trinitarian self-communication of God in salvation history, that she not only sums up what the faithful believe but also *teaches* that which they *have* to believe.[230] As we remember, this formal deduction, as it were from above, of the Church's teaching office is a postulate to be accepted along with our faith in the Church. But, facing the meaning of the Magisterium, Rahner will point out, along with the necessity of its existence, its ambiguity in the concrete life of the Church. To a Catholic theologian nothing is more evident than his faithfulness to the Magisterium of the Church, although, as Rahner admits, 'the nature of this teaching office is more obscure than is commonly supposed.[231]

After more than fifteen years since Rahner's death and in a post-conciliar time when events have confronted the members of the Church with the repeated intervention of the Magisterium, it is most interesting to follow his understanding of and his struggle with the concept of the Church's teaching office, with its relationship to the creed, with the *de facto* belief of the faithful and, above all, with the work of the theologian. We should recall his reminiscences in the 'wintry season' of the Church, with which I introduced his ecclesiology: it was his unconditional love for the Church, to the service of which he dedicated his life, which made him both accept and criticize that teaching office. Rahner's view of the Magisterium is the touchstone of his 'Churchmanship'.

(A) *The concept of the Magisterium*

From Rahner's many writings on the teaching office of the Church I first want to look at his lexicon articles in *LTK* and *Sacramentum Mundi*.[232] To start with, Rahner does not derive the basic notion of the Magisterium 'from the transference of formal authority from God' as granted to a person or to an organized body. He rejects this approach on the ground that such a formal authority coming from God should have been present in God's guidance of his people in the Old Testament: Why did not God, he asks, in his will to save his chosen people, the Israelites, entrust a prophet or even a body of rabbis with such an authority in the synagogue of the old dispensation?[233] The existence of the teaching office is a novelty in the history of salvation. It is derived from the faith of a community which believes in and is witnessing to the eschatological victory gained by the event of Jesus Christ. Faith and trust in a self-revealing God existed before this event, it had even formed and united a people in expectation of their hope, but it is the new people assembled by the guidance of God's Spirit that can believe in and witness the *irreversible* fulfilment of their salvation. Hence, an irreversible faith in Jesus is the ultimate basis,[234] the main source from which the authority of the teaching office can be derived. Rahner's approach to the Magisterium always presupposes this starting point.

However, in itself it would not be clear how this faith in an eschatological event implies the Magisterium, unless another aspect of the same faith were taken into consideration. Thus, the second, complementary approach to the notion of the teaching office is the social constitution of the Church. To whit: the word of witness to Christ is first uttered by the whole community of Christian believers, it is *their* truth not only at the fleeting moment of its making but throughout the history which has been opened by the Christ-event. The historical permanence of this truth and of that first testimony is precisely due to the ongoing action of the Spirit which, 'from the beginning to the end is directed to this Church as a whole,' and this Church is 'preserved in the truth of Christ by the Spirit.[235] The Church is the continuing presence of this truth – not only in the faith and testimony of individual believers constituting, as it were, a 'meta-historical' fellowship, but rather in a 'historically structured society with the [common] confession of faith and doctrinal authority' – a truth ever to be testified.

What, then, is to be understood by this 'historically structured society'? For Rahner, the Church is of an eschatological nature, which means that her doctrinal authority is not derived from the faith of her single members or their totality, but from the 'implementation of God in Jesus Christ by which he willed that the salutary truth of the Christ-event should remain historically present in the world.' From this it follows that 'the Church would not be the eschatological community of salvation if it were not in "infallible" possession of the truth of Christ.'[236]

In other words, the Church is the bearer of 'God's creative word', she is an effective reminder (*anamnesis*) of the truth of a past event of Christ's salvific deed and, at the same time, the *prognosis* which anticipates the promised future in hope. With this presupposition alone can the Church claim doctrinal authority: not to teach an abstract truth for its own sake, but to pronounce the salvific word of truth under the guidance of the Spirit in each historic situation. In brief:

> The real nature of the Magisterium derives from the Christ-event which is eschatological triumph and possesses in the Church and in its confession of faith its permanent presence.[237]

With this, however, only the condition for the possibility of the Magisterium is stated. It gives, at the very most, a definition of the formal authority of the Church in doctrinal matters. This means that in interpreting divine revelation the Magisterium can and must demand absolute assent of faith from the members of the Church (and not from outsiders). Thus the Magisterium, precisely in performing this task, belongs to our belief in the Church; what and in what way it authoritatively teaches is her own decision. 'The Magisterium is itself the judge of its own authority,'[238] and the only and sufficient guarantee that the Magisterium does not transgress the limits of its competence is the promised assistance of the Spirit. Now, this formal authority to teach, to preserve and to defend the truth entrusted to the Church as a structured society, belongs to the stewardship of the bishops and the Pope. They are, in practice, *the* Magisterium: the assembly of the bishops in Council or its head the Pope defining *ex cathedra* a doctrine is called the *Magisterium extraordinarium*, whereas the teaching of the sovereign pontiff, most of the time with the aid of the Holy Office (Congregation for Faith and Doctrine), is the *Magisterium ordinarium*. Their competence, and to a certain extent power, is restricted to the contents of divine revelation and whatever seems necessary to preserve and defend it. In authentically teaching the truth of divine revelation the Magisterium is also delimited by the nature of the truths to be announced: some are revealed truths *per se*, that is, not for the sake of revealing other ones connected with the former. The sum of these truths about faith and morals is called the *depositum fidei*, the acceptance of which with an absolute assent of faith is the *sine qua non* of being a Christian. Beyond the contents of the deposit of faith (a notion which, as we shall see, is not clearly definable) there are truths logically connected with it. These are dogmatic facts without which the truths of the deposit could not stand. Again, there are true doctrines which, though not implied in the deposit, can be taught with absolute binding force for the safeguard of faith. To guard and teach these truths is in the competence of the teaching office. The material authority of the Magisterium consists in teaching *this truth*.

Rahner, though, in faithfully explaining and documenting the teaching of the Magisterium about itself, sows also the seeds of possible dissent, concerning the Magisterium and its authority. For there are truths which, as proclaimed by the Magisterium, do not claim the same obligation of faith but only a qualified assent. These are *authentic* but not irreformable statements which, as stated in *Lumen Gentium* 25, require the 'religious assent of the mind' or 'of the will and intellect'. These, too, are to be respectfully acknowledged according to the mind of this supreme teaching authority and according to the nature of the truth repeatedly proclaimed.[239] The assent to these authentic teachings of the Magisterium is not a matter of faith but of religious obedience. Their truth, unlike that of an irreformable dogma,[240] is not ultimately binding. Yet, on the one hand

> the Magisterium must be able to put forward . . . provisional, more or less problematic and . . . non-binding statements, since without these the Christian faith . . . cannot be vividly conveyed and really assimilated by the faithful in a particular situation.[241]

These statements, on the other hand, 'may turn out later to be in need of completion or even to be erroneous' – not only in principle, but 'in the course of history' they often have been.[242] Furthermore, there are not always clearly defined criteria to separate defined statements from these authentic teachings of the Magisterium. And this is why the very notion of the Magisterium 'is more obscure than it is commonly supposed.'[243]

(B) *The 'obscure' nature of the Magisterium*

This possible 'obscurity' arises on several scores:

(i) From the nature of common faith which is, after all, composed of many individual subjective convictions (the *fides qua*) assenting to that main belief (the *fides quae*) which, from the sociological point of view, is the basis of the Magisterium.

(ii) It can be 'obscure' concerning faith's absolute assent to the deposit which, as we shall see, in the course of history was expressed in manifold propositions.

(iii) The nature of the Magisterium can be 'obscure' as regards the ultimate bearer of the infallible teaching office, whether it is stated by the Pope's announcements or those of the College of Bishops.

(iv) Lastly, a similar 'obscurity' can occur as to how this teaching authority is put into *praxis*, how its pronouncements, its decisions are formulated for the assent of the faithful: does an appeal to formal authority suffice to stress the truth of a statement or decision, or is the Magisterium obliged to explain how this truth is 'discovered' as a part of divine revelation? That is, how it arrived at this decision[244] and to what degree does it relate to God's salvific word.[245]

In his lexicon articles, Rahner merely indicates these difficulties inherent in the nature of the Magisterium. Later, especially in the 1970s and towards the end of his life in 1982, he will be less reticent about them; for example, he summarily puts the doctrine of the Magisterium in its proper place by stating that the recognition of the Church's teaching authority is 'dependent on the 'authority' of revelation which ultimately . . . sustains the teaching authority – and is not sustained by it.[246]

From this it follows that assent to the Magisterium is *not* an absolutely *primary datum* on which faith can be founded. We believe in the Church, because, as Augustine said,[247] we believe the gospel and not the other way round. We believe in the essentials of faith (*depositum fidei*) not because the Magisterium tells us, but the other way round: we accept and obey the Magisterium, because we believe in the deposit of our faith. This latter approach is, of course, based not on the formal authority of the Magisterium, but on its material content.

Furthermore, a similar difficulty arises nowadays against the Magisterium from the nature of faith. How can the Church demand an absolute assent of faith from her members to truths which in the conscience of the individual are by no means acceptable? In the same way, the question is also asked: Why is such an absolute assent demanded from our contemporary faithful, when faith is a free act and any grown-up person is entitled to his or her own opinions even if these throw doubt on the teachings of the Magisterium?

Rahner in almost every essay concerning this or similar subjects tries honestly to face this problem. In 1968 he explicitly admits 'that to us today the assent of faith . . . does not come easily'.[248] Speaking on behalf of contemporary Church members he uses a language by no means complimentary to Church officials wielding doctrinal power; they too often appear pitiful and narrow minded, their teaching old-fashioned and out of date, their outlook is restricted and pettifogging – and precisely these individuals demand of us in the name of the gospel and of the Church an unconditional assent. No wonder that some members of the Church find their assent to the Church as she exists in the concrete a heavy burden.

In awareness of these difficulties in which the subjective conviction of the individual concerning the Church and her authority seems to be at loggerheads with the content of what this authority says, Rahner tries to re-assess modern man's attitude to the authority of the Church in general and to the teaching office in particular. As to the first, he honestly admits that

> a certain unity between a radical criticism at the fundamental level, on the one hand, and a spirit of unreserved trust in that which is yet untested by criticism, on the other

can coexist, provided we are prepared to endure the tension which thereby is inevitably introduced.[249] With an appeal to Newman 'a thousand difficulties of faith do not constitute a doubt of faith,' Rahner assures modern men and women that such an attitude need not destroy a person's basic commitment.[250] The constant reappraisal of our commitment to the Church

> gives us the promise and the hope that what in her is still alien, and incomprehensible as well, can be[come] meaningful for us and can gradually, albeit always in an asymptotic process, be assimilated.[251]

The approach of contemporary faithful to authority in the Church, according to Rahner, is immensely aggravated when he or she is confronted with the Church as 'the accredited messenger of God's revelation and as such endowed with the authority to teach.'[252] By fully acknowledging this difficulty he uses two sorts of argument against those who may come to grief on this point.

First is the argument that truth is never a private matter, but it should occur in inter-communication with others. In order to overcome the isolation of our own subjectivity we are always referred to a socially instituted fellowship:

> Truth, and that truth precisely in its specific force as illuminating and sustaining human existence as a whole has something to do with institution.'[253]

Secondly, in arguing with the doubter in the Magisterium, one has to point out the process character of faith in assimilating the doctrines of the Church. In doing so Rahner can appeal to his own personal experience. In an essay published in collaboration with other authors, Rahner's contribution emphasizes a fundamental identification with Christianity which 'does not imply agreement with each and everything that is done in the Church.'[254] In any case, there are teachings of the Magisterium which remain absolutely binding; yet, concerning these, critical questions are not excluded. In facing such doctrinal statements he admits:

> I as a theologian have not infrequently had to make an effort to discover what was really meant by a particular statement put forward as a dogma by the Church's Magisterium, in order to give my assent honestly and confidently. But I have never known an instance in the course of my life where it became impossible.[255]

Although this may or may not be a consolation for the doubter, the question remains: Which statements of faith as taught by the Magisterium are of a permanent and irreversible significance without which Church membership is annulled? The traditional answer would be: everything that belongs to the *deposit* of faith.

The explicit notion of the deposit as such is never clearly defined by Rahner. He is, of course, aware of Vatican II's hints on this subject. It is said in the Decree on Revelation (No 10): 'Tradition and Scripture together form a single sacred deposit of the word of God, entrusted to the Church,' and explained in No 8 with reference to 2 Tim 2:15 as 'whatever is handed down by the apostles.' This deposit 'includes everything that helps the people of God to live a holy life and to grow in faith.'[256] In 'Crisis of Authority' (1970) Rahner understands these points in the sense that the Magisterium, which is bound to the deposit of faith, does not directly derive all that it teaches from Christ but learns also from the common faith of the believers. The bearers of this authority depend on the history and development of common faith.[257] In a later essay, the same deposit gains a function other than its verbal objectification in statements. Arguing for the congruence of the official doctrine of the Church as pronounced by the Magisterium and the common beliefs of the faithful, Rahner states:

> The *depositum fidei* is not first and foremost a sum of statements
> formulated in human language. It is God's Spirit, irrevocably
> communicated to humankind, activating in persons the salutary
> faith that they really possess.[258]

This same Spirit, he says, brings together the faithful, cares for
their unity and assists the objectification of faith in statements
which can be the content of Church teaching. However, the
deposit 'infinitely transcends the most sublime objectification of
the faith'.

In 'Certainties' (1971), Rahner anticipated his later views on
authority (expressed in 'Crisis of Authority' in 1981); this, let us
say, *formal* function of the deposit is still maintained as a basic
and ultimate trust in the meaning of existence and the 'possibility of a full, all-embracing and definitive salvation.'[259] It is subject
to human decision and at the same time the hidden work of the
Spirit's grace. Now, if this quest after ultimate certainties is pur-
sued by a believing member of the Church in his or her act of
faith, that person can accept the Church herself and trust her
Magisterium. Of course, this trust in the Church does not dispense us from the task of further interpreting her teachings in
single propositions, from further overcoming those doubts which
assail our assurance in their acceptance. The Church cannot give
us such assurances and certainties, 'because no such assurances
and certainties can ever exist in human life at all.'[260]

Nonetheless, there are statements through which that attitude
of trust can be nourished. For an individual in certain circumstances there are religious propositions that are medial for his or
her decisions by which this basic trust can be confirmed.[261] These
statements give an objective orientation to such a person's attitude of trust. Thus, for instance, statements about Jesus Christ the
crucified and risen Lord can confirm our ultimate trust in the
grace-given meaning of existence. The first half of this statement
refers to a historical fact which in itself is insufficient without the
other: only acceptance and trust in correlation participate in the
sureness and certainty of which we are in quest, ' . . . it is impossible to have any real faith in Jesus in history without the
grace-given acceptance of the meaning of existence.'[262]

From this it follows:

> . . . that from the basic statements of Christianity about Jesus Christ we cannot truly expect any other certainty or sureness than that which is inherent in that ultimate basic attitude of trust.[263]

So far we have one or a cluster of propositions which for us Christians can mediate that ultimate certainty which the Church can objectively give us, provided these can be connected with that subjective trust – the basis of all our certainties. Along with the content of this faith in Jesus the Christ, its indestructibility and permanence are also given. To this 'certainty' about Jesus Christ belongs faith in the Church and her official creed. Now, it is obvious that the Church 'must at least recognize certain propositions as belonging to the true and indestructible propositions constitutive of her own faith.'[264] These are the objectifications of her ultimate and basic self-understanding and of her basic attitude of trust which she can propose as true and abiding.

The Church, however, can dogmatize certain statements other than those concerning Jesus the bringer of salvation and these statements, too, can mediate that grace-given trust which supports our certainties in life. They are equally to be believed, for no one can live *only* on basic and ultimate convictions assented to as final and definitive. The same, however with a proviso, applies to the Church

> . . . in her life of faith in the concrete she also inevitably and necessarily has propositions which are merely provisional, which, under certain circumstances will later come to be recognized as erroneous.[265]

To these propositions, if they are pronounced at a certain time at least a respect is due, for they are meant to prop up and sustain the main convictions of the Church. The only difficulty is that these secondary or derived statements, unless they are explicitly named as such, are often amalgamated with true and abiding propositions of faith. There is no precise line of distinction between these kinds of statements. And if we admit with Rahner that, 'The Church has *de facto* very often made mistakes in the past in propositions of this [secondary] kind,'[266] it may aggravate man's obligatory assent. In this case the individual will be permitted to leave these propositions respectfully alone until he or she can connect them with the ultimate religious trust of faith. This is also valid for the teaching office of the Church: she is not obliged to proclaim all the derived statements she ever made in history.

This last statement, however, does not seem to refer to truths dogmatized by the Church. What about these defined statements? Can a dogma be changeable? Do all defined dogmas belong to the deposit? Rahner's affirmative answer is immediately qualified. The reasons for this have already been hinted at: in 1971 he summarily appeals to the 'hierarchy of truths',[267] the understanding of which is then explained later the same year.[268] According to Rahner, this hierarchy can and must be affirmed on two scores. First, there is a coherent structure among defined truths and if the essence of this is assented to, its more peripheral statements, which may not have reached the awareness of the believer, are covered by the same assent. Secondly, this objective hierarchy of truths can and must be accompanied by a *subjective* one. This comes from the various aspects under which a Christian discovers the saving significance of a true statement to which one unconditionally assents. In searching for such essential statements, one may also discover that, at the moment, one is unable to cope with some related, but equally defined truths. While 'objectively' speaking the individual Christian must not 'get rid' of some tenets of the Church's defined teaching, he or she can avoid facing these by failing to notice them, or can 'postpone' a problematic question to a later time, and so on. In this way the individual works out their own *subjective* hierarchy of truths and can

> confidently live in an untroubled sureness of having been redeemed without having to endure all the darkness and anxiety about his salvation or being lost in guilt.[269]

The same can follow from the structure of our coming-to-faith which is, as we have already seen, a process directed to its objective totality. Once faith on this basis has come to be, it can go on assimilating other objects equally defined.[270] The single basic act on which this process is built is a belief in the self-communication of God, the Holy Spirit, and the surrender of the individual in hope and love to the self-revealing God.

Besides the hierarchy of truths, the partial changeability of dogmas can also be argued by pointing to the historical and cultural contexts in which the definers produced them.[271] They are often stated in philosophical concepts which have their own horizon of development. Thus, even defined dogmas should be read in the totality of their particular historical context from which the true kernel, the abiding meaning, could be re-expressed in oncoming new situations and with different conceptual models in new formulations. Although what they intend to state is permanent, in their formulations there are no 'chemically pure' dogmas.

This permanent element contained under the surface of a past language is not subject to change:

> Rather it implies an element of decision at the level of faith and hope such as cannot in any adequate sense be verified merely by the investigation of historical facts.[272]

This is the very nature of a dogma: a statement with changeable and unchangeable elements. The task of dogmatic theology is to find and re-express the unchangeable in a new formulation which remains changeable in its own turn.

However, whether *all* the defined statements belong to the deposit or only those referring to Christ and our salvation in him, is a question which Rahner has not yet explicitly answered. The first alternative – their verbal definition once upon a time – cannot function as a criterion in discerning the orthodoxy of one's faith. For instance, the existence and use of indulgences is a defined dogma of the Church, yet one could hardly defend the view that ignorance of this fact, or abstention from using it would impair anyone's commitment to the faith of the Church.[273] There is more likelihood that Christological statements are part and parcel of the deposit. But can they become criteria in judging the orthodoxy of propositions dogmatized; for example, in matters of morality. It is much more likely that by the deposit of faith those propositions of our Christian inheritance are meant which, according to individual circumstances, are able to mediate that basic trust in the self-revealing God of which Rahner wrote in 'Certainties'. If this should be his ultimate position about the propositional content of the deposit, he must safeguard it from an exclusively subjective and individualistic understanding. Up to this point, the only way to do so is to regard those propositions which are acceptable to an ecclesial communion as belonging to the deposit. And who else determines these statements if not the *infallible* Magisterium of the Church?

(C) *The 'infallible' statements of an 'infallible' Magisterium*

In 1970 Hans Küng published his redoubtable *Infallibility?*, which was intended as a challenge – an *Anfrage* – about the dogma of Vatican I.[274]

It was the even more redoubtable encyclical of Pope Paul VI, *Humanae Vitae*, which gave rise to Küng's book provoking a number of reactions both from the Holy Office and from the Euro-American theological confraternity.[275] Rahner's reaction was not amiss; yet, that he would attack head-on Küng's denial of infallibility was a surprise to those who knew his ecclesiological views. In 1968 he had published his own critical remarks on *Humanae Vitae* in an article which was, at least in part, taken over by a number of Euro-American publications.[276] Küng's book used the teaching of this encyclical and the world-wide reaction to it to show that the infallibility of the Pope *in practice* is null and void. Hence, what really belongs to our faith in the Church is that, in the long run, owing to the promised assistance of the Spirit, the Church will not go astray in her teaching, she will never abide in error. The Church is *indefectible* in maintaining the essential truth of man's salvation in Jesus the Christ. But this indefectibility does not imply that her single pronouncements, her doctrinal or moral statements are also infallibly true. Thus with the bath water the baby also has to go: from an erroneous statement (such as the prohibition of artificial means of contraception) and from a number of other erroneous teachings of the Magisterium in the past, the principle of infallibility has to be denied.[277] It was this argumentation of Küng that provoked Rahner's criticism. In fact, Rahner sums up Küng's position, saying that his:

> . . . publication contests the defined doctrine of the First Vatican Council. In doing this, however, the book does not confine itself

merely to the teaching authority of the pope, but rather refers quite in general to *all propositions of faith whatsoever*, whether contained in Scripture or put forward by the Councils or the teaching authority of the pope, with the intention of making an ultimately binding statement.[278]

The main difference between the two theologians does not lie in Küng's argumentation from the history of errors (Rahner is more than aware that the Magisterium often erred[279]) nor is Küng's pretension that the pontifical ban on artificial contraceptives is *de facto* an infallible statement (Rahner holds to the very end that it is *not*):

> . . . the statements of Vatican I would have no meaning at all, if the doctrine of the Council about the infallibility of the Church (the Councils) and of the pope on occasion of a definition referred not to statements but to a quality of indefectibility and permanence in the truth of the Church.[280]

This is why Rahner holds out for the definition of infallibility as proposed at two Vatican Councils which means that an *ex cathedra* decision of the Magisterium, even if it can be interpreted, cannot be straightaway denied. If Küng perseveres with his denial, he has transgressed the limits of Catholic orthodoxy. The voice of the Church in matters of faith and morals is and remains a *norma normans*.

Rahner's case against Küng is obvious. If Küng's thesis about the Church's indefectibility in truth is valid by itself, one can also suppose that all or a number of her statements, *as statements*, can be erroneous. If this holds true, then no human statement which is pronounced out of a basic conviction (*Grundentscheidung*) could be true.

> One lives in the truth only through true statements, although to-be-in-the-truth, and to make true statements are not identical. Even he or she can in principle be in the truth who otherwise pronounces a number of erroneous statements.[281]

Küng's long and repeated reply to Rahner's criticism endeavoured to show that, save for the explicit denial of the Vatican I dogma, his view on *ex cathedra* definitions is practically the same as that of Rahner. In a further debate, Rahner gingerly admits an *operative agreement* with Küng, however with a proviso:

> ... there remains between our positions an essential difference. It is because for me an inadequate, dangerous and one sided dogma, on the one hand, and an erroneous doctrine which is nonetheless proposed by the Magisterium for the unconditional assent of the faithful, on the other, are essentially different.[282]

What Rahner hints at is that Küng's main examples for erroneous statements (especially the one, *Humanae Vitae*) are indeed not defined dogmas but authentic teachings supporting dogmatic definitions. Had Küng formulated his main thesis in such a way that some dogmas *appear* to be erroneous, because they are connected with supporting doctrines which in concrete circumstances are wrong,[283] his *Anfrage* would have been justifiable.

But what is Rahner's view on infallibility? In the same year, 1971, he tries briefly to asses his own approach to infallible statements.[284] If we restrict ourselves to this essay we are going to meet some characterizations of infallible statements which would surprise a conventional ecclesiologist. It is obvious to Rahner that an infallible definition is not an external intervention in the process of truth-finding which would render any further reflection superfluous. Nor is it a means of imposing truths in a totalitarian way. Even a definition central to the message of Christianity presupposes the free assent of faith – it is a matter of our free decision. It would follow from this fact that 'an *absolute* assent to [such] a proposition and an abiding attitude of criticism with regard to it are not mutually exclusive.'[285]

Infallibility, however, as a dogmatic statement is secondary insofar as it presupposes our general faith in the assistance of the Spirit which entails an attitude of (eschatological) hope 'that the Church will *de facto* never fall victim to the danger which is really immanent in her very constitution.'[286] When this general faith, regardless of possible error, is present, *then* it is valid to assent to the Church's infallible statements.

The other presupposition is connected with the former: just as in human knowledge all dogmas are historical – that is, in a process of a deeper understanding, so is the dogma of infallibility no exception. The statement about infallibility is a historical proposition and, as such, not only tied to its past but open to continuous and steady development in the future. And this means not only a slight change in its formulation, but also in its very meaning.[287] And, indeed, Rahner will sketch the development of the dogma of infallibility from 1870 to Vatican II and after.

This indicates also the logical status of the dogma of infallibility. Its position as compared with other dogmas is odd: whereas the *ex cathedra* pronouncement of a theological subject renders a statement and a number of connected ones infallible, this dogma of the first Vatican Council cannot in turn be based upon itself, that is upon the infallibility of the Magisterium. It is a statement within the system of faith and not the foundation of the system itself. We accept the truths of faith taken as a whole not because of infallibility. It is one statement among others

> ... applicable to secondary cases of conflict, and in this it depends upon the system itself as a prior condition. Thus one can say that this dogma is not infallible (that is, not sustained by the infallible authority of the Church *quoad nos*) but merely renders other propositions infallible.[288]

From this follows that faith in the system of revealed truths must be prior to and accepted without any *logical* appeal to the declaration of infallibility: 'one has to be a believing Christian even before, and without *ipso facto* having to believe in the infallibility' of the Magisterium.[289]

In short, infallibility is a proposition which is ultimately sustained by something outside itself rather than one which sustains the system of faith as a whole. As Rahner elsewhere says:

> The existence and justification of the Church's teaching office [including its infallible propositions] is something which each individual must in fact recognize and accept as such without being able to base himself on the authority of this teaching office.[290]

This logical position of the dogma of infallibility renders its meaning and use bound to historical circumstances. For us, after

Vatican II, it has a different sense than it used to have in the times of Pius IX: it now emphasizes the ecclesial relation of all the other statements of faith. Otherwise, the word 'infallibility' shares the analogical nature of all dogmatic propositions. This means that they are pointers to ultimate truth. From this it follows that its contrary (that is, not contradictory, a simple negation) is not necessarily false.[291] If this is so, then in the future we may hit upon an unknown, apparently contrary, interpretation of the same dogma. Rahner's courageous approach to the dogma of infallibility does not, in my view, imply that the linguistic regulation brought about by its solemn definition ceases to be obligatory, until a more adequate formulation is found: we shall have to speak of infallibility, even if its sense and application have changed.

This explains Rahner's conviction that in the future there will be no 'new' dogmatic definitions as proposed by the infallible Magisterium – that is to say, statements which would appear for us to be beyond the present system of defined dogmas.[292] Though this view would run contrary to nineteenth-century expectations, in our time no one would expect *ex cathedra* decisions of the Pope to be published in the daily edition of *The Times*. Nor could anybody argue that a certain power correctly attributed to the Magisterium has to be put into practice at any given time. No, Rahner does not expect a *quantitative* increase of magisterial definitions. The latest Marian dogma of the Assumption was *not* quantitatively added to the others as a new epithet of Mary: it put explicitly what was already implied in our hope of bodily resurrection.[293]

The main reason for the Church's (according to Rahner, obligatory) abstention from 'new' definitions is the well known and constantly referred to topic of *pluralism* prevailing in regional cultures, philosophies, terminologies, outlooks and, above all, theologies which 'cannot be reduced to any one synthesis'. Though we shall return to this, here it is enough to note its consequences for, what he calls, 'New Dogmatic Formulae', were they ever put forward by the Magisterium:

(i) Any such 'formulae' should be one of the many interpretations of previous dogmas as produced by their development. On the one hand, in view of the fresh formulation of a dogmatic statement 'the past dogma does not retrospectively disappear' – it is newly interpreted. Yet, on the other, the new historical circumstances in which it now emerges may influence their wording – different from those in which it was first formulated.[294]

(ii) If the 'new' is an interpretation (and not straightforward negation) of the 'old', it is among many other possible ones, and none of these can be regarded as false. From which it follows that, in view of other interpretations which were bypassed, the new formula is neither false nor true. Such a new 'dogmatic formula is no longer capable of being false.'[295] It is just one of the many interpretations in a process towards God's truth. It is no advance upon former or even contemporary formulations, but another aspect hitherto not considered.

(iii) The above characteristics are not only valid of statements about transcendent or metaphysical realities, but also hold true of propositions of moral theology. They do not belong to an altogether different category for they, too, are intended to be propositions of faith insofar they imply a relation to God the absolute mystery never to be grasped in its entirety. Propositions in moral theology, which impose the duty of a real assent of faith, can be asserted in the present under different dimension of reality than at the time of their previous announcement. It can also be that such statements are norms aiming at the goal of human behaviour, which is constant, but the means of fulfilling them has emerged recently. This is why similar norms can be proposed in different ways: 'new' norms in the field of moral theology can introduce a plurality over and above their previous formulations.[296]

In all these qualifications Rahner emphasizes the role of Christian *memoria* 'that embraces and expresses the totality of the past pregnant with the future prior to all plurality of different interpretations of the present.'[297] And this is indeed what makes him recommend abstention from new definitions but, if there have to be new quasi-definitions of the Magisterium, then Rahner advises caution in a situation marked with insuperable pluralism.

Can, however, a theologian in this way play schoolmaster to the Magisterium? As we saw, Küng's book did so in suggesting the scrapping of the dogma of Vatican I. Rahner seems to do something similar, although respecting and keeping the dogma. One wonders, however, whether through all these qualifications he, the theologian, does not in effect do just what Küng did. An answer to these questions may emerge from Rahner's view on the relationship between theology and the Magisterium.

(D) *The teaching office of the Church and the theologian*

Ever since the late 1960s, Pope Paul VI's encyclical, *Humanae Vitae*, has become an ecclesiological watershed. To be more precise, its publication and the reaction to it has put the authority of the Magisterium to the test *within the Church*. Apart from the question of the morality of artificial contraception (which furthermore belongs to experts and moral theologians), it has caused the faithful to revise their attitude towards the teaching office and its infallibility. This changed attitude has found its defence in the writings of theologians not always conforming to the official teaching of the Church. As we saw, it has provoked Küng's radical rejection of the principle of infallibility, as well as the more moderate anti-Küng reaction of several theologians, including Karl Rahner.

Beginning with *Humanae Vitae*, there arose more generalized theoretical questions concerning the relationship between what Catholics actually believe, what the theologians publish and the official teaching of the Church. Karl Rahner already had his cards up his sleeve: his own critical reaction to the encyclical[298] deals with the prohibition of the pill, as a non-defined but authentic teaching of the Pope which in principle may prove to be erroneous.[299]

With due respect to the Pope's decision against the majority of an expert commission concerning contraception, Rahner, too, summarizes his own difficulties. In this, his view seems to coincide with the German bishops' interpretation of the same in their Königstein declaration. Rahner holds their not-literal understanding of the encyclical as legitimate. This leads him to the further, more generalized, question about the interpretation of statements connected with the deposit of faith.

The main problem in this, even after Rahner's death, proved to be as he had put it in 1977:

The Roman magisterium itself can hardly be said to have spoken at all hitherto about the precise question of how the acknowledgement of a certain binding force of a purely authentic declaration . . . can co-exist with the necessity and possibility of allowing for an error in that declaration.[300]

Thus the Königstein declaration on *Humanae Vitae* arrived at its slightly deviant conclusions from the encyclical through the way, as Rahner says, of 'theoretical consciousness' of theologians and of the believer. The theologian's function as regards the teaching of the Magisterium cannot be that of a further and more subtle interpretation of its teaching, and of defending it, by showing that it is 'indeed' contained in the original sources of revelation. As far as the authority of such authentic teaching goes, we shall have to regard it as a *provisionally valid* statement – however, with the reservation that a later and better insight may lead to its revision.

To buttress this attitude Rahner appeals to the fact that any dogmatic definition and other authentic statements connected with it *are already theology*, for 'The dogma is inevitably always formulated with the aid of theology.'[301] It is a synthesis of divine revelation and human reflection. Even if this 'synthesis' is affirmed by the authority of the Magisterium, despite its inerrancy, it 'is open to the future for a new form of expression, to be worked out with the tools of a different theology.'[302] This is why we can speak of a pluralism of theologies even within the Bible, and all the more during the development of dogma. Without an ongoing theological reflection, we could not envisage a development which is not only a subsequent reflection on the defined dogma, but affects its contents. In defining a dogma or buttressing it with an authentic statement, the Magisterium sanctions a development in the Church's sense of faith which has been stimulated and sustained by unofficial theology *before* this sanctioning.[303] To conclude: the Magisterium always depends on the work of the theologians, its declarations, as Rahner puts it, do not come from a 'magico-mechanical process on the basis of its purely formal authority'.[304]

To go a step further: theology does not only assist in the making of magisterial proclamations, but it has the task of reflecting upon what has been taught by the Magisterium. This kind of theological activity, apart from its theoretical aim in developing the statements of the Magisterium, has the purpose of adapting these to different horizons and different realms of parlance. Added to this, the teaching of the Magisterium, valid for the whole Church, is inevitably traditional: it activates the Church's memory of past (mainly) theological reflections. It is the task of the theologian to arrive at a 'synthesis of the old faith and the present-day understanding of it.'

What is asked of the theologian is constantly to re-examine this synthesis with a view to its concrete acceptance in the consciousness of the faithful. To this belongs the pointing out of expressions which, though apt for the understanding of statements in the historical circumstances of its making, have lost their significance in the present. If these no longer 'get-across' today, the theologian is supposed to find new ways of expression more easily accessible for the present. For any declaration of the Magisterium, including defined dogmas, are but a beginning of a continuous and never ending process of approaching the mystery of God's self-revelation. In this, Magisterium and theology are mutually dependent on each other: their relationship is a reciprocal causality in their ongoing history.[305]

From this basic position concerning the relationship of Magisterium and theology Rahner makes a number of suggestions for putting this relationship into practice. In a way he too, as Küng did, 'schoolmasters' the Church's Magisterium. The first of these obviously follows from the nature of this relationship: it is the need for a *dialogue* between the two. Contrary to this would be the view according to which the Magisterium 'does not discuss, but decides.'[306] True enough, the two have different functions, but inasmuch the Magisterium is dependent on theology (and today even on the plurality which prevails in it), then the mutual exchange of insights, of terminology, of philosophical assumptions, etc., is inevitable. A Church facing the multiplicity of theologies with an 'official theology' fully supported by the formal authority of the Magisterium would impair, if not totally impede, the possibility of this dialogue.

It was perhaps the lack of this dialogue which motivated Rahner to write his 1980 essay in the style of an imaginary letter of complaint to the Magisterium.[307] As a theologian he admits that the Magisterium cannot tolerate 'theologians, who publicly, in direct confrontation, reject [defined] truths of the divine and

Catholic faith.'[308] They can and should be censured. However, has Rome the right, Rahner asks, to force the dissenter 'in the old feudal way' to submit and withdraw a view contradicting a defined dogma or even an authentic statement of the official teaching? What Rahner had in mind in speaking of the 'old feudal way' is then covertly hinted at some aspects of the still prevailing practice in trials against dissenting theologians: 'In such things Roman authority violates human rights which the Church claims to defend.'[309] A sincere dialogue presupposes from the theologian acknowledgement of the Magisterium and from the Magisterium respect of the theologian's freedom.[310] This latter is pre-eminently valid regarding non-defined, but authentic, statements of the Magisterium which, as we saw, may turn out to be erroneous. In cases like this, a so-called *silentium obsequiosum* (an obedient silence) is not always the right attitude of an apparently 'dissenting' theologian. Rahner often refers to magisterial pronouncements during the reign of Pius X concerning the interpretation of the Bible in which, for example, it was forbidden to speak about different sources of Old Testament literature. Had not Catholic exegetes disregarded this ruling there would not have been any development in biblical scholarship. As Rahner points out, the present Pope, John Paul, speaks today of 'Yahwist', or 'Priestly' authors of the book of Genesis without any reference to the, at that time, authentic rulings of the Magisterium. At certain points in dialogue, the theologian has the *right* to contradict the declarations of the Magisterium and maintain his or her opposition:

> The magisterium could tolerate this contradiction and use it to improve its own arguments without suppressing the theologians that side with it. The best policy would be to let the question of which side is right by ongoing discussion and by the future history of the faith.[311]

From this postulate for a dialogue follows that the Magisterium should clearly qualify its own statements, by referring to the arguments that led its representatives to prescribe not only the contents but also the degree of binding force of such statements. The dialogue, however, is not closed after an absolutely binding decision of the Magisterium. There remains in its rulings what Rahner calls a certain 'amalgam', where the dogmatic kernel of a statement is expressed or covertly connected with alien elements. Thus, for example, the Tridentine term of 'transubstantiation' does not bind the dogma of the real presence in the Eucharist to an Aristotelian-medieval philosophy of substance; and the dogma of original sin, in the way it was defined at Trent, is hardly defensible without an implicit affirmation of monogenism (the whole human race descending from one and only pair).

The conflicts between Magisterium and theology usually arise about these 'amalgams', where the Magisterium is not willing to give up a terminology or an implicit world-view valid at the time of definition, and the theologian, thinking in and for another situation, is in search of a new terminology or different expression for what is no longer understood in the statement. Even if a magisterial decision puts an end to the present-day conflict (as happened concerning the Eucharist where the term 'transfinalisation' was not officially acceptable against the old transubstantiation), the theologian is not bound to defend the view of the Magisterium at all costs. Although the Church is not a debating society, as Rahner acknowledges, the dialogue must go on even after the decision of the Magisterium, however, by pointing out new assumptions. The argument that the ordinary faithful in this period of unresolved conflicts are left in a state of uncertainty and doubt is parried by the fact that it was frequently so in the history of the Church: tolerance is demanded not only on the part of the partners in dialogue but of those who witness it.

Especially in his later writings, Rahner does not forget this third, and mostly silent, partner in this dialogue. It is the people of God. First, however, his concentration is restricted to an intellectual milieu. In 1969 Rahner compares the intellectual presuppositions of a theology in the past with the present situation.[312] Today, the specialization of various scientific disciplines has reached a stage where a synthesis, prevalent for example in the Middle Ages, has become impossible. Neither the contents nor the prevailing methods of our modern scientific mentality are such that a theologian can presuppose any firm conclusion to ground his or her contemporary theology. And if any one of the intellectual and technical achievements of a modern world-view are taken over, the ensuing theology will be one in a plurality of other theologies.

In this situation one interpretation stands against another without either being able to exclude the other's statements and conclusions.

A feature which was not possible in the past.

> The pluralism of which we are speaking here . . . consists precisely in the fact that it is quite impossible to reduce the theologies and their representative theses to a simple logical alternative in this manner [namely, to their intellectual foundations], in the fact that they exist side by side with one another as disparate and mutually incommensurable.[313]

If a theologian in discussion with contemporary Catholic intellectuals should discover a firm conviction of faith on their part, but its expression and emphases are entirely different from what he or she is used to, then it cannot simply be rejected on the suspicion of heresy. It is the theologian's duty to *learn* the context of the other in order to be able to enter into conversation. For a dialogue *a readiness of mutual learning* is presupposed which is, of course, applicable to the relationship of Magisterium and theology. The Magisterium, therefore, is dependent on theologies as well as on their unsurmountable pluralism. Its main function ultimately lies not only in censuring or rejecting propositions of an alien theology but in seeing

> . . . how in, and in spite of, a situation of theological pluralism which is consciously being reflected upon and recognized as insuperable, we can maintain the unity of the creed in a form which is at least partially new.[314]

If Rahner stresses the importance of learning even for the Magisterium, he does not restrict himself to theologians and intellectuals, but also to whatever is actually believed by the faithful. Nowadays we cannot say that any rulings of the Magisterium will unquestioningly be accepted by the average Catholic. Nor can we say that the, often implicit and unreflected, creed of the so-called 'simple faithful' literally coincides with the official teaching of the Magisterium. Rahner can even go a step further: what people actually believe as a content of their faith is no longer fragmentary owing to ignorance 'but coexists with positively contradictory elements in a kind of mostly unconscious and schizoid state.[315] Can the Magisterium learn from this state of affairs? Could that be regarded as the *sensus fidelium*, which is still a source of our common Catholic faith?

At first sight, the Magisterium does not seem to acknowledge this discrepancy between official and not official teaching. As it seems, it goes on writing and speaking in a language which for most people remains esoteric. And, if the so-called 'average' faith is not able to assimilate this language and the truths pointed out by it, then an anathema from the Magisterium is at hand. On the other hand, in our day, we have to see the positive side of this ('gnoseologically concupiscent', as Rahner puts it) situation. In spite of contradictory elements, the average faithful stands in relation to the faith of the whole Church.

> The faith of the average Christian is not just a pitiable sketch of the official faith. It is *a salutary faith borne by God's self-communication*. It is really the faith that God's grace wishes to bring forth and keep alive in the Church.[316]

Obviously, Rahner refers here not to the objective verbal contents of average faith, but to that saving faith which is God's and his Holy Spirit's gift to the sincere believer: 'It is God's Spirit, irrevocably communicated to humankind activating in persons the salutary faith they really possess.'[317]

Rahner's above statement, however, entails more: this average faith can also be normative for the rulings of the Magisterium.[318] His arguments for this statement are not quite convincing. First, he seems to fall back on the relationship Magisterium-theology, for after all the theologian too is one of the people of God. Then he refers to the eschatological nature of the Church which should obediently be accepted. 'That is why this obedient faith is also a necessary and rightful source for the preaching of the faith, and not the other way round.[319]

Of course, the Magisterium with its 'official' faith is the ultimate norm. But should not this Magisterium shift its emphasis in listening to and learning from the common faith of the average Catholic? This shifting of emphasis is, of course, not to be understood as meaning that the Magisterium should withdraw a defined doctrine because a considerable part of the faithful has refused to accept it. Should not, however, this refusal induce the Magisterium to re-think and re-express the same doctrine? Though the example Rahner gives for this case is rather problematic, it is worthwhile quoting. In the old times the keeping of moral precepts was regarded as ultimately decisive for salvation or damnation. Nowadays, when this fear of one's own salvation is less predominant, there is another kind of anxiety, or even guilt, which makes us co-responsible with God who also has to answer 'for the dreadful world he created' (*Gott müsse sich wegen seiner von Ihm bewirkten Welt verantworten*).[320] Would not this observation induce the Magisterium to shift its emphasis in the proclamation of Christian truth and of morality? However dubious this argumentation, it has an ecumenical significance.

§§§§§§

It will be up to Rahner's readers to decide whether his treatment of the relationship between Magisterium and theology, the actual faith of the people of God and the official teaching is a genuine defence and modern reassertion of the Church's teaching authority.

Or is it only a lip-service that, though postulated on theological and sociological grounds, does not leave any practical room to an infallible teaching of an infallible Magisterium? To answer this question (among many others) will be the task of the next chapter.

Chapter 4

Comments and Questions: The Church in the Power of the Spirit

> The community and fellowship of Christ which is the Church comes about 'in the Holy Spirit'. The Spirit is this fellowship. Faith perceives God in Christ and this perception is itself the power of the Spirit. . . . The church is the eschatological creation of the Spirit.[1]

The sub-title and the above quotation from Jürgen Moltmann's ecclesiology, will guide our reflections on Rahner's writings about the visible Church. My previous Comments and Questions (1.4) emphasized the basic tension in speaking about the Church: between her empirical shape and her image in the interpretation of faith. For we experience the Church and at the same time we believe in her, just as we believe in the blessed Trinity. She is part and parcel of our creed.

I have tried to present Karl Rahner's approach to the empirical aspect of the Church: to a visible community or society, the historical counterpart to that which we know through revelation. He spoke of the origin of this Church, of her self-realization in the structures and institutions which are the living experience by members and outsiders as well.

Rahner's picture of the Church is not only the analysis of this empirical phenomenon, but at the same time a reflection of faith which interprets this experience through the charismatic power of the Spirit. This reflection in faith does not set aside the empirical reality of visible structures, institutions and the organs of the

168

Church, but understands them in a new dimension. They do not cease to be what they empirically are, yet they are now 'raised' to be something beyond direct experience. The Church always remains a two-faceted reality.

Apart from the *Handbook* and the short summary of *Foundations*, Rahner never produced a formal systematic ecclesiology. Yet my detailed presentation of his insights into the practical life of the visible Church and her theological foundation could certainly yield a coherent system. His mosaic-like writings about the Church suggest an underlying system, when his throwaway insights and hints are critically collected, expanded and discussed in the construction of a scholarly ecclesiology.

I do not feel myself competent to fulfil this task in my Comments and Questions. Rather, inspired by Rahner's writing, I shall try to expand his ideas concerning the Church bearing in mind our different situations. Our present experience and our theological reflections are different. Rahner's own historical setting of the 1960s was dominated by Vatican II. Before that, many of his writings foreshadowed the teaching of the Council. After it, during his most prolific period, he was writing in the euphoria of a theological renaissance which lasted until the 'wintry season' of the Church. Thinking back, now, after more than 40 years to that post-conciliar epoch, when Rahner's 'wintry season' was refused passage to spring, I could welcome most of his ideas and suggestions concerning the visible Church. This is, however, no longer our situation today.

Thus, my Comments and Questions will be proposed as an essay in its own right yet always reflecting Rahnerian insights from other points of view. A dialogue is not only a critical confrontation, but also a way of thinking together towards a common vision. Whether or not my own contribution would be acceptable to Rahner and his followers is left to the judgement of the reader.

In order to give some structure to these Comments and Questions, I shall presuppose the 'message' of Chapter 3: the Church is both an empirical fact to be experienced and a mystery to be believed. These two aspects are distinct yet inseparable. The correct image of the Church keeps them in harmony and strives at their synthesis which can only be made if the two are genuinely correlatives and not merely parallel approaches to the Church.

So, in this chapter, I shall try, first, to tease out the coherence of these two: the empirical and the mystery aspects of the Church. It is this approach which, in the *first part*, I reflect on and extend. In the *second part* I discuss in more detail the empirical aspects of the Church and in the *third part* I search for a more synthesized view of the Church's ministry in the communion of the faithful.

4.1 The Relevance of Sociology

In this section, first, I discuss (A), the relevance of social sciences for the Trinitarian foundation of ecclesiology; and, secondly, I propose (B), a pneumatological reinterpretation of our faith in the Church.

(A) *The analogy between sociology and ecclesiological beliefs*

Unlike Bonhoeffer, Rahner offers no explicit discussion about the suitability of social sciences for ecclesiology. Although his discussion of the individual and institution (see 3.1.1) and his introduction of the charismatic element into the 'constitution' of the Church (see 3.1.2) could be read as a kind of sociology, he never speaks as a sociologist and never tries to apply the various systems current in modern sociology of religion. In Bonhoeffer's *Sanctorum Communio*, and much more in Medard Kehl's *Catholic Ecclesiology*,[2] there is an explicit discussion about the relationship of these two disciplines. Kehl opts for the sociological horizon of the *Frankfurter Schule*, the leading ideas of which can be ascribed to the analysis of man's communicative action (*kommunikatives Handeln*) by J. Habermas.[3]

In these two ecclesiologies, where social sciences seem to play an important role for the understanding of the Church, reservations are expressed about their suitability. Bonhoeffer doubts his own attempt to understand the structures (*structural zu verstehen*) of the Church in terms of social philosophy:

> What is essential in the Church can only be [*cum ira et studio!*] understood from within her and never neutrally from the outside. Only those who take seriously the challenge of the Church coming from the gospel have a chance of understanding her.[4]

Kehl, on the other hand, appeals to the 'incarnational structure' of the history of salvation in which failure to face and analyse empirical realities would misrepresent those known by revelation.[5] Hence, Kehl assumes an *analogy* between the Church as known by faith and a society as structured by the 'communicative action' of her members. Not only the parallelism between these two but their very convergence proves the suitability of that sociological system, to which Kehl appeals for a better understanding of the Church.[6]

However, in assuming the analogy between the empirical and the revealed aspects, he does not want to deduce the Church directly from the incarnation. Kehl's analogy is between the *whole of salvation history* and the concrete Church. He takes the definition of Chalcedon as an example. The empirical and the revealed aspects of the Church, like the two natures in Christ, are one yet distinct and unmixed; nonetheless, there is an interaction between the two. For Kehl argues that, if the analogy is valid, certain features present in the sociological aspect are also theologically valid and therefore ought to be present in an integral image of the Church. The *Frankfurter Schule* speaks of a society in which there is a strict equality of members who are therefore capable of communication without violence (*gewaltfreie Kommunikation*). The other quality of this communication is that it is not authoritarian. (This is, I believe, the best translation of the original German *herrschaftsfrei*.) Should these sociological features be applied to the Church?

Aware that such an analogy between the notion of the Church and the findings of the *Frankfurter Schule* should not be taken for granted, I will proceed more cautiously. It is true that the experience of living in a religious fellowship was obviously different in a world in which the financial basis of society was slavery, or in a society under a feudal system, no theological reflection on religious fellowship can avoid interpreting the Church in the light of the actual shape of contemporary secular society. It is clear that almost all the problems and even crises in the self-understanding of the present Church derive from the desire for proper communion, realized through consent and non-authoritarian communication as well as by the ideals of a democratic society based on the freedom and equality of its members. Is this desire admissable for our contemporary notion of the Church?

One wonders, however, whether this relationship can simply be characterized as an analogy between the Church as known from the gospel and the ideas of a certain social system. Analogy presupposes a fairly well-defined main concept, an *analogatum princeps*, to which the other concept exhibits noticeable similarities which are not merely verbal. Kehl's 'fraternising' with the *Frankfurter Schule* can betray that for him the *analogatum princeps* is on the side of one sociological system which rules the analogy with the consequence that the revelation aspect is simply assumed, or, in the end, thoroughly modified. Can a theologian, as a theologian, afford to follow Kehl's approach? Should not he or she rather convert the approach and start from the revealed notion of the Church and then ask what can be learnt for *theological* ecclesiology from various sociological systems? Thus, instead of analogy, I prefer to speak of a *parallelism through dialogue*. I am aware that the correspondence between the two can never be complete, yet there is *perichoresis*: the empirical 'concretises' the revealed aspect of the Church, while the latter always remains a critical element for our social life.

If we follow the description of the experience and the definition of the Church, as proposed in Chapter 2, our starting point should be the direct and natural experience of living in a religious fellowship. For, I believe, all religious experience, even those tending to individual mysticism, bear a reference to community. Being religious implies at least a loose consensus of beliefs shared with our fellows, and this consensus is the first characteristic of a society. If, to a certain extent, we want to go along with Kehl's analogous application of the theory of communicative action, we should also hold that each fellowship or community has a utopian element which holds its members together in anticipation of a common aim and its final fulfilment at the end. A religious system not based on eschatology at its background is hardly imaginable. Any religious association with these two distinguishing marks can become the space in which the commitment of faith can arise. Hence, my primary question is: How do we modify this basic experience when we interpret it in the light of our faith in Christ's salvation?[7] This should be our *analogatum princeps*.

(B) *The pneumatological structure*

In the previous section, I have only cursorily referred to faith in the Blessed Trinity as the central mystery supporting also the integral notion of the Church. It is the teaching of Vatican II and no modern ecclesiology can avoid addressing the questions implied by this. Rahner points out that it is an advance on the earlier ecclesiology based on apologetics. This apologetics defends the founding of the visible Church, with almost all her structures and institutions, by the pre-Easter Jesus. Though this has not lost its importance, it has become today a secondary question. It is more important to ask in what sense belief in the Trinity can be relevant for the understanding of the Church of Christ.

The parsimony of Rahner's texts explicitly dealing with this question does not mean that he was not aware of it; in 1971 he outlined the way in which the three 'powers' of the hierarchy derive from the inner life of the Trinity (see 3.2.2). Nevertheless, for Rahner it is more important to envisage the actual life of the Church under the guidance of the charismatic gift of the Spirit. The biblical notion of charismata helps Rahner not only to face the problem of the relationship between the individual and institution (see 3.1.2), but they become the dynamic force in an 'open Church': 'The first and the ultimate among the formal characteristics . . . in the very nature of the Church as such.'[8] The emphasis on the charismatic element which, at times, Rahner regards as the essence of the Church, will produce dividends in the attempt to characterize the concrete historical Church. Indeed, at times, he writes of two structures within the Church: the charismatic and the institutional. Rahner's appeal to the charismatic is an insight of faith which prevents the Church from becoming either an absolute monarchy or a popular democracy. It is indeed the charismatic that brings us to the knowledge of Christ and of the triune God; its basic power is the Holy Spirit.

Yet, in spite of his concentration on the charisms, Rahner's image of the Church is not really *pneumatological*. One has the impression even that the charismatic gifts of the Spirit are used as incidental to both the theoretical and to the practical account of the Church. It is the Spirit that saves the Church from becoming a tyranny under the paramount authority of the Roman Pope. It is the Spirit as the source of novelty and unrest, that opens the Church to a world-wide dialogue. Innovators therefore can always appeal to the charisms of the Spirit. Since Rahner seems to blur the historical borderline between Divine revelation in Jesus Christ and the ensuing tradition, there is a certain ambiguity in the role of the Spirit: Is the Spirit merely a stand-by or a personal contribution in the coming-to-be of the Church? None of this yields a genuinely pneumatological image of the Church. It remains the continuing presence of the Incarnate (a truly *incarnational Church*) helped at certain points by the Spirit in her life here and in her eschatological fulfilment.

A genuinely *pneumatological* image of the Church presupposes a change, an insight into faith in the blessed Trinity and our salvation; a change which, I believe, is implicit in Rahner's theology. It concerns the *relationship between Christology and Pneumatology*.

No one would deny that these two disciplines are inseparable, but this does not establish a relationship. The theology of the Western Church envisaged the Spirit's role through the biblical concept of *mission*. The Son asks the Father to send the Counsellor to his disciples as the Spirit of truth, as the pledge of unity now and of the reality of the fulfilment then. This Spirit sent by the Father is, of course, Christ's Spirit who cannot be and do more than Christ, if he had remained with us. The theory of the, so-called, immanent Trinity reflects this concept and leads to the conviction that the Spirit proceeds from the Father as well as from the Son, *patre filioque procedit*, a point of faith that still divides the Western from the Eastern Church. For those who concentrate especially on the Church as a society, this point of contention between Orthodoxy and Western theology is only speculative *quisquilia* as is the question of precedence between Christology to Pneumatology in salvation history.

I believe, however, that these speculative questions have a significance in an ensuing ecclesiology: we should distinguish between an epistemological and an ontological priority in discussing the precedence of the Spirit. An appeal in faith to the power of the Spirit of God can reassure us that we can believe and understand who the Christ is. For 'no one can say "Jesus is Lord" except by the Holy Spirit' (1 Cor. 1:3b). The power of the Spirit is presupposed by faith in knowing the Christ-event, and where faith in the Christ-event occurs, there the Church can emerge.[9] In spite of this epistemological priority, Christology often precedes Pneumatology. This latter precedence, however, which is, incidentally, characteristic of Paul's epistles, leaves Pneumatology undeveloped, a handmaid of true Christology. The theology of the West in particular uses this concept for ecclesiology. Jesus founds *and* constitutes the Church in her originality and the Spirit is the historical stand-by to the eschatological fulfilment of both the community and the individual. Perhaps this is why Père Congar warns Western theology of the Church against a certain *Christomonism* in which only a secondary role is attributed to the Spirit.[10]

In contrast to this epistemological priority, I shall propose an ontological one: Pneumatology before Christology. By this I do not mean that there is a *difference* between the divine nature(s) of the Son and the Spirit. This would lead to tritheism. By 'ontological' priority I mean, first, that the *content* of the Spirit's work in the order of salvation history is *different* from that of the Son. Secondly, this difference is not only in their respective works, but is rooted in their very *personal being*.[11] For ecclesiology this means that *not only the existence or life of the Church, initiated by Jesus the Christ, but her very nature is the 'creation' of the Spirit.* With this sentence we come nearer to the position of Eastern Orthodoxy, well expressed by the words of J. Moltmann:

> Orthodoxy understands the history of Jesus itself pneumatologically. . . . His incarnation, his mission, his anointing, and his resurrection are the works of the Holy Spirit. . . . The Holy Spirit is the divine subject of the history of Jesus. For that reason the Son of God is also present in and through the Spirit in his Church, . . . [just as] it is at work in creation. Pneumatological Christology leads to a charismatic ecclesiology.[12]

Two trends in assertions about the Spirit exist in the New Testament. On the one hand, the Spirit is given *by* the risen

Christ, '. . . for as yet the Spirit had not been given, because Jesus was not yet glorified' (Jn 7:39) and, on the other hand, it is the Spirit who is at work at Jesus' biological conception and at the beginning of his public mission (baptism, Mt 3:16 and parallels; temptation, Mt 4:1 and parallels). As for the second trend I would agree with J. D. Zizioulas: there is no *Christ* 'until the Spirit is at work, not only as forerunner announcing his coming, but also the one who *constitutes his very identity as Christ.*[13] To be precise: I do not assert the priority of the Spirit in the so-called 'essential' Trinity, but of his priority in the realm of history. Even H. U. von Balthasar wrote of a 'Trinitarian inversion: not only *after* the mission of the Spirit at Pentecost, but *before* in the whole earthly life of Jesus: the Spirit rules, holds sway in God's history within the world.[14]

The priority of the Spirit in the economy of salvation should thereby be established. But there is more to it. It is true that the work of the triune God *ad extra* (outside of the life of the Trinity) is one and indivisible: wherever the Spirit is there also are the Father and the Son. Yet, the contribution of these divine Persons is marked by their own distinctive characteristics.[15] Their work *ad extra* is one but not undifferentiated. It is the Son who becomes one singular person within *history*, but it is the Spirit who in raising Jesus from the dead (Rom 8:11) makes him a living spirit (1 Cor 15:45; 2 Cor 3:17). The particularity of the event of Jesus thus becomes a universal *eschatological hope* for all mankind (1 Cor 15: especially 20–28). It is through the Spirit that this particular Man, Jesus, becomes universal, one and many, an individual *and* a corporate personality. It is through the Spirit that we can identify the one Body of Christ with the Church. This is the significance of the *ontological distinction* which emphasizes the priority of Pneumatology over Christology.[16]

Ecclesiology provides another distinctive characteristic attributed to the Spirit: the antithesis between the *one and the many* finds its balanced synthesis through the power of the Spirit. Jesus the Christ is at the same time *one* individual and *many* as a collective person by the power of the Spirit. We can safely hold that the universality of Christ's message is due to the Spirit. In the history of Trinitarian speculation it is the Spirit that enables the two other divine Persons to be one, yet keeps them as three ('many').

In God there is a *pluralism* in the complete harmony in the unity of the Persons. And this divine oneness is the *communion* enabled by the Spirit.[17] This unitive function which, at the same time, upholds the distinction of the 'many' (the Father and the Son) is the Spirit's contribution both to Christology and to ecclesiology. The Spirit empowers a group of believers to use the first person plural in reciting the Creed, 'We believe.' The Spirit, too, moves believers to interpret that which they confess in common in many different ways. The Spirit who dwells in the particularity of the one Church and at the same time works from the beginning of creation everywhere where humans are in search of their own and the world's salvation.

I am aware that my argument for the priority of the Spirit in salvation history can be misinterpreted as a *pneumatomonism* over against Père Congar's Christomonism. Apart from the practical danger for the unity of the Church that early in her history promoted a pneumatological enthusiasm and created exclusive communities of the elect proffering deviant doctrines and ecclesial discipline, there is the danger, too, of destroying the strict unity of the Trinity. This was, I believe, one of the reasons that by the *filioque* the Western Church, as it were, 'closed up' the model of the one God in three persons and postulated one Divine nature for God's work *ad extra*. Though Western theology starts from the, so-called, 'essential' Trinity, but could not we, for a better understanding of salvation history, retain the statement of the Orthodox creed: From the Father through the Son to the Spirit? By means of this the Spirit's action, though one with that of the Father and Son, can acquire his own personal character in history. The Spirit can in this sense be the 'space' where the Church can emerge. The farewell speeches of Jesus in John's gospel contain two statements which support such a theology of the Spirit:

> But the Counsellor, the Holy Spirit, whom the Father will send in my name, he will teach you all things, and bring to your remembrance all that I have said to you. (Jn 14:26)

One wonders indeed if 'all things' are already implied in Jesus' teaching which the disciples are going to remember, or whether there are insights not so much implied but in harmony with Jesus' words. And further:

> When the Spirit of truth comes, he will guide you into all the truth; for he will not speak on his own authority, but whatever he hears he will speak, and he will declare to you the things that are to come. (Jn 15:13)

The 'not speak on his own' here seems to restrict the power of the Spirit to Jesus' eschatological message, meaning that he merely interprets the teaching of the Son. Yet, in interpreting the whole of the Christ-event, the Church could be guided to truths that could not logically have been deduced from the words of the Lord.

This is why I am inclined to attribute an ontological dependence of the Church on God's Holy Spirit. Vatican II comes near to this position:

> The same Spirit *makes* the body one through himself and by his power and by the inner cohesion of the members, and *produces* and urges charity among the faithful.[18]

Is not this a step towards a truly pneumatological ecclesiology? In such a doctrine of the Church, the Spirit is not only that which 'makes', 'produces' something within the already existing Body of Christ: the Spirit *constitutes* the Church in *existence*. We are about to adopt a similar opinion as that of John Zizioulas:

> Pneumatology does not refer to the well-being of the Church. It is not about a dynamism which is added to the essence of the Church. It is the very essence of the Church. . . . Pneumatology is an ontological category in ecclesiology.[19]

From this point of faith, I shall try to understand the constitution and social institutions of the Church.

4.2 The Constitution and the Institutions of the Church

If the Spirit has to do with the very essence of the Church and if she is formed to the analogy of the blessed Trinity she should not be anything else but a communion. And in a communion type of human association the equality of its members, their mutual love and consent in their diversity are expected. Nor is there an external goal clearly definable in this corporate personality in order to hold its members together: their very communion as interpreted by faith is the meaning and – to some extent – the fulfilment of their association. United in faith, love and eschatological hope is already their salvation.

This is, however, not our everyday experience. The Church appears most of the time as an organized society. It is, then, understandable that in Rahner's ecclesiological writings one finds elements of some sociological considerations without which the mystery of the Church cannot be grasped. We shall now turn to these.

A) *Sociological aspects of the Church*

In my long presentation of Rahner's ideas about the foundation (see 3.2) and the organs (see 3.3) of the Church, I could not fail to point out some sociological features. Rahner was in search of the Church's basic constitution without which no society can achieve any stability. He spoke (and not always consistently to boot) of structures within the Church which are supposed to regulate various institutions – taking it for granted that the visible Church exists in her institutions and trying to indicate their origin. If we take these three, constitution, structures and institutions, without a certain amount of sociological reflection, we are unable to gain an adequate image of the Church.

There is no doubt that the Church as a society should have a basic constitution. Secular legislation answering problems arising out of everyday situations must have an ulterior criterion in order to safeguard its own validity. In most societies it takes the form of universally valid laws (*Grundgesetz*) which in their permanence are at the same time a court of appeal for the ambiguities in the everyday application of secondary legislation.[20] Rahner was, in principle, ready to assign certain features as belonging to the basic constitution of the Church as society. Most frequently he referred, as something fundamental, to her hierarchical nature and even to her Petrine and episcopal regiment. Yet, when facing the Spirit's charismata he could not regard these 'constitutional' factors as the last platform of appeal. Here, Rahner's search for a Church-constitution had to abandon a purely sociological level and appeal to the trust and faith of the believer in the guidance of the Holy Spirit. Hence, in this respect, he admits that in a secular sense the Church has no basic constitution. The Spirit is the last criterion, as it were, the 'supreme constitutional court' of appeal.[21]

In Rahner's writings, however, there are some attempts to speak of the Church from a sociological point of view. In referring to structures and institutions within the Church, he comes to a quasi-definition of each of these terms. Earlier (see 3.1) I quoted:

> . . . all institutional factors constitute, in a social sense, the outer periphery and the . . . secondary . . . realisation . . . of that which is called structure and order.

As a counterpart, by 'structures' Rahner means everything that exists in fact in the Church – permanently and universally as a reality determining the action and decisions of Church members, especially that of her office holders.

All that we can take from these remarks is that while structures ought to be permanent, institutions can change. We could then assert that structure and order are what could be, in *praxis*, taken for the constitution of the Church.

What are these permanent structures (now taken as the basic constitution of the Church)? Let me try, first, at least a descriptive definition of permanent structures. By social structures I mean *the build-up and the inner articulation of a human grouping as a whole in which the diversity of its members, as well as their unity among themselves and with the group as such, are safeguarded.*[22] The origin of these permanent structures presupposes certain conventions among the members which can become normative within the group and, after a time, it can even become an institution, taken for granted by subsequent generations.

Thus *some* institutions can be part of 'permanent' structures which rule and pattern the others. Nonetheless, according to my first quote, they remain only 'peripheral and secondary realisations'. For instance, if the papacy and the hierarchy are such institutions which rule the subsequent ones, then they can be regarded as a quasi-constitution of the whole Church.

This is, however, only one aspect in approaching permanent structures. There is, however, another one which takes these institutions not in their concrete form of appearance, but as a *principle* ever-present in the society which regulates the emergence of any possible institutions, also that of the hierarchy under the Pope. I believe that both alternative aspects are present in Rahner's thought: it is, in the first place, possible to assume one, and apparently central, 'institution' of the Church as a permanent structure – even on anthropological grounds – and apply it as regulative for subsequent ones.

In his essay 'Hierarchy', Rahner discusses what is its meaning and takes it as an institution which gives sense and meaning to all supervening ones (see 3.2.2). In this case one of the permanent structures (the hierarchy) could regulate subsequent institutions: in their origin and function they would be dependent on the power and care of its ordained officials. This could, for instance, imply that in the Church nothing could be institutionalized without the initiative of the hierarchy. Although Rahner dutifully repeats that the hierarchical structure is a constitutive principle of the Church, I believe that nothing is further away from his mind than the above conclusion. Otherwise, how could he speak of the diverse trends among the people of God without mentioning the hierarchy?[23] How could he point to a sinful manipulation of human freedom by the hierarchy.[24] How could he speak of the misuse of power even by representatives of churchly institutions?[25]

In 'Hierarchy', Rahner can assert the emergence of the hierarchy as a *natural human need* within the Church as a society which would also imply the authority of its officials. However, for example, in a chess club (an analogy Rahner likes to use) the supervening institutions require the free consent of its members. Thus, what Rahner seems to understand by hierarchy as a permanent structure, as belonging to the quasi-constitution of the Church, is not only *one* of the institutions (that is, the hierarchy in its concretely realized form), but also a *regulating principle*.

By this regulating principle I understand a recurrent mode of social action by means of which the various elements of common living are ordered. This act of 'ordering' is the structural principle common to all societies, including the Church and her hierarchy. Rahner often uses similar considerations in explaining the build-up of the Church as a society. He could argue that institutions are necessary, because subjective convictions about beliefs can only become objectified as they are caught in the net of official, communitarian professions. 'Truth has something to do with institution.' The structural element is here an objectivization of subjective convictions. Something similar is valid for freedom: a free acceptance of beliefs is only then concrete, if it is engaged, if it adheres to the common task shared with others. The structural element here is this concretization of freedom, its engagement in society's striving to its goal. Instead of taking the institution of the hierarchy as the permanent structure (that is, the social constitution) of the Church, Rahner regards it, in the second place, as an active principle at the basis of all external manifestations, of all institutionalizations of a society.

That the hierarchical structure is of essential importance for the Church is not only Rahner's conviction, but is repeatedly reasserted from a legal point of view. As K. Mörsdorf states, 'The hierarchical structure is constitutive of the people of God . . . ' and:

> In an ecclesiastical legal language the hierarchy is the structure [of the Church, but], in an objective sense is the institutional order within this structure, and, in the subjective sense the totality of those holding sacred authority. [For] The hierarchical structure is constitutive of the people of God.[26]

When we take this basic structure for an active principle, we refer also to an anthropological fact of human society creating its own ordered build-up, often leading to further institutionalization. The concrete hierarchical order and those holding office in it are products of the same active principle.

It is a tenable view that the word 'hierarchy' (sacred dominion) was introduced into ecclesiastical usage only in the sixth century by Denis the Areopagite. In his neo-platonic thought, the hierarchy of the Church, consisting of bishops-priests-deacons on the one hand and monks-lay people-catechumens, on the other, is a mirror of the similar (3+3) hierarchy of the angels in heaven.[27] With this, what sociology may call, 'legitimation' of ecclesiastical hierarchy, a descendent order from Pope to catechumens can be introduced into the people of God. Today, we find this sort of 'reasoning' questionable. Even more questionable is, from the point of view of the gospels, that it is also associated with a (sometimes ontological) subordination to higher power which excludes not only a partial democratization of the Church, but also could and can hinder a genuine brotherhood within the community. It is suggested by Kehl that in our modern circumstances, it would be better to abandon the word 'hierarchy' with its possibly misleading meaning: it may refer to stable stratification of the Church with an almost inevitable reference to power structures.[28] This, does not exclude a reasonably ordered distribution of tasks and roles within the brotherhood of equals as based on, what I have called, a regulating principle in society, which can be equivalent to hierarchical structures.

As we see, the basic structure (that is, the quasi-constitution) of the Church is connected with the emergence of institutions. Rahner seems to have been either unaware of theories in modern social sciences or never explicitly used them. They would have helped him in their ecclesiological application; their common question is to work out what it is in human nature, in human groupings, in human culture, that makes institutionalization inevitable. Since Rahner's quasi-sociological approach to the Church was an attempt to answer the same (or very similar) questions, he could have applied these to illustrate his structural principle within the Church. It is a task that Kehl tried to fulfil. In his dissertation on the Church as institution, Kehl attempted to sum up the current theories of the coming-to-be and role of institutions.[29] He speaks, however, as a theologian, of the origin of institutions with regard to the findings of sociology.

For myself, I see especially three aspects in these anthroposociological sciences which a theological ecclesiology should take into consideration. I discuss them below.

First aspect

There is a distinction current in social sciences: a difference between an original, or primary, institutionalization and the objectification of the same for future generations.

As for the first: it is the community and its members which, by trial and error or by consent, freely opt for norms of behaviour, of communication, of different roles and their authority or power in their communitarian life. The results of this process are the different institutions and their structural coherence with which individuals of later generations are confronted. Sociology's proper study is this second aspect: an institution is such a system of norms (and values) which have their own objective reality to be confronted by the members of a group as an outward 'necessitating' factor.[30]

Had Rahner applied a similar pattern for social institutions in the Church, it would have been easy to find strict parallels with the first generation of Christians (*die Urkirche*) in which creative human freedom brought about its primitive institutions. This first generation laid the foundations of a developing tradition in which some of these were firmly established. Individuals of further generations are born into a, so to speak, ready-made world in which one has to be 'socialized'. The community lives out of and with the dividends of their ancestors, whose freedom was different from theirs; their knowledge will presuppose (or even will be biased by) the insights, the values, the beliefs and the customs of the initial institutionalization. They demand acceptance and, if it is done in freedom, ancient traditions and formerly established institutions inevitably gain a new shape. After the first Christian generations this is the world of Church members.

On the other hand, the unquestioning acceptance of these traditions, as a rule, results, in what Rahner would characterize as a *Volkskirche* or (which is worse) in an ossified and fundamentalist sectarianism. 'Internalization,' as Berger and Luckman would call it,[31] goes parallel with strict questioning, putting to test a tradition (and the institution conveying it) from the point of view of a different world with its own questions, with other social structures of a community the members of which are equally as Christians as their ancestors were. The testing and questioning of inherited traditions and institutions were not always felicitous. Think of the time in the reign of Constantine the Great and his successor, when the Church paired up with the Empire. She remained Christian, yet she had 'interiorized' her beliefs with barely Christian elements taken over from the surrounding secular society. The same happened in the Middle Ages, when the feudal system and its mentality penetrated the beliefs of committed Christians: many of the Church's ancient institutions were re-shaped according to feudal taste. We could apply something similar to our present situation, where Rahner's Church in an 'open society', is about to take shape (see 2.1.2).

Second aspect

The second way in which the social sciences (or rather social philosophy) may help in construing an ecclesiology are the various theories about institutionalization. As we remember, Rahner held this latter inevitable in the life of the Church. Here he could have applied A. Gehlen's theory which postulates it as a 'discharging' mechanism (*Entlastungsfunktion*) inherent in every human culture.[32] Or, he could have appealed to N. Luhmann's theory of social systems according to which institutions emerge as answers to communitarian need and remain as stable mechanisms for reducing the complexity of communal knowledge or social behaviour.[33] We could go on by pointing out various (and sometimes diverging) theories of social institutionalization. More important is, however, to see their possible application to the *Urkirche*.

It is clear that, from the viewpoint of anthropo-sociological sciences, a kind of primitive institutionalization or something similar happened at the beginnings of the Church. A group of people, living with the common belief of their risen Lord's memory, will try to find their way in their social context. The more their number increases the more the need for self-organization and eventually for stable institutions. It is a free human process not of individual persons, but of the community. When the group of the twelve found its cohesion in a shared belief in Jesus' dramatic presence in their midst and in his teaching about the Kingdom and Rule of God or, when each of them experienced his risen and spiritualized body, when they had perceived their Mission for the whole world (Mt:28,18–20; the much debated Mk:16,15–16; Jn:20, 21–23) their beliefs and their common tasks were bound to hold them together as a group.

Already before that happened, they had to fill the gap left over by Judas Iscariot. Matthias is elected 'by casting lots' into an already well-established 'institutional body', calling themselves the twelve (Acts:1,21–26). This 'institution' is now launched on the road of history. There develops a certain network of personal authorities: Peter and John, and, later, the other James. They become natural leaders and when Paul comes with the almost scandalous idea of the heathen-mission then, quite naturally, a kind of synodal institution comes to be. The difference between strictly judaistic Christians and Paul's party is ironed out in Acts:15. This proto-synod decides in favour of Paul, legislates for the newly converted and sends missionaries into the field with its blessing. By that time they have already organized the institution of deacons – and Acts:6 refers to a good number of them, as it seems, with Stephen, the martyr, at their head. They have certainly come together to break bread and remember the Lord's passion and resurrection. Although we have no evidence of it, it is easy to guess who presided at their assembly. Later, in the Pauline churches, the words *presbyteroi* and *episkopoi* emerge. The two words have meant the same thing and there is not the slightest evidence that they were also regarded as *hiereis*, priests in the analogy of Jewish sacrificing priesthood. Last, but not least, as a result of their missionary activity we have a score of newly-founded churches within the one Church. These will have their own leaders appointed or elected; and they will, according to need, found new institutions and initialize their own traditions. Roughly, this was the Church's primary institutionalization in the *Urgemeinde*.

Third aspect

There is a further point, which could be taken from the social sciences. In the process of this early institutionalization the community must have come to new insights and taken important decisions for their communal life. In these, their appeal to the Holy Spirit (and much less to the 'ordinance' of the Lord), can be regarded as a *legitimation* harking back to the origin of their beliefs. 'For it has seemed good to the Holy Spirit and to us,' as their 'synodal decree' in Acts 15:28 states.

By legitimation, of course, I do not understand an appeal to an ideology which, under certain circumstances, means the exercise of a non-legitimate power (a feature which has, regrettably, happened at times in the history of the Church). Legitimation is simply an answer to the question: Why do we act in this way and take this and not the other decision? This is reinforced by their belief in the 'gift of the Spirit' which may also explain the conversion of an individual or a group to the gospel of Christ.

It is remarkable that Luke, who is believed to have been in contact with Paul, does not explicitly refer to this 'gift of God' as a charisma which 'to each is given . . . for the common good' (1 Cor. 12:7). It is a notion not unknown in sociology. There, a charisma is an unlearned spontaneous psychic power not dependent on any objective institution which, in certain historical circumstances, enables its possessor(s) to change the structure of an established society.[34] Whilst the charismatic in Acts can often be regarded as an attempt to wean the new community from its Jewish background, the Pauline notion of charisma in 1 Cor. 12, as I see it, understands the same psychic force *also* for the unity of an already established fellowship. I stress the word 'also', since at the same time, as Rahner emphasizes, the charisms are a power of innovation. In both cases, however, an appeal to the Holy Spirit's charisms functions as a legitimation of important events and decisions in the history of the emerging Christian community.

To sum up: I believe that Rahner would agree with my hypothesis that the Church as a society, its coming-to-be, its initial self-organization with the resulting basic institutions, could, in principle, be explained by merely anthropo-sociological means. Indeed, this is what he seems to do in his 'Hierarchy'; he argues for the viability of the hierarchy on the anthropo-sociological level and then appeals to the blessed Trinity as its background. From this mystery he seems to have 'deduced' the threefold office and the threefold power of the hierarchy. Did he do it as an analogy from the side of the mystery to natural processes? Did he want to confirm his reasoning with the content of faith as regards the sociological construction of the Church? Or did he *interpret* this latter from the dimension of faith? Can such an anthropo-sociological construction add something or correct the faith in the Church?

B) *Institutions and the founding of the Church*

A merely sociological viewpoint of the Church never yields a theological ecclesiology. Though such a view is freely examined on the level of Church sociology, it has to be confronted with what the Church is believed to be through her members' act of faith. What we mean by an act of faith is independent of the events of a social group-building. It refers rather to the members' common experience of Christ and his Spirit, to their own, individual, decision to follow him within the fellowship of the equally called in order to announce to and realize his message to mankind.[35]

If we take this as the minimal content of faith, then for Church members the task of legitimizing the sociological event of the Church's coming-to-be and her organization becomes an existential need. It is a matter of final salvation. This is why, beyond grounding the existence of the community and its institutions by natural need, there is an appeal to *divine authority*. It is true, even on the sociological level, that man's dependence on an already established social system and its institutions (secondary institutionalization) is accepted on the authority of the group and its representatives. In sociology, however, the question of any society's origin is secondary, and living with its institutions in principle the task of man's free consent or dissent. On the other hand, from the point of view of faith the question about the origin of the Church is of decisive importance. If it cannot be shown that the Church is of divine origin, then one's belonging to her can eventually prove to be a fatal mistake. This is why any religious association (or even every religion) claims a divine origin. Either this claim is embedded in man's original group-building, as some anthropologists assert,[36] or it is an appeal to a revelation wherein a person or a group is supposed to be in immediate contact with the Divine. What is then experienced is transmitted by oral or written tradition. Hence without this (even) vicarious experience of divine authority and without a decision for or against it we cannot speak of a genuine act of faith. Nor is this faith valid if it does not convey any content: a message, a new way of life, a promise, or even an information (however primitive it might be). Once this security of faith is given, it is easier to deal with religious institutions.

Leaving apart other religious traditions, Jewish-Christian revelation certainly had this claim to divine authority. One had to justify the very existence of Israel, as the elected people of God, and within this the authority of the Torah, of singular institutions (for example, the kingship after it was introduced against the will of Jahweh), of cultic actions, and so on. To be a member of Israel meant commitment to the authority of Jahweh, living in accordance with the laws and customs of the elected people, obeying its anointed leaders, belonging, on any level, to the Jewish community and its cult – all this meant the security of living in possession of Jahweh's promises: all these decided one's temporal and even eternal well-being. The Jewish *kahal*, translated in the Septuagint as *ekklesìa tou theou*, claimed her origin from Jahweh and was built on his divine authority.

It is now understandable that also the first groupings of Christians strove to justify (or, which comes to the same, to 'legitimize') the existence of their fellowship by an appeal to faith, this time either in God's raising Jesus from the dead or in his teaching, which had been an existential experience as well as the message entailed by it to subsequent generations as an authoritative revelation. Their belief in it was at the same time a sociological factor which enabled their community, the Church, in her coming-to-be.

Rahner in his access to ecclesiology in *Foundations* wisely avoids entering into the debate of the exegetes about the founding of the Church by the pre-Easter Jesus. Exegetical literature concerning this topic is immense and it is most difficult for a dogmatic theologian to find his way in the labyrinth of diverse interpretations. The only explicit words of Jesus are in the pericope of Mt 16:16–19 where not only the tacit intention of Jesus, as Rahner correctly argues, but his explicit will to found a community of his followers under the leadership of Peter the Rock is documented. 'You are Peter and on this Rock I shall build [*oikodomesw*] my Church.' (Mt 16:18). The tag, 'my Church' (as against the hitherto used *ekklesia tou theou*) seems to mean that, on the similarity of the Old Testament's *kahal*, Jesus, after his departure, will have his own organized assembly within or apart from Israel.

Leaving aside the rest of the pericope concerning the role of Peter which is, as we shall see, its most contested part, the question emerged, whether indeed the coming-to-be of the Church is due to these words of the Lord. W. G. Kümmel questions such a conclusion: with Jesus announcing the imminent arrival of God's Kingdom, his concept of a Church with her institutions in this aeon before the end of the world is logically unacceptable.[37] The

Church as she has become must find her origin somewhere else, for instance, in God's raising the crucified Lord and, above all, in his eschatological gift of the Spirit. Hence, as Kümmel states, the Church is an entity after the Resurrection and Pentecost. Accordingly, one cannot argue for the intention of the pre-Easter Jesus to establish a Church in the time between his death and the second coming.

Even if – with most Catholic scholars – we disclaim an error concerning the parousia on the part of the man Jesus, it is difficult to see what he really intended in the logion of Matthew 16. Can his future 'church' be taken for a continuation of the assembly of the Old Testament, or something entirely new?[38] If we consider that Matthew alone adds these words to an account also present in Mark (8:27–30) and Luke (9:18–21), where there is no reference to the founding of the Church, then, despite all dogmatic assertions to the contrary, the doubt in exegesis is justified. It is, however, probable that Matthew was writing for an already established local church. In this case, Matthew's version of this event presupposes the gradual separation of Christians (begun already in the time of the *Urgemeinde*) from the Jewish community.[39] This separation indicates the newness of the Church over and above the Jewish *kahal*. Whether or not this Matthean addition repeats the genuine words of Jesus, it certainly serves as a kind of etiology[40] with which Matthew justifies the existence of his addressee church for subsequent generations of believers. Only in this mediated sense can we speak of Jesus' Church-founding intention in Matthew 16.

If Jesus indeed meant to institute yet another, new and rival, *kahal*, one should ask whether only the rest of the Jews who accepted him as Messiah belonged to this, or to an all-embracing universal church with its basic organization to which the whole of mankind should be converted? Although *after* the Resurrection he gives an universal mission to his apostles and their followers (Mt 28:17ff), in his lifetime he seems to have meant something different with the call of the twelve and with their mission. It is evident that the pre-Easter Jesus sent his disciples *only* to Israel and seemed to have forbidden the mission to a pagan world (Mt 15:24.26; 10:5f). From this J. Jeremias concludes that between Jesus' departure and the parousia he had no intention of instituting a community separate from Israel. Yet it is certain that he intended the renewal of the whole of Israel at the end and not only a small part of it. We can admit, therefore, that Jesus' own mission was *at first* explicitly restricted to Israel. To this he gathered the twelve around himself in order to symbolize and to anticipate the eschatological consummation of history in the realized Kingdom.

Yet the refusal of his message by many of his contemporaries created a new situation: hence, his words and parables in which not only Israel, but outsiders also, are named as heirs of his mission (for example, Mk 13:10; Mt 8:11f; Mt 21: 33–45; Mt 24:14). This lets us surmise that Jesus must have thought of a period in between his death and the parousia. Did he, however, envisage that a number of his followers, Jews and pagans, would organize themselves as a group in expectation of the end? Otherwise why should he have predicted persecutions for his disciples from the Jewish authorities also? Why did he, before his death and Resurrection, 'institute' the Eucharist as the remembrance of him, if he had not reckoned with a time in between? And even if we do not take Matthew's explicit Church-founding words (Mt 16) as genuine, Jesus must have made provision for the (gradual) grouping of his followers around the twelve: as reported, he gave to the group, as a group, the power to bind and loose (Mt 18:18) and repeated it (Jn 20:23) to the twelve.

It is, therefore, difficult to deny that Jesus could have sent his disciples and empowered them to an all-embracing task before the end of history. Since this task was given to them as a community they have become, as such, an organ capable of aiming at the consummated Kingdom of God. As an organ empowered to convey Jesus' salvation to the world, he must have meant – at least in generic terms – that their future organization is more than the *kahal* of the Old Testament. In this sense we can assume, at least indirectly, a Church-founding intention in the mind of our Lord,[41] just as Rahner did in *Foundations*.

(C) *The Pentecostal roots of the Church*

Arguments for an intention by Jesus to found his Church can only conclude to a probability. This is why Rahner can say that in the words of Jesus we can only argue a rather vague sketch of a

Church to come, the rest is left to the history of the community under the guidance of the Spirit (see 3.2.1). Can we then say that the realization of his alleged intention is believed to be the work of the Holy Spirit in the miracle of Pentecost?

If this is possible, then in the events of Whit Sunday we do not see the continuation of Christ's history, but in it we face a new beginning in the whole history of salvation. Tillich was right when he saw in Pentecost the 'impact of the Spiritual Presence' now not in an individual person but in a community.[42] There, a spiritual community is grasped by the Spirit and finds firm faith in the risen Christ. It begets the spirit of love for one another and for strangers who are about to join the original group. This spirit of mutual and self-surrendering service overcomes the linguistic division of mankind at Babel and becomes truly one and universal. With these characteristics of the Pentecost experience, Tillich lays down those conditions without which no spiritual community, that is the Church, can exist.[43] The Spirit, in enabling these characteristics within a community, is at the roots of the Church of Christ. He is the one who *constitutes* the Church.

This Church is now launched on her way in history; she already has structures – perhaps other than that which any anthropo-sociological analysis could point out. Instead of speaking with Rahner about charismatic and institutional structures of the Church, I would prefer, with John Zizioulas,[44] to envisage an historical and an eschatological structure within her self-realization. The first is based on the concept of *mission*. The disciples with the twelve have to continue the mission of the living Christ (Jn 20:21–23 and Mt 28:19, and perhaps Mk 16:14–18): just as Christ is sent from the Father so are they sent by Christ. So they disperse in the world to fulfil their task. As individual missionaries they possess the authority and the charisma of preaching the gospel. Although the mission was entrusted to the twelve, it applies to all those who are going to follow them and are witnesses of the Resurrection. For this is, as I have already mentioned, the new definition of apostleship: there is a link between Christ who sent the twelve and those who on their part send others to transmit his message by establishing churches and ministries.

On the other hand, one should not forget the original sense and meaning of the twelve disciples: theirs was an *eschatological* function – that is, one representing, anticipating, the presence of the fulfilled Kingdom. This is the nature of John's realized eschatology of the Johannine *nûn* where, within the flow of history, the ultimate judgement and life eternal is already present (for example, Jn 3:18 and Jn 36; Jn 5:39f; Jn 17:3). It is not any of the twelve, but the twelve as a corporate body which is the effective sign of the *eschata* amongst us. And the *eschaton* is the end-state, a new creation not achievable by human striving. One cannot aim at it, yet one can symbolize, one can anticipate it. This is exactly what the 'apostolicity' of the Church means beyond the 'apostolicity' of preaching the kerygma, by which she strives to embrace the whole world. There is, therefore, a twofold structure, permanent in the apostolicity of the Church.

First, the historical approach underscores the Church's *societal* organization which also is open to anthropo-sociological analysis, whereas the eschatological structure of the Church posits her in the category of a *sign*, a symbol that makes the consummation present. Indeed, the founding of the Church can be envisaged from its historical origin and at the same time from the end of the process. Thus, the Church is not the Kingdom: the one is the sign, the other is the signified. In the Church, the eschatological Kingdom of God is symbolically present.

Secondly, whereas the historical approach emphasizes the Christological foundation of the Church, the eschatological one is built upon a *pneumatological* Christology. It is the Spirit who not only guides the organization of the Church, but makes the risen and glorified Christ present *hic et nunc*. The glorified One, made present by the Spirit, is not only an individuum with his past history but a person who is capable of uniting his followers into one body, into a corporate personality.

Thirdly, whereas the historical approach to the Church's apostolicity emphasizes her *societal* nature, the eschatological presents us rather with the Church as a *communion*. It is, indeed, the last and definitive convocation, the gathering together of everyone who believes in his Name. It is this end-state which symbolically is made present in and through the Church.

John Zizioulas repeatedly refers to the unity of these two in the celebration of the Eucharist.[45] It is here that the historical and eschatological features of the Church come to their unity in distinction. By remembering the life, death and resurrection of Jesus and by ardently expecting his second coming we are in the lineal, historical approach. Yet, by celebrating the presence of Jesus after the *epiclesis* and participating in a communion with him and with the others present, we are beyond history and define ourselves as a local Church from the end-state of history. This, of course, does not exclude any of the anthropo-sociological explanations of the Church as a *historical* society, which, however, are always under the correction of her eschatological nature. Though distinct, the two go together.

To conclude: there is an analogy of *correlation*[46] between the revealed structure and the sociological understanding of the historical Church. It is an analogy between the historical coming-to-be, the development, the gradual self-organization of the Church and secular societies. Their relationship is *mutual*, that is, while the revealed, the 'mystery' aspect of the Church is in control of social practice and sociological theories and these latter can give a concrete pattern to belief. On the one hand, no anthropo-sociological explanation can deal with a human gathering which builds on an anticipated future state which is accepted on faith in the Church. This future state is, so to speak, humanly 'not constructable'. It is a gift of God. On the other hand, Church-sociology can pattern the *de facto* institutionalization of the Church.

Rahner's query, for instance, about the monarchical *versus* (partly) democratic organization of the Church would have been meaningless in a feudal system of the Middle Ages. Then, equality of all human persons was acknowledged only before God, but it was unheard of in secular society. The Trinitarian model of the Church, if applied then at all, would there be a subordination among the Divine persons and the obvious pattern of the Church, would have been a strictly hierarchical society. Emphasizing, however, Trinitarian equality one will be inclined to a 'communion' model of Church.

In such a Church there are mutual dependencies among the members which, however, can be changed by different functions and circumstances. Perhaps in the Church as a communion, the sociological ideal of the *Frankfurter Schule* and of Medard Kehl, at least as an aim, could be realized. There is a correlationship between the revealed unfolding of the Church and her social reality. She is divinely revealed and at the same time, as we say in the liturgy of the Offertory, it is that which 'human hands have made'.

In these reflections on the structures and institutions of the Church I have abstracted from another aspect of her concretization, namely, the ministry in an apostolic succession. To this we are about to turn.

4.3 Ministry and the Communion of the Church

In the expository part of Rahner's ecclesiology (see 3.2.2 and also 3.3) I have tried to sum up his ideas about the structures of the Church, as it were from below upward: from the laity to the hierarchy. I also summarized the approach taken by Rahner to the genesis and the meaning of the various grades of the one Ministry within the Church. To reflect upon all of these features would take us too far afield. In retrospect I find, with some insignificant exceptions, Rahner's insights are not only theoretically important, but, to a certain extent, already realized in practice. This is why in this following section I shall develop some of them. Whether or not Rahner himself would agree with the positions I take, indeed under *his* inspiration, is unimportant. It is not what Rahner *de facto* says, nor his often heavy-going argumentation that is decisive, but the vistas he has opened for those who care to study his writings.

The particular question which will mainly occupy us is founded on Rahner's own thought: What is the origin of the one Ministry of Jesus Christ and how does it develop into a variety of ministries within the society and the communion of the Church? In this formulation, which is of course my own, I have presupposed that there is no other Ministry within the Church but that of Jesus the Christ. He is the apostle (Heb 3:1), the only master (Mt 23:8f), the only (high) priest (Heb 3:1; 5:6; 8:4, etc.), the only bishop – *episcopos-poimené* (1 Pet 2:25; 5:4, etc.). Christ is even the *diakonos* (Rom 15:8; Lk 22:27; Phil 2:7) in the service of our bodily and spiritual need.[47]

How then can the various sorts of ministries share in the one ministry of Christ? From a sociological viewpoint this variety can be regarded as a *system* developing since their beginning. To give an account of these, to point out their legitimation is just as much the task of ecclesiology as the discussion of the Church's divine origins. Here, too, we have to do with a two-faceted Church.

Apart from the tension between, what I have called, the 'mystical' (or revelational) and the empirical side, there is another kind of duality in the Church: she presents herself both as a communion of the faithful and as an organized society of her believing members. Considering the active life of the Church, we could re-name these two aspects as her task *ad intra* and *ad extra*. To the first belongs everything that builds itself up towards a genuine communion, whereas the second, as we have already seen, is intent on the common goal, a task in which each member of the Church ought to take a share. Looking at the ministries from this aspect it will be easier to understand the meaning of certain offices and their functions as integrated into the life of the Church. Thus the office of leadership within the community is first of all a task *ad intra*, whereas Christ's missionary mandate of Matthew 28 which holds every Christian to the evangelization of the whole world is a task *ad extra*. Which of these two aspects rules its counterpart is a further question.

With these methodological premises in mind, I shall single out in Rahner's ecclesiological writings four insights for further consideration.

(A) From the *consecration* of each and every member of the Church I shall conclude to the ministerial function of all Christians.

(B) Then I shall reconsider not only the unanimity, and even unity, of these ministries, but also their *origins*, which under a certain aspect are identical with the origin of the whole Church.

(C) To underscore this double conclusion I shall, first, take up and discuss Rahner's theory of the *divine right* (*Jus divinum*) as a possible legitimation of a Church which, though built on the apostles, lives in her historically changing institutions. One of these is the sacramentally ordained Ministry.

(D) Secondly, without going into detail about the various ministries, I shall reflect on Rahner's view, according to which the Church herself is not so much an institution as an event.

These four insights are discussed below. From them, I hope to be able to re-define the nature of the *one* Ministry to be shared by the various ministries, and to gain a workable foundation of a systematic view for the whole reality of the Church.

(A) *Consecration*

In Section 3.2.2, on the laity within the open structures of the Church, I have ventured to call Rahner's approach 'revolutionary'. In the essays there quoted we could see that he was working his way towards a new and more meaningful image of the Church. One important aspect of the Church now belongs to the past: it is the concept that the merely passive laity is subordinated to the active and often dominating hierarchy. The borders were drawn by the fact that persons belonging to the clergy are sacramentally ordained to be ministers and thus they alone share the one Ministry of Christ. If we re-read Section 3.2.2 we can see how Rahner demolishes this, for many still valid, distinguishing mark and introduces a notion worthy of further reflection. Especially in his essays on 'The Consecration of the Layman to the Care of the Souls' (1936) and in 'Consecration in the Life and Reflection of the Church' (1976) Rahner speaks of 'sacraments of Consecration'. These are the three so-called 'lay-sacraments': baptism, confirmation and marriage. Through the grace of these sacraments every member of the Church is already allocated to the 'dimension of the sacramental and sociological reality of the Church'.[48] These persons, regardless of any further ecclesial appointment or commissioning, have a certain function in the community, whether sacramentally ordained for it or not. An additional sacramental ordination does not add anything to their being a Christian, but lends to it a specific way of being a Christian.

Thus according to Rahner, in a genuine Christian community every member has his/her proper place in the sociological and sacramental reality of the Church. By 'proper place' in this, apparently, commonplace sentence, I presuppose membership with its active and passive function, with its rights and duties in sharing the being and mission of the Church. Even if this participation is not actively put into practice it is, in principle, implied in the calling of every already consecrated Christian. Take away any aspect of this consecration and the person ceases to be a Christian. Add any new dimension to it, and no one becomes more of a Christian than he or she ever was by being a member of the Church.

It seems, however, that for Rahner the membership of the Church is not exclusively through the sacrament of baptism. As I shall later discuss in more detail, the person's consecration happens in the very fact of belonging to, of having a place in the sociological and sacramental reality of the Church. This basic 'sacrament' of consecration is ratified by the cultic sacraments of baptism, confirmation and, eventually, through the sacrament of marriage. In this sense, baptism is not the 'cause' of membership, but an existential mode of living out God's gift in the grace of explicitly becoming a Christian. Baptism irrevocably incorporates the believer into the life of the Church *ad intra* and confirmation irrevocably assigns him/her to the mission of the Church – *ad extra*.[49]

With this last line of thought I have already begun extending my own reflections beyond Rahner's explicit words. By my statement 'ecclesial consecration happens simply by belonging to the community', I have tried to give up causal thinking, an undertaking at times implicitly aimed at by Rahner though, as a rule, with not much success.[50] To ask the question, What made, 'caused', me to become a member of the Church? is just as meaningless as to ask, What made, 'caused', X to leave the Church? None of the possible answers is adequate, because we cannot ever grasp the inner process that leads to either of these decisions.[51]

Furthermore, Rahner, though he speaks of the Church's sacramental *and* sociological reality, does not seem to apply this non-causal way of thinking to the question of membership. In a *sociological* sense it means either to be situated in or freely taking up one's responsibility for the whole community and sharing the task allotted to it. At the same time, 'the place of the person within the Church' can also be affirmed in her sacramental reality. It is a qualification which we can understand in two senses: it could mean either that the person who shares in the being and in the tasks of the community can receive or dispense the sacraments which enable full membership *or* that the community of the

Church is already the sacred space in which consecration of the individual member becomes an event – even without the person's awareness of it.[52] Membership, indeed through the person's consecration, is obtained by belonging to the 'sacred place' of the Church. This is what I shall understand by Vatican II's (and Rahner's) insistence on the notion of the Church as a (Proto-)sacrament. She is not such, because she dispenses the seven sacraments, but she can dispense the seven because she is the Proto-sacrament of mankind's salvation. If this is the case, then the obvious conclusion is that belonging to her is identical with that basic consecration of the believer which may precede the cultic administration of baptism. This is what Rahner must have meant by his 'sacrament of consecration'.

This approach, however, belongs to the treatment of the sacraments proper in drawing a distinction between ministries which presuppose a sacramental ordination and those which do not. Therefore, I am inclined to conclude that *any member of a Christian community* is *ipso facto* 'ordained' to a *certain ministry within the Church*. To participate in the social and sacramental reality of the Church, to be a consecrated member within the being of the Church is at the same time a service in building up the community into a genuine communion of redeemed in Christ (*ad intra*) and a contribution to its common goal, the evangelization of the whole world (*ad extra*). On the sociological level we may, or may not, become aware of these tasks, yet in our commitment to faith, we believe that, as Christians, we are meant for this entirely new dimension of ministering others. For one does not live for oneself but lives like Christ who became a slave for us all (Phil 2:7). To this kind of service we are all called, and even elected, by God. The grace of membership is ultimately one of the mysteries of our faith.

(B) *Origins*

The Ministry or the ministries are interchangeable ideas. There is a basic unanimity or even an inalienable unity among the many offices of the Church. A biblical illustration of this manifold oneness is the twelfth chapter of Paul's first epistle to the Corinthians. His 'thesis' is:

> There are varieties of gifts, but the same Spirit; and there are
> varieties of service, but the same Lord; and there are varieties of
> working, but it is the same God who inspires them all in every
> one (1 Cor 12:46).

Paul is speaking here about the one and the many, and his
vision discovers the origin of divergent gifts of the one Spirit.
The end of this small treatise on the charisms gives us a clue that
makes the manifold unanimous and the many one: Paul speaks
not only about the unity of these services in their divine origin,
but also about the ground of their unanimity among themselves.
Their oneness is affirmed both in the vertical and horizontal
dimensions. Chapter 13 with its hymnal praise of love *belongs* to
Paul's teaching on the charismata. Verse 30b speaks of the
'higher gift' that shows us 'a more excellent way'. It is the one
and pre-eminent charisma of the Spirit, comprising all the others.

Rahner never loses this purview of the oneness of the Ministry.
He repeatedly comes back to the teaching of *Lumen Gentium* 28.
This speaks of a 'divinely established ecclesiastical ministry'
which 'is exercised on different levels by those who from antiq-
uity have been called bishops, priests, and deacons'. The Council
obviously meant the one and the same Ministry by means of
which the successors of the apostles become 'partakers of the
function of Christ the sole mediator'. The oneness, in spite of its
manifold gradation, is ultimately secured by the one and only
office of Jesus the Christ in whose consecration and mission, as
the same decree says, they participate.

At first sight, the teaching of the Council of Trent,[53] is repeated,
which envisages the hierarchy (the clergy), but we can follow
Alois Grillmeier in *Commentary* (as Rahner certainly did) who
extends it to the general priesthood of all the baptized.[54] If my
view is acceptable, namely that owing to the basic consecration
of every member in the Church, all the faithful are 'ordained'
(whether later receiving the sacrament of *ordo* or not) to share in
Christ's ministry, we can extend the notion of the one Ministry
beyond (or, if you like, below) the confines of the clergy. To be
partakers of this one Ministry is not their privilege alone.

Now, according to Grillmeier, *Lumen Gentium* 28 avoids
speaking of the origin of this one Ministry and of the unity of
ministries in the plural. It will be the task of this section to point

out the origin and meaning of this twofold participation, namely the Church's share in the one ministry of Christ and the participation of various ministries (in the plural) in the one Ministry of the Church.

I adopt two valid views or rather thought patterns, for a possible answer. The *first* typifies a causal thinking characteristic of the Roman Catholic tradition: Christ, at least implicitly, wills the Church to be and this entails not only her one Ministry, but also her office holders (the ministries). In this sense, he is the origin and 'cause' both of the Church's one Ministry and the ministries implied in it. It is also his founding will that the Ministry of the Church should be committed to the twelve apostles under the leadership of Peter. In the eyes of this tradition it is clear that this Ministry originates in the alleged intention of Jesus.

There is, however, no evidence from the words of Jesus for the origin of the variety of ministries within the one Ministry. Thus one appeals to the rest of the New Testament and so to the development of the early Church which, very soon after Christ's departure, produced a plurality of ministries within the one Ministry. Their origin is ascribed to the guidance of the Holy Spirit who authorized the early Church to create and to define a variety of ministries.[55] With this the causal or historical line is complete: Christ—the Church—the apostles and their associates —leaders of Christian communities under the guidance of the Holy Spirit resulting in a plurality of various ministries. For these latter Christ's founding will is indirect, yet he is ultimately the origin of a hierarchically structured order within the communities of the Church.

The *second* view in answering the same question about the origin of the one Ministry and the ministries could be characterized as *eschatological*. In this, there is no causal chain, but a unity already achieved between Christ and the Church, between the Church and her ministries in their unanimity. This answer does not attend the beginning, but the final end which also explains the origin. In this sense, this second approach to our faith in the Church is *eschatological*.

Let me illustrate this pattern of thought through an excursus. John Zizioulas understands the participation of the Church's one Ministry in the ministry of Christ as an identity. There is no distance, as he says, between Christ's and the Church's ministry, not even that of a cause and its effect.[56] One can speak rather of a 'mystical unity' of both subjects (Christ and Church) and consequently of their ministries. This mystical identification is worked out against the background of a Trinitarian theology and in terms of a pneumatological Christology. This means that the mystery of Christ is

> . . . initiated by the Father who actually sends the Son in order to fulfil and realise the eternal design of the Holy Trinity to draw man and creation to participation in God's own life.[57]

The Holy Spirit is the principal agent in the fulfilment of Christ's ministry both in Jesus' human life (born of a virgin!) and in what follows after his resurrection. Christ's ministry is then identical with that of the *Church*:

> What, therefore, the Spirit does through [this] ministry is to constitute the Body of Christ *here and now* by *realising* Christ's ministry as the Church's ministry.[58]

Since the Holy Spirit is the origin of the Ministry and the ministries, he is also the origin of Christ's intention to found a church. In other words, the identity of Christ's and the Church's ministry is not so much *by*, as *in* the Spirit. Of course, Zizioulas, like Rahner, assumes that there is no difference between Christ's essential being and his functions and likewise between the Church and her functions. In both cases function and agent coincide. According to 1 Cor 12, the unanimity, if not the coincidence of the ministerial functions are active in building up the communion of the Church.

In projecting this image of the Church one cannot appeal either to empirical or interpretative evidence. It relies on the promise of final salvation. This is why Zizioulas qualifies this one Ministry common to Christ as well as to the Church, *first* by taking the Ministry of the Church out of the flow of *Heilsgeschichte*: its unity with Christ's ministry is not just a passing, contingent episode, but anticipated salvation.[59] *Secondly*, this ministry in common is *soteriological* – a quality which he understands not so much in its Western sense of reconciliation or satisfaction, but in the terms of realized *theosis*, deification of the persons believing in it.[60] In this anticipated fulfilment (realized eschatology) there is no longer the history of cause and effect, but eternal present, the coincidence of origin and result.

At first sight the two approaches to the origin of Church and her ministries seem to be incompatible. The first is historical: it starts from the cause and concludes to its effect. The other is eschatological: it begins with the result and ends with the understanding of the origin. In the first the ultimate cause is Christ's founding will and the effect is a historical process (the visible Church) that leads to an eschatological fulfilment. The second proceeds from this latter in order to grasp the ultimate meaning and essence of the Church, as we experience her in history. Whilst the principal agent in the first is Christ with the help of his Spirit, it is the Spirit who accomplishes that which is still happening in history to unite the Church with Christ and his ministry with the ministries.

Despite this apparent divergence I shall defend the complementarity of these two views: the causal-historical needs the eschatological-pneumatological and *vice versa*. First of all, I have to stress that both views project a Church in which we believe and not the Church as the object of our everyday experience or of our sociological environment. For even if we declare Christ to be a founder of a religious society, we have to believe that he is somehow one with his Church, that his ministry is the same as his Church's service to mankind. Secondly, in experiencing the Church as allegedly founded by Christ in a historical process towards her future, we have to believe that this goal in a sense is already reached. This eschatological anticipation is an essential property of our faith. For eschatological realities of the future have a retroactive function on the present. In the form of divine promise they are already here and yet to come – a statement to be further explored in dealing with eschatology. We may recall Rahner's oft repeated statement: 'The Church is on her way to the end, by being already at the end.' Christian faith without this eschatological anticipation is void.

If I may add here an insight of Vatican II, as I understand it: something similar could be said about the two metaphors of the Church, equally present in *Lumen Gentium*. The Church is the Body of Christ as well as the people of God which, guided by the Spirit, is on its way towards fulfilment. The first is the promise already acting in the second – it is the future already present. Were the Church only the people of God wandering in the pathless desert in hope of the promised land without the security of eventually finding it, our belief in her would be incomplete. On the other hand, were the Church to be viewed only as the (mystical) 'Body of Christ' we would tend to see her as an unchangeable ideal that has nothing to do with our experience. The two metaphors are complementary, just as the eschatological view is with the historical.

If our faith in the Church did not have this eschatological anticipation, we could not stand by the traditional predicates: *una sancta apostolica et catholica*. For any assertion of these attributes applied to the historical Church would prove to be a lie. On the other hand, Rahner's dialectic, simultaneously affirming the sanctity and sinfulness of the same Church would be obviously invalid. Even in believing the Church we are confronted with a double-faceted reality. This reality is asserted not only of the Church that we experience and believe, but also of that communion of redeemed mankind living in firm belief of a future consummation. The future shape of the Church is already with us and makes its presence felt.

Zizioulas has an obvious preference for the eschatological view over and above the causal one[61] and, by not neglecting this latter, I am going to apply it. From this approach to the mystery of the Church there follow a number of important conclusions. The first of these may be surprising for some: *the origin of the Ministry coincides with the origin of the Church and her communities*. This means that there is no Church without the ministries in the one Ministry, and there is no Ministry without the Church; that is, without the community of Christians. It also follows that the existence of the ministries in the one Ministry is now dependent on Christian communities and Christian communities on the Ministry, for along with these the Church is set. Thus, I believe, we can contrast: in the beginning there was the communion of the faithful and *then* its Ministry, with: in the beginning there were the various ministries in the one Ministry and *then* the community. We can affirm the priority of the community over and above the Ministry as well as the priority of Ministry over and above the community. There is a *simultaneity* of the 'two' constituted in the Spirit sent to us by the Father through the Son. The origin of the Church is not relegated to a particular act of foundation, she is 'recreated' each time she receives new ministers in her bosom.[62]

The practical consequences of this apparently theoretical conclusion are significant for our present ecumenical situation. To put it bluntly: the much over-estimated principle of *apostolic succession* is alien for a Church living in anticipation of her final destiny. The transmission of a special ministry by the symbolic act of imposition of hands is no longer required in order to assure historical continuity: a Christian community lives, in a real sense, already at her eternal consummation. If indeed this eschatological image of the future is part and parcel of our faith in the Church I can embrace fellow ministers of other denominations, provided their ministry has its origins in their Christian community. Furthermore, in such a Church, the 'essential distinction' between a sacramentally ordained minister and his lay counterpart has no significance.[63] Nor has the principle of hierarchy as actualized in determined and exclusive authority and power: their service to one another is interchangeable and exercised in the Spirit's highest gift of mutual love (1 Cor 13). Our belief in the Church is only viable if we can believe in her identity with Bonhoeffer's *communio sanctorum* as more fundamental than the present images of the Church.

Before, however, one smilingly discards the above as a dream or ignores it as a beautiful but useless vision, there is the other side of our belief in the Church to be faced. Indeed the causal explanation of origins cannot be omitted. Rahner and Zizioulas have passages in which elements of both are present. For considering the Church as a visible and ordered society, we cannot grasp her origins except as a causal and historical manifestation. The Church is due to Christ, and the ministry owes its existence to the will of the Church. Though we believe that our service and ministry participate in Christ's function and ministry, though we trust that in the variety of ministries the one ministry of Christ is realized, yet the actualization of the same is always according to her human and historical possibilities.

This is indeed part of our belief in the Church, in which the previously summarized conclusions seem to be reinstated. In this historical Church, Jesus the Christ is the founder of a new community, and the inspiration of the Holy Spirit is the guide in the compiling of sacred scriptures and in establishing permanently effective traditions for an ongoing history. The same Spirit is the safeguard in creating an (unwritten) constitution with its structures and subsequent institutions in order that Christian communities may become an ordered society. In this Church of concrete history the hierarchical principle will become a permanent structure and various forms of ministry will be established. Rights with corresponding power with defined obligations will be existentially inevitable. We are back to the Church of our everyday experience.

If our faith in the Church cannot accept the dialectical unity of these two images, we are left with either a dream of a 'heavenly' assembly of the elect or an 'earthly' society in which certain features are legitimated by the transcendent power of divine ordinance. On the other hand, our commitment to the Church will be an integrated whole if we accept both. It is important to stress the *priority* of the eschatological, because this offers us a communion-Church, which can already alleviate the struggle in building up the society of the Church on earth. T. S. Eliot's unforgettable words from his *Four Quartets* could be the motto of this integrated faith: 'In my beginning is my end.' The people of God wandering in the pathless desert is already at the promised land. They are the Body of Christ.

I must now return to this wandering people of God and consider how their faith in the Church develops her earthly existence from society into communion.

(C) *Divine right*

It is characteristic of almost all historical religions, including Christianity, that doctrinal, disciplinary and organizational matters have to be expressed in statements, ordinances, structures and institutions, which are believed to be outside the flow of history. Although proposed in human terms, they are claimed to be of divine origin. God is believed to communicate his will with mankind through them. Consequently, human whim must not interfere with what they purport. Yet the theologian has to show *how* these positions are part of God's self-revelation or, at least truths entailed in the same. He or she has to justify statements proposed in history as something parahistorical and hence irreversible.

This dilemma was obviously the background of the rather complex article, 'Jus divinum' – Rahner's theory of the divine right. As far as I can tell, this category, although known before,[64] was used specifically by the Council of Trent in controversy with the Reformers' *sola scriptura*: any irreversible position in the Church has to be grounded in the Bible. For example (as mentioned by Rahner) Trent asserts that sinners *ex jure divino* have to submit all their mortal sins to a priest's judgement in order that their confession be integral.[65] In order to justify the divine origin of this ordinance Trent quotes James (5:16) and 1 John (1:9) where confession of sins is recommended *in general*. Trent, of course, is thinking of auricular confession which had become customary in the Church toward the end of the first millennium. Neither is it clear that the distinction between mortal and venial sin was known at that time. What is here taken for granted is the intervening tradition which gradually shaped the penitential *praxis* of the Church up to the sixteenth century. During this time the Church determined the manner in which this *praxis* developed. Roughly the same could be affirmed about other instances in which the Church appeals to a divine right in order to defend her contemporary *praxis*.

Rahner's 'Jus divinum' was an attempt of a systematic theologian to make this and similar claims intelligible. He had to show that such a claim to divine right can only be established if its relationship to revelation can be proven. Hence, to maintain this category, one has to prove that even a concrete and historical position can be irreversible. Thus the real problem of theology is to point out the criteria for this irreversibility.

Of course, the easiest way would be a direct reference to the Bible where divine right could be documented. Trent's reference to the statements of James and John about sinners' need of and obligation to confession is nowadays no longer valid in the light of historical and exegetical scholarship. It would also be relatively easy to maintain the same claim, if an instance of divine right were logically implied in a biblical text. In this case a logical deduction could show that the essential kernel of a present *praxis*, though different in shape, was already implicit in the awareness of the primitive Church.

Such a 'logical' deduction would, almost certainly, take into consideration non-logical elements. And these elements are historical decisions by the Church (for example, the later emergence of a clear-cut distinction between mortal and venial sins, the hierarchical principle determining the dispenser of sacramental absolution and so on). If these are really positions of divine right, then they are (as Rahner correctly asserts) not of the essence of the revealed word, but *in conformity* with the nature of the Church. Yet even if this conformity is present, it remains the historian's task to show that the   decision of the Church in time was meant to be permanent, hence irreversible. In 'Jus divinum' Rahner concentrates on this latter case; his argument is that irreversible positions, ordinances and institutions of the present originate in the (collective magisterial or juridical) decisions of the Church in the past and therefore of divine right.

Even if a detailed and critical assessment of 'Jus divinum' would take us too far afield, something has to be said about the nature of Rahner's argumentation. Its basis is obviously anthropological: it depends on the analysis of the human act of decision. This in itself would not be enough: it would mean that anything decided by the Church in the past, present or future could be held to be of divine right. There must also be a theological element, at least to show how the Church's certain decisions conform to and are coherent with divine revelation.[66]

In my Volume 2, on Rahner's fundamental theology I tried to sum up the kernel of Rahner's theory. There the context was Rahner's approach to the concrete content of God's word (in his terms, to the 'categorial word') from man's transcendental experience which he, in the situation of 'supernatural existential', equates with 'transcendental revelation'. In this the word of God is mediated by the Church.

If I may quote my own summary understanding:

> . . . he [Rahner] asserts that there are two 'moments' of God's intervention [in history]. God wills absolutely the coming-to-be of the Church in general, and with it he also wills its main constitutive elements in particular. One of these is the genesis of the inspired Bible. . . . Thus the Church becomes a mediation not only for subsequent tradition and teaching but also for the Bible,

in which we ought to recognise the categorial word of God in history.[67]

Of course, in the New Testament this word centres on the under-standing of the Christ-event in the Bible, yet it extends its range to the testimony of its immediate witnesses, to the primitive Church. Do we, however, draw a line at the demise of the last apostle (as generally accepted), or can we refer to a post-apos-tolic revelation? (Incidentally, in the last part of 'Jus divinum', Rahner does not seem to exclude this possibility when he warns 'not to dismiss unreflectingly the possibility of a post-apostolic revelation'.[68]) Can this extended concept of revelation, relying on the decision of the primitive Church, be transferred also to later decisions? If the answer to this question is positive, then we have also a theological justification of Rahner's theory of divine right. The burden of his argument, however, falls back on an anthropological analysis of the nature of communitarian deci-sion. This decision is always selective: it is a choice from alternative possibilities, all conformable to the constitution of the Church which is the mediator of divine revelation. Hence, he comes to this final definition for irreversible facts for which divine right is claimed:

> Such a selective, historical decision of a juridical nature, which is made in conformity with the nature of the Church and which reveals itself as such an irreversible decision in the primitive Church *by a proper revelation*, may rightly be called '*iuris divini*' in its creation of law.[69]

Though it is not clear whether the choice of the primitive Church or the content of the irreversible ordinance, institution, etc., that is conformable to revelation, Rahner certainly requires this revelatory background for the divine right. Divine right must either be grounded on a post-apostolic revelation or on infallible definitions of the later Church. As I see it, this question is left open in Rahner's theory of 'Jus divinum'. He obviously excludes both of these alternatives. 'Divine right' is something in between post-apostolic revelation and infallible definition.

The situation remains ambiguous: what about the Tridentine

integrity of confession, institutions like the cardinalate or other organs of Vatican's *dycasteria*, including the Congregation of Faith (formerly the Holy Office of the Inquisition) and so on? It would be vain to attempt to reduce these to the *praxis* of the primitive Church and deal with them as something revealed. Likewise, it would be false to argue from the long tradition in which some of these institutions arose: the number of years or even centuries cannot make something 'revealed', which never was implied in the awareness or *praxis* of the primitive Church. Hence each decision of the present Church puts us in the dilemma: Is this a fact of divine right (somehow revealed) or is it not? Yet there *are* statements, ordinances and institutions which are *more* than temporary opinions, rules and arrangements, even if one cannot establish their divine origin.[70]

Nevertheless, to establish the origin of stable institutions in the Church and her ministries in the one Ministry, I need Rahner's theory of divine right, or something very similar. Otherwise we shall be unable to give account of several irreversible norms of behaviour, of laws, of institutions which in their present state can hardly be found in the primitive Church.

My own suggestion is indeed inspired by what I have called Rahner's anthropological argument: what is of divine right is dependent on the Church's decision. The Church here can be taken as a collective person who at a given time had *freely* to choose between *alternatives*. An alternative before the actual choice is a possibility (x^1) which *per definitionem* is related to other possibilities (x^n).[71] At the moment of decision both x^1 and x^n, as long as they all conform to the nature of the Church, are eligible. What happens to x^n after the actual choice for x^1 has taken place? Has the foregone possibility perished for ever or does it remain (perhaps modified) as a possibility? Let us suppose that in the primitive Church both a monarchical or (what we now call) a synodal or conciliar structure were possible. At that time they were alternatives, still undecided. If at a given time there has to be a choice for one of these (for instance for the monarchical episcopacy), the question is whether its alternative (the synodal government) will then be suppressed for ever, or whether it will remain an open possibility for the future. When the Church opted for a monarchical episcopacy it is most likely that the synodal structure remained a real alternative. Were this alternative resurrected, the monarchical structure of the Church would become a latent, but by no means a defunct, possibility in a future situation.

If we can familiarize ourselves with this, still hypothetical, suggestion, then we ought to understand irreversibility of facts in a more flexible way. A 'discarded' alternative remains an open possibility and, in a certain sense, has its own life and own efficacy. Thus, for example, the possibility of a synodal and collegial Church, even under a strict monarchic regime, survives in the mind of some of her members and can revive. (Think of religious communities without a monarchical or even with a democratic constitution under a strict monarchical regime of the Church.) This fact should be obvious, because the 'discarded' and the actually chosen alternatives always remain in relationship: the development of the one draws with it the other's evolved understanding.[72]

It would then be possible to extend this principle to most post-apostolic decisions. I suggest that the decision for the ministries in the one Ministry (including the classical triad of deacons, presbyters and bishops) is such a decision which could have taken other forms. This, however, does not apply to the one Ministry of the Church, since, as I affirmed above, there is a certain identity between Ministry and the Church as revealed. There has never been an alternative to the one Ministry. In facing divine revelation (that is, the Christ-event) the community had to grasp the 'institution' of the one Ministry in order to exist as a church. And in this sense we can speak of the one Ministry as a primary *Jus divinum*.

Now, in accepting the one Ministry as such there immediately emerge alternative possibilities for the ministries. This choice, however, can only be taken with total trust in divine revelation in which the active assistance of the Spirit is also revealed. Hence, deciding for one alternative presupposes *conformity* with divine revelation (that is, with the Christ-event as believed in the Church). This 'conformity', however, is not only an objective fact, but also an act of the Church: she actively makes such a fact conform to divine revelation. Yet the human act that makes a post-apostolic decision 'conform' is not only that of the society of believers but also that of the Spirit who, as Zizioulas would say, not only constitutes the Church, but is the divine force of her concrete life and action.[73] We can call the content of these decisions *secondary* divine right, since they were taken at a later time, not necessarily by the twelve or even after the time of the *Urkirche*, and often under the pressure of historical circumstances. Hence, they do not become irrevocable decisions *for good*, nor can they be called *revealed facts*. Yet the Spirit's assistance is needed even for these. If his presence were only a promise in the past and not an active help in the present, our trusting faith would be vacuous. Hence it is feasible that the chosen alternative at the moment of decision is also 'inspired' by the Spirit. If this is so, could we not suppose that the same Spirit, under altered historical circumstances, can inspire that possibility which was at a previous moment passed over?

The main objection against this interpretation of divine right is similar to that one raised against Rahner's *Jus divinum*: if it is correct, then any ordinance or rule and any statement about them at any time is *somehow* revealed, *somehow* decided by the primitive Church and exists *somehow* as a one-way, irrevocable position. My response is: why not? Unless we rigidly maintain a theory of verbal revelation, we can hold that though the Church acts in a human way, her action is not only *about*, but *because of* an irrevocable revelation. In this sense, of course, revelation is mainly the significant event in the history of salvation and any statement concerning this event is always a *human* assertion[74] (even if it comes from the mouth of the man Jesus!). God speaks to us only through humans in a human language, God acts in the world only by means of his creation. Hence it is no wonder that the Church can become uneasy about some of her decisions (whether or not they are explicitly proposed *juris divini*, is not important) and feel herself obliged to return to the point of original decision. In retrieving her steps to the origins she does not follow her own whim, but obeys the dictates of history in the belief that it is the Spirit of Jesus who leads her. The Church's one-way decisions become in certain situations, revisable. The irrevocability of one-way decisions is always temporal: it means that *at a given time* there is no real alternative until historical circumstances suggest a salutary revision.[75]

These reflections present the Church as a collective unit, and the content of her various decisions as doctrinal, legal, disciplinary or pastoral. This Church is a dynamic *agens* in the history of salvation. It is she who accepts the one Ministry as a primary object of revelation; and it will be she who will have to determine its stratification. Whether or not the traditional triad, deacons-presbyters-bishops in their hierarchical order is *jure divino* in a primary or secondary sense, is still to be decided.

(D) *The event*

Although all the members of the Church share the one Ministry of Jesus Christ, there are specific ministries within the community of the faithful. To these I turn now by implementing those insights by means of which I have tried to represent the life of the Church in her historical circumstances. Whether or not these (relatively new) insights are acceptable depends also on their verification or, rather, on their verifiability in the present Church and the future *communio sanctorum*.

Let me sum up briefly what I believe I have gained in my dialogue with Rahner's theology. Like him, I started with the universal priesthood of all the members of the Church, the community of salvation. Following his search for her basic constitution I adopted the hierarchy not so much in its present shape but as a principle on the basis of which the Church organizes herself both as a society and a communion of the faithful. This principle was then maintained as the origin of the Church herself and of her one Ministry shared with that of Jesus the Christ. I have insisted that her one Ministry and the Church herself are one: in their origin these two are interchangeable realities. Their origin is the Holy Spirit and love, her highest gift (1 Cor 12 and 13) which, on the one hand, prefigures Christianity's ultimate fulfilment in the life of the blessed Trinity and, on the other, in accordance with the principle of hierarchy, enables the various ministries in the actual life of the Church. Whereas the first of these insights relies on the eschatological anticipation of faith, the second relies on belief in the guidance of the Spirit in the action of the ministerial community. These two aspects of faith are the same and yet different, insofar as the second, the genesis of the variety of services, is subject to the dynamic of human sociology.

In order to understand this latter process, which I shall call stratification, I have adopted and appreciated Rahner's insight: the realization of the Church's constitution is due to the decisions of the Church. She actively establishes the various ministries within the circumstances of history. Or – in a reversed sense – the development of the Church herself in the history of past, present and future is a dynamic event, a dramatic history of self-realization.

The idea of a communitarian decision as a continuing event is by no means a self-evident notion. The decision of a single person is easier to analyse, because introspection can indicate its stages and assign a result. Thus in an absolute monarchy there is one person who, as representative of the whole (*l'état c'est moi*), assigns others to various services to implement his or her decision. This is certainly not the way the Church has developed. Nor is she constituted by democratic vote (by simple majority), but by the laborious process of several persons who reach a unanimity, for which they are all responsible *in solido*. Let us suppose that this is practicable. In my opinion, the result of their decision cannot yet be regarded as an event. It will be an event through the persistence of its dynamic nature. Rahner speaks of the charism of the Spirit as a 'dynamic unrest', which characterizes both an individual and a collective decision as an event. Whoever decides chooses one from a variety of possibilities: the possibility now decided upon is not just a static *fait accompli*, but something which opens a new set of possibilities available for further decisions. If we accept this characteristic of dynamic decision the act itself becomes the source of an ongoing drama in the very history of the individual and the community.

The very history of salvation both in the Old and the New Testaments illustrates what I mean by a dramatic event. I can follow Rahner insofar as he regards the genesis of the Church as the continued incarnation of the Logos. Yet the incarnation is not a static event, but a history enacted by the man Jesus in autonomous decisions responding to actual circumstances (see my approach to Christology in Volume 3). From the miraculous healer and teacher destined to renew his own people Jesus becomes the apocalyptic prophet of the coming Kingdom of God who then accepts his fate by dying on the cross. Thus the incarnation is not a fact but a dramatic event, which is then understood, by him or rather by his followers, as the anticipated *soteria* of mankind. This process is not continued in the Church:

she is rather a new beginning that can follow the pattern of the incarnation, but has her own autonomous history as a dramatic event. The event of the Church is the event of a developing drama and the *dramatis personae* are the community of the faithful in rapport with the Holy Spirit as they gradually develop their assembly into an organized society in the hope of becoming a genuine communion here on earth and within the life of the blessed Trinity in the future.

Against this background I have tried to understand both the stratification of the Church's constitution and her future possibilities. Given the acceptability of this approach, there are two inevitable consequences to be verified: first, the institutions actively decided and passively accepted by the community are themselves sources of new possibilities of development; and, second, the institutionalized ministries which these generate are *not of a substantive but of a relational nature*. They are not 'substantive' in the sense that they have a definitive reality. They are 'relational' in that they relate to the community of the Church and in respect of their mutual functions in the service *ad intra* and of the world *ad extra*. This implies that the special 'ministries of the Church' (a *genitivus objectivus*) are not 'possessed' by the Church and her ministers as the result of her decision. They are (along with the ministry of each Christian) the Church herself. They only exist insofar as they correlate between themselves for the benefit of the whole.

In this sense, therefore, the Church is an event whose historical decisions recreate her unchanging faith in mankind's ultimate destiny. As a result of century long reflection this eschatological consummation is believed to terminate in communion with the blessed Trinity. Of course, this conviction of faith, on which alone the Church can be built, is the ultimate mystery of Christianity. Even if human reasoning and speculation underpin this mystery, the believer has no clear-cut image through which to anticipate the nature of this desired end. One image is that the three Persons exist through their mutual relationship: *In personis nulla differentia nisi in relatione*. If this is indeed the pattern of the Church on earth then the Ministry, which they all share, is one and the same. There is no substantial difference, a rupture between special and general ministries, unless in the relationship of their respective functions. The basic and unchangeable conviction of our faith in the Church betrays the relational character of all ministries in the One Ministry.

Faith, however, can assume another aspect in the same image of the Trinity. This was thought out in analogy with the processions of the Trinitarian persons. The Father as the source of the other persons can be considered as holding a certain primacy: 'The Father is greater than I am' (Jn 10:29) and 'When all things are subjected to him [the Son], then the Son himself will be subjected to him . . . that God may be everything to everyone' (1 Cor 15:28, where Paul dreams of the end as the final victory achieved by the Son). And, that the Spirit proceeds from the Father and through the Son suggests a gradation. In other words, there is a hierarchical order within the blessed Trinity. I believe this image was operative in historical genesis of the Church when, though maintaining an equality, an ontological difference was introduced between the special and general ministries of the faithful.

This view of the ministry (still very much in vogue in the Roman Church) prevailed throughout the Middle Ages. I am obviously not able to present the theology of it in all its historical detail. It is, however, right to say that this ontological difference between 'special' and ordinary ministries was a common feature. Vatican II adopts this difference as 'essential' and not only 'in degree'.[76] I believe, however, that this statement does not apply to an extra-sacramental access to the ministries. In the Middle Ages one could hardly think of the ministries apart from the sacramental ordination of some persons: the Ministry of the ministers was conceived as the effect of a sacramental act. The customary analysis of a sacramental process applied: conferring the outward sign (here, the laying on of hands) and the imparting of corresponding grace, as the basis of rights and duties of the ordained. An objective reality is postulated between the sign (cause) and grace (effect). The ordained is now set apart from the rest of his fellow Christians, by something which was called *character indelebilis*. To be a minister involves an ontological *plus*, an increase, so to speak, in one's being. This concept introduced a profound division into Christian communities. It is still hard to overcome: clericalism is mainly due to this medieval approach to the nature of the Ministry.

The diversification of the one Ministry (and with it the 'special' ones) is not yet sacramental theology, but an account of the historical genesis of the Church. My limited exegetical acquaintance with its early history finds no traces of this medieval development. Recent biblical scholarship, however, enables us to form a picture of what had happened at the birth of the Church.

The forty days between the resurrection and Whitsunday must have been a period of gradual understanding for the twelve apostles. They, as a group, like the two on the way to Emmaus, had appreciated more and more the significance of the Christ-event as well as their own role in it. Yet at that stage the twelve were *not* the Church; they were gathered together by Jesus, not so much to be launched on a world mission, but mainly to represent Israel's twelve tribes in the ultimate blossoming of God's universal rule at the end of time. The twelve apostles were pledges of this eschatological fulfilment, which would become the central belief on which the Church was to be built. Theirs was a ministry of a kind, but not yet the one Ministry which would emerge along with the Church.

With the conversion of Paul the very notion of apostleship[77] undergoes a change. The twelve's very personal experience could not be transferred to future generations. Yet with the emergence of the Church the ministry of the twelve is extended to a group also called 'apostles'. There is, however, a difference between the ministry of the twelve and the ministry of their followers and collaborators. No doubt, both groups had gained their faith in the Spirit by accepting the resurrection of the man of Nazareth. Yet their insight must have been different. Paul's vision of the risen Christ (identified with the Church that he was persecuting) was not the same as that of the twelve. In 1 Corinthians 15:5-8 this fact may be indicated by telling the story of Jesus' appearing first to the Cephas and to the twelve, then 'to all the apostles' and to a 'multitude' the last of whom was he himself. If Paul indeed recognized a difference between the twelve and the rest of the newly converted faithful, then he had introduced a new twist to the meaning of apostleship. Whereas Luke, believed to be Paul's future companion, applies the word apostle almost exclusively to the twelve and not to others, Paul generously attributes it to anyone who is preaching the Christ-event and who is somehow witnessing Jesus to the emergent communities.[78] The role of the twelve apostles is now completed.

If this understanding of the twelve's role is correct, then it is legitimate to assume a certain novelty in the situation of Christ's followers. When Peter, on behalf of the twelve, began to preach the Jesus-event to the multitude at Pentecost, at that moment he discovered himself to be a minister. His ministry was to share his mature faith with the group, that is, in the Church of Jesus the Christ. At this moment the Church and the ministry were born. Indeed, *Ubi Petrus ibi ecclesia* – but the later saying is convertible: wherever there is Church there must also be a leader in Peter's stead.

It is not surprising then that most of the original apostles fade away into the realm of legend: with the exception of Philip and perhaps John (Acts 8:4–17) we hear practically nothing from Luke about their further apostolic works, but he explains the unfolding of the Church by the 'apostles' – now in the Pauline sense. This latter group of 'apostles' indeed will determine the institutionalized structure of the Church as she sets out on her path through history. The Rahnerian decision, as exposed in this section, is now operative.

The Church quickly chooses the first deacons (Acts 6:1–7) and the emissaries to foreign parts and Paul (supposedly with others) begins to spread the gospel, by establishing new assemblies from Samaria to the heart of the Roman Empire. After they had left to continue their mission elsewhere, there was a natural need to look after and assign persons to the new communities and it was a dictate of their faith to recommend these persons to the assistance of the Holy Spirit. The sign of this was the prayerful imposition of hands – an ancient signal of blessing and entrusting someone to God. At this stage, however, it is not yet clear whether their assignment to a function was due to the respective communities or to a messenger, as in the case of Stephen and the other six deacons in Jerusalem (Acts 6:5). Nor is it evident that the ministry of a new minister was attributed to this blessing. It will be the result of later reflection (also, incidentally, another decision of the Church) that the imposition of hands is regarded as one of a grace-conferring sacrament.

At this stage the stratification of leadership within the local churches is an accepted fact: the leadership of the churches by bishops, priests and deacons becomes crystallized, and establishes the traditional basis upon which the Church builds her inner organization. This 'decision', however, did not take place from day-to-day: it was a process through repeated experiment which eventually reached definitely the triad.[79] This is the situation in which the one Ministry will become shared with the ministries. And this process, though founded on the apostles' faith and teaching, is (at least partially) subject to sociological rules.

The concrete (and perhaps general) realization of this triadic structure seems to have occurred only in post-apostolic times. The pseudo-Pauline pastoral epistles of Timothy and Titus surely helped. Whereas the three are mentioned in Acts and 1 Peter[80] as ministries, the so-called pastoral letters refer to them as more or less established offices. In these epistles the authors introduce themselves as Paul's disciples (without ever using the name 'apostle' for themselves), but their image of the Church is different from the Pauline notion of the Body of Christ which, to my mind, is an eschatological concept. The ministry now, as a concretely defined office rules the coherence and unity of the churches and of the Church. Various grades, and apparently descending ones now structure the faithful and their 'church'. The simple faithful are no longer the main element in the community: this position is assumed by those entrusted with the office of the ministry, as representatives of the apostles and as leaders of the communities.[81] Indeed, the pastoral epistles are not only guided by the principle of the hierarchy, but gradually introduce its concretization.

By the middle of the second century, with the first letter of Clement the classical triad, bishops-priests-deacons, are church functionaries, even if not always in a constant hierarchical order.[82] This obviously presupposes the stabilization of corresponding structures and a more stable stratification of leadership, introduced partly to secure continuity and preserve the original deposit of faith against heretical tendencies. Above all, it was the unanimity of the faithful within the local communities and with other local 'churches' that motivated this increasing institutionalization. This process not only preaches the direct testimony to the gospel of the crucified and risen Lord, as it was in the time of the 'apostles' of the first generation, but also helps to preserve received doctrine intact.

I believe that this represents another hiatus on the development of the Church similar to the change from the twelve to the later apostles of the early generation. This hiatus, too, came about by a 'Rahnerian' decision both by the community and then more and more by the ordinance of their leaders. And if we return to his theory of divine right we could agree that this development is 'somehow' related to divine revelation. This 'somehow' is an event of the Church. In view, however, of *my* understanding of divine right the question is justified: Was the fixed establishment of hierarchical order of primary or secondary divine right? It can surely be explained by sociological rules, but is it indeed the manifest will of a self-revealing God? That there is a ministry in the Church is certainly an irrevocable fact *de jure divino*. But can we affirm the same of this later development? My conviction is that a concrete and fixed hierarchy in the Church is of *secondary* divine right. And if it is so its existence opens up to a new set of possibilities to be chosen and to be realized later.

However this may be, even a secondary divine right, as Rahner requires, can express the nature of the Church. The Church that is the depository of divine revelation as well as of the apostolic teaching (*depositum fidei*) including ministries has in fact existed ever since those early days. The presbyterate and the office of priests is only later discovered to be different from the ministry of the bishops. It is not easy to state whether the priesthood started as a collective body or a group of single individuals. Nevertheless, this societal fact together with its background in revelation had to be transmitted from one generation to the next. How this succession was exercised in *praxis* is again one of the possibilities, which is an institution of secondary divine right. The question for this decision was either the integrity of personal faith and/or the appointment by a 'higher' authority accompanied with a rite. Whereas in the first the main requirement was the acceptance of the irrevocable mystery of faith, the other emphasized also the readiness to preserve the developing teaching of an ecclesiastical tradition. We now know that the actual decision was for this second alternative. It is, however, difficult for historians to demonstrate an unbroken line between present-day ministries and their apostolic origins. A *secondary* divine right leaves the question open as to whether or not a once discarded alternative could be revived in the current decisions of the Church.[83]

The question of apostolic succession becomes even more acute in the case of the Bishop of Rome. For this office, too, was due to a later decision of the Church. Throughout my presentation and comments I have already hinted at the problems implied in a continuous link between the apostle Peter and present-day papacy. No doubt Peter had an eminent role in the history of Jesus and the twelve. He must have been the hot-headed initiator of many of their undertakings, a kind of busybody throwing his weight around in the company of the twelve. Jesus must have had a certain liking for the man, who had first denied him, then repented. He was later to become the one to *strengthen* and not to *judge* his fellow apostles' faith (Lk 22:33). There is, however, no solid evidence that he was put in charge by Jesus to *lead* the assembled disciples during his life, and much less that he became the sovereign leader of the first Christian communities. Even if he was their appointed founder and the acknowledged leader, his 'rule' was short-lived and was soon assumed by James the brother of the Lord and his body of presbyters. Peter, like Paul, very soon took to the road and ended his life in martyrdom in Rome, as tradition reliably documents.

The biblical texts of Matthew 16, John 21 and 1 Peter 5:1–4, referring to Peter's 'primacy', are mirroring a post-apostolic situation and are valuable documents for the tradition of already established local churches. None of these puts him forward as the *locum tenens* of the departed Christ. In Matthew he is the rock (a linguistic play on his newly-obtained name), a symbol for the unanimity of future communities built on the faith in Christ and his Holy Spirit. In addition, Peter's competence seems to have been limited by the assembly of the faithful, which plays an equally decisive role in the life of the community. Matthew 18:15–20 is one of the customs taken over from the Old Testament *kahal*, and apparently practised in Matthean communities. As Peter himself in Matthew 16, and the twelve in John 20:22, the assembly in Matthew 18 have the same power of 'binding and loosing': the one in doctrinal the other in disciplinary matters. Jesus says nothing about Peter's wide-ranging power in managing a young assembly of the faithful. In Acts, of course, Peter does use his authority and power; but we have no evidence how this authority and power inherent to his person was later exercised on the path towards Rome and how much of his authority was inherited. I cannot therefore affirm that the mystery and the real existence of the Church is identical with the papacy. Yet I can agree with Kertelge:

> The possibility of such a development as a legitimate interpretation of the Church's power to be exercised by Peter is not to be excluded. For the fullness of power and authority (*Vollmacht*) granted, according to Matthew 18:18 and 28:18–20, to the whole Church, needs also the singular office and official who puts (*wahrnimmt*) this full power into practice.[84]

Kertelge is speaking of a *possibility* and not the necessity of such a development. It was one of the alternatives available in history, by which the monarchical and paternalistic leadership could soon develop with all the paraphernalia of a papal regime. Could we then ask whether a discarded possibility can reassert itself at a later stage of history and become a real alternative, though in another form?

This is how I understand Rahner's approach to the papacy and so do modern ecumenical consultations concerning the Pope's primacy both in doctrinal and jurisdical matters. W. Pannenberg asks on behalf of other Protestant theologians:

> Apart from the leadership of the local, *regional* and also *universal* level of the Church, is the service of a particular office and a singular person necessary? This person would be able to speak for the world on his own behalf and not only in the synodal form of ecumenical councils in which the regions of Christianity are represented by their bishop.

His answer is yes: 'If any of the bishops can speak up for the whole of Christianity . . . it is most likely to be the bishop of Rome.'[85] As Pannenberg insists on a future papacy as the universal sign of the unity of all Christian communities, so Rahner regards the supreme function of the papacy: to be the *symbol of unity* of a Church, which in herself is nothing other than the sacramental sign of eschatological fulfilment of mankind.

In our present circumstances, however, it is evident that the primacy, whether it is exercised in a monarchical or more and more in a synodal way, entails first of all a magisterial competence in matters of doctrine, of jurisdiction and of discipline. I use the word 'competence' on purpose in order to avoid authority and power, which are, in the present discussion often either pitted one against the other or used interchangeably. To my mind competence implies both; a right to be head on account of the office and the capacity to execute. This competence belongs first of all to the Pope himself, but it can be delegated, as it has been today to the Roman congregations. Thus conceived, competence is a relational word: it presupposes the competence of a person or of a collective unit in relationship both to the subject matter to be dealt with as well as to the persons who do or ought to accept it. In doctrinal matters, past and present, this competence has been often exercised by the *Magisterium* in statements either rejecting an opinion or affirming another official standpoint. The truth of affirmative statements is, however, by the very logic of their nature is arguable and controllable.[86] It is a requirement that was repeatedly proposed by Rahner. Truth, apart from being conformity to reality has a social perspective: it has to be rooted in the community in which it exists.[87] Whether or not infallibility should be attributed to the magisterial competence of the papacy and to the reigning Pope will remain within and without the Roman Catholic Church the most debatable as well as the, logically, most negligible predicate. Nonetheless one thing is certain: no one within the Church dare fail to take up the challenge of a magisterial statement. It is at least an existentially inevitable question to which the answer is the responsibility of every faithful Catholic in word and deed.

To sum up: the irrevocable mystery of the Church and the Church that is our day-to-day experience is an event. Her life is lived out in all her consecrated members. Their consecration is actualized in apparently stable ministries in an institutionalized form. Since, however, the Church herself and her ministries are interchangeable in their origin they are not substantial but relational realities: the single ministries in themselves, including those 'special ones' of our present considerations, cannot be envisaged without their manifold relations. They are part of a process towards a humanly incomprehensible consummation. While the object of our faith in the Church is this fulfilment in the communion of the *Body of Christ*, the pilgrim way of the *people of God* is ruled by our belief in the guidance of the Spirit in building up an adequate society of the faithful. That this society may become the sign of the salvation of mankind is our unshakeable hope.

Once we have accepted that neither the established ministries nor the corresponding offices in a structurally developed Church are substantial realities, but relative to the community and to Jesus Christ, then the following thesis should also be acceptable. *Owing to the event character of the Church and because of the basic oneness of all ministries in her, the difference neither between their various grades (deacons, priest, bishop, pope) nor between the so-called clergy and laity can be fixed in an objectivised, ontological definition.*

I believe that the verification of this *negative* part of my conclusion is, at least provisionally, sufficient. The *positive* side of the same thesis should be a basis of hope – for many contemporary believers. *Although the one Ministry of the Church and the variety of her ministries are of irreversible divine right, their actualization in history is part of an ongoing process and open to an unforeseeable future development.*

§§§§§§

There is, however a legitimate objection which can be raised: how could I deal with the origin, the consecrated membership, the structures and organs of Church-leaders without referring to the sacramental nature of the Church herself and to her seven traditional sacraments? I have assumed that as a promise of salvation, faith and beliefs can be operative on a pre-sacramental level. It will be the task of sacramental theology to reconsider the same also of their God-given actualization in individual men and women.

Epilogue

There are topics in theology the treatment of which cannot be exhausted. Instead of concluding my dialogue with the ecclesiology of Karl Rahner I am going to abandon it, for the time being. The full reality of the Church is not itself complete; although many practical questions were touched upon in my long-winded presentation and reflections, my treatment has been mostly at the theoretical level of Roman Catholic theology; a treatment that deals with the essence or nature of the Church without discussing its existential reality. To use Rahner's own word: up to now I have not faced seriously her *Selbsvolzug*, her self-realization or self-actualization. The Church is present in the world as a concrete historical existence: in her preaching of the Word and in administering the sacraments to each and every individual member of the people of God. I have tried to show, furthermore, that the Church, in contrast to the Old Testament assembly of the elected people, the *kahal*, is the crowning event of a common history of salvation. And yet, she can only be truly a *new* initiative of God with mankind if she believes that all the promises of God are irreversibly fulfilled in Jesus Christ under the guidance of the Spirit within the assembly of the faithful. Without this eschatological faith all that was said about the Church would be vacuous. In other words, a theology of the Church needs a treatise on the sacraments and on the eschatological future of mankind. It is this aspect which is still outstanding in my dialogue with Karl Rahner's theology.

Nonetheless, a brief account of this present volume would be necessary in order to see the tree within the wood. At this stage, however, it would hardly be possible to sum up Rahner's views with succinct clarity, and even more difficult to point out those elements in my own reflections which try to correct or develop his thought. Our two versions of the Church are inextricably interwoven; in what I have tried to add I have never been sure whether my own insight was due to his tacit inspiration, or whether I was deviating substantially from the Rahnerian mind.

One thing, however, is certain: I am not prepared to accept that premise of Rahner which I label 'transcendentalism'. By this I mean those *a priori* elements in his ecclesiology, at least, that endow the human spirit with a non-conscious, anticipative idea of the Church. I ventured indeed to sum up one of the first steps in Rahner's approach as 'transcendent ecclesiology' (see section 1.2). I grant that human nature is basically social, but I doubt that this sociability alone makes men and women capable of living together in that solidarity of personal communion which the Church really ought to become. The human lot *de facto* imposes the constraint of living together as separate individuals and involves the accommodation of one's own interests to those of the unavoidable other. The encounter with the self-revelation of God in Jesus Christ *as something given in history* alone enables the insight that human existence should be basically relational, and in essence for others rather than the self. It is no mere chance embellishment that the *Urbild*, the prototype of the Church is the blessed Trinity. Hence my repeated insistence on the difference between the 'self' and the person: the one referring to each separate individual and to *society*, and the other to a human existence living out an encounter in *communion* with the entirely other. The task of theology is not to verify that which we, aware or unaware, already possess, but through belief in the Word of God, to reinterpret what we already are, and to learn what we ought to become.

I was constantly confronted therefore with the 'two-faceted' Church, the need to reconcile the elements of human society with God's 'destiny for mankind'. That is, communion with one another and with God: the one is apt for the analysis of social sciences; the other something similar, but now subordinate to the word of God. We can speak about the Church both as another human society and as a mystery already foreshadowing the Kingdom of God. The longest and central chapter of this book proposed discussion in detail of the correlationship between these two aspects. True, it may have implicated both writer and prospective reader in the manifold characteristics that two thousand years of Church history have exhibited (an understandable development in any human society), but the ultimate purpose was always to appeal to the Word of God or, more especially, to the trust grounded in our faith in the guidance of the Spirit. On the one hand, the assembly of the faithful, whose membership of the Church is by no means uniform, can only avoid anarchy by being organised with a certain stratification, by creating institutions and a more or less stable structure, by producing various organs and accepting an authoritative rule under the service of a hierarchy. Yet, on the other hand, to escape the pitfall of a uniform collectivism and of a tyrannical absolutism they need the charisma of the Spirit in order to understand these structural elements in their nature, transient in their function and open to be absorbed in the mystery of an ineffable communion. Beyond the inevitable hegemony of a Roman Pontiff whose infallibility shared with the Church redounds in his person, and the necessary coherence of all the local ordinaries whose College enjoys the ultimate power in a worldwide Church, and a Magisterium which can lay down the details of our beliefs and enforce the norms of Christian behaviour, there is no human organ of appeal unless our faith and trust in the guidance of the Spirit. I believe with Karl Rahner in the social necessity of some organization among members of the Church, yet I also believe (at least, as implied in his approach) that one can and must live with the real tension involved in this two-faceted Church, since all social structures are transitory and will yield to the mystery of the future.

Theology (as Karl Barth's words in the Preface tell us) is never an entirely free science: its context is the Church, it is dependent on the Church. Even in these troubled days of ecclesiastical disorientation, I still believe that the best expression of this dependence is the Magisterium of the Roman Catholic Church. All other attempts to preserve unanimity are ambiguous and produce a history of divisions within the people of God, in itself already the one body of Christ. This, of course, does not mean that the theologian is the mouthpiece of an 'official theology' as is often advocated by this central organ. I am of the same opinion as Karl Rahner concerning the relationship between the Magisterium and the theologian. Without repeating his well reasoned views I add the following two observations only.

First, the truth of certain doctrines and often their verbal expressions which the Magisterium of today strives to free from all contemporary relativism. It is true that a merely secular culture must not influence truths apparently essential to our faith. Human circumstances require us to assert and reassert them as absolute, even if they are relative with regard to the Word of God's promises whose fulfilment is still outstanding. If I may so put it: the truth of Christian revelation is, and always remains relative to, the mystery of God in its vertical coordinate; but this is not true of its horizontal coordinate. This notion is valid, I believe, even when applied to the Church and to the doctrines about the Church. Although we may not enjoy the absolute security of a truth, we are entitled to affirm it with absolute certainty in face of other secular or religious convictions. To believe that the Roman Catholic Church and her teaching is the absolute and exclusive way to salvation (as asserted throughout past centuries) is correct, but it does not exclude *absolutely* other approaches to God's unfathomable mystery. A contrary affirmation would be the *hubris* of pretending to be God. If we accept this obviously dialectical statement, we cannot avoid taking seriously convictions that dissent from the 'official doctrine'. *Mutatis mutandis*, something similar could be said of the moral and ethical standards of Christian behaviour advocated by the Magisterium. Any other attitude than this dialectical tension would land us with an unsavoury compromise.

My second observation on Magisterium and theologian finds me in full agreement with Rahner; he insists on the autonomy of the theologian in relation to the teaching office of the Church. Autonomy does not exclude dependence. Proper dialogue involves dependence on the other party. I am bound to learn by listening, even if I abide with my own basic conviction. To say that the duty of the theologian is only to explain and defend precisely defined doctrines would yield a monistic image of the assembly of the faithful and *that* the Church is definitely *not*.

The autonomy of the theologian should mean that one partner in the dialogue is in encounter with the Magisterium: both are ever in constant pursuit of God's ultimately mysterious truth. Granted that the equality of the partners is not at the same level in every aspect of their confrontations but we ask: what could the teaching Office of the Church achieve without the autonomous teaching of the theologians? And what could the inevitable plurality of theologies achieve without the lead of directives from the Magisterium? Let me apply to this tension Rahner's analysis of the structures of Church-membership: even the marginal believer and the everyday Christian in a *Vokskirche* are not only represented within the Church but also consecrated to the service of God's Word, just as much as is the so-called hierarchy. The theologian with his or her co-workers belong to the same ecclesial structures (see Rahner's article 'Structure' and my references to it); they may represent a marginal group from the viewpoint of 'official' Christendom as imagined by some of the doctrinal congregation, but this does not diminish the value of the task they fulfil within the solidarity of the whole Church.

In this respect, too, Karl Rahner is *a man of the Church*, and especially in his ecclesiology.

Notes

Preface

1. See K. Barth, *Church Dogmatics*, Edinburgh (1968), p. ix: 'When the word "Church" replaces the word "Christian" in the title of the book . . . I might point to the circumstance that dogmatics is not a "free" science, but one bound to the sphere of the Church, where and where alone it is possible and sensible.' Barth wrote this unforgettable foreword to the very first volume of his book one hundred years after the second edition of Friedrich Daniel Schleiermacher's *The Christian Faith*.
2. Cf., Vass, Vol. 1, pp. 1–17. Although the first chapter is mainly philosophical (*A Theologian in Search of a Philosophy*), I began with, I believe, good instincts by pointing out the framework of Rahner's faith and by analysing his attempts at new and contemporary formulations of that faith.

Introduction: The 'Wintry Season' of the Church

1. There exists in the German-speaking world, an extensive secondary literature on the practical trend in the whole of Rahner's theology. The best summary is that of K. Neumann, *Der Praxisbezug der Theologie bei K. Rahner*, Freiburg-im-Breisgau (1980). This should be compared with N. Mette, 'Zwischen Reflexion und Entscheidung, Beitrag K. Rahners, zur Grundlegung der praktischen Theologie', *Trierer Theol. Zeitschrift* 87 (1978) pp. 26–43 and pp. 136–151. See, however, Rahner's own admission in an interview in 1984: 'I've never theologised just *l'art pour l'art*. I must say the publications are altogether another of my pastoral concerns.'
2. H. Vorgrimler, *Understanding Karl Rahner. An Introduction to his*

Life and Thought, New York, NY (1986) and London (1986). By a coincidence, the German original is published under the same main title as that of my own analysis of Rahner's theology.

3. Cf., P. Imhof and H. Biallowons, *Glaube in winterlicher Zeit, Gespräche mit Karl Rahner aus den letzten Lebensjahren*, Dusseldorf (1986). Although a partial translation of this volume was published by H. D. Egan, *Faith in a Wintry Season*, New York, NY (1990), I shall often use the original with my own translations. Hence, in what follows, the first is referred to as '*Glaube*', the second as 'Egan' (the first use of this arrangement occurs in the next note and see also the Table of Abbreviations).

4. Cf., *Glaube*, pp. 16–18 (Egan: missing). Imhof and Biallowons describe Rahner's interview with Walter Tscholl at Innsbruck in 1984. See also *Glaube*, pp. 44f (= Egan, p. 32), noting Rahner's comments that same year in the journal *Vida Nueva* in Madrid: 'Actually that ecumenical Council has not really been put into practice in the Church, either according to its letter or according to its spirit. In general, we are living through a "wintry season" as I have often said. Still there are unquestionably communities in the Church where the charismatic element is very much alive and offers occasion for much hope.'

5. Cf., *Glaube*, p. 245 (= Egan, p. 200): ' . . . and so I think it's part too of Christian hope that we do not interpret these wintry times as a prelude to ultimate death.'

6. Cf., *Glaube*, pp. 178f (= Egan, p. 146). My own translation of an interview Rahner gave in 1983.

7. Ibid., *Glaube*, pp. 174f (= Egan, p. 142).

8. Cf., *Glaube*, pp. 214 (= Egan: missing); an interview with E. Gutheinz.

9. *Glaube*, pp. 175f (= Egan, p. 143).

10. *Glaube*, p. 174 (= Egan, p. 142).

11. *Glaube*, p. 175 (= Egan, p. 143).

12. Cf., *Glaube*, p. 202 (= Egan: missing); see here Rahner's remark on humanism concerning the absolute validity of the Christian religion for all cultures.

13. *Glaube*, pp. 181f (= Egan, p. 148).

14. Cf., Rahner's early writings. For example, 'Die öffentliche Meinung in der Kirche' in *Kirche in der Welt*, Munster (1952), pp. 137–42, an article motivated by a statement of Pius XII. Rahner elaborated on the same topics in a later work: see his *Free Speech*

in the Church, New York, NY (1959). See also his ever recurring dictum, 'Do not stifle the Spirit' (*Löscht den Geist nicht aus*), first published in *Münchener Kirchenzeitung* (1962) and later corrected and reformulated up to its publication in *TI* 7, pp. 72f (= *ST* VII, pp. 77f); the theme of courage to change in the Church appears in *Die Furche*, Vienna (1962); the same motif appeared in the short study, 'Wagnis oder Trägheit? Die Kirche und die geistige Situation der Gegenwart' in *Universitas*, Stuttgart (1963), pp. 1202–14, and others.

15. Cf., Vorgrimler, op. cit., especially chapter 10 and pp. 87–92.
16. Cf., *Glaube*, p. 37 (= Egan, p. 11); an interview with D. Müller, (1984). See also, both Rahner's 'Die öffentliche Meinung in der Kirche' in *Kirche in der Welt*, Munster (1952) and *Das freie Wort in der Kirche*, Einsideln (1953).
17. Cf., *Glaube*, p. 119 (= Egan, p. 96): 'No Christian is obliged to a blind, that is, corpselike obedience which only says yes and amen. On the contrary, there is within the Church something which is necessary to its very being, that is, a critical relationship to a specific way of life, to particular rules, and the like, even of this Church. Since it is always the Church of the pope, the bishops, the priests, and the laity, there is an obligation to criticise these persons.'
18. *Glaube*, p. 191f (= Egan: missing).
19. See *Toleranz in der Kirche*, Freiburg-im-Breisgau (1977), especially pp. 34–7. The English translation was published the same year; cf., 'Toleration in the Church' in *Meditations*; here, pp. 75ff.
20. *Glaube*, p. 19 (= Egan: missing).
21. *Glaube*, p. 32 (= Egan: missing).
22. *Glaube*, p. 94 (= Egan: missing).
23. *Glaube*, p. 32 (= Egan, pp. 94f and p. 238).
24. *Glaube*, p. 221 (= Egan, p. 180). See also *Glaube*, p. 95 (= Egan, p. 76).
25. *Glaube*, p. 90 (= Egan, p. 71).
26. *Glaube*, p. 91 (= Egan, p. 72). See Rahner's study 'Demokratie in der Kirche?' in *Gnade als Freiheit*, Freiburg-im-Breisgau (1968), pp. 113–30 which was first published in *Stimmen der Zeit* 182 (1968), pp. 1–15. The English translation was published a year later, cf., *Grace in Freedom*, London and New York, NY (1969), pp. 150–69.
27. *Glaube*, p. 100 (= Egan: missing).

28. *Glaube*, p. 209 (= Egan, p. 171): ' . . . in regard to Anglicans, a Catholic in good standing can certainly hold the opinion that the declaration of Pope Leo XIII concerning the presumed invalidity of anglican orders [1896] is incorrect, even according to the Catholic understanding of the sacraments.'

29. *Glaube*, p. 124 (= Egan, p. 101): 'The Congregation of the Faith has declared, in an authentic, but non-defined way, that according to the will of Christ women may not be ordained in the Catholic Church. I have openly presented my own opposing views. That is, I am not bound to declare the teaching of the Congregation of the Faith, for which I have great formal respect, as absolutely binding and obligatory for me. We must leave open the question of who really is right.' See also *Glaube*, p. 199 (= Egan, p. 163): 'And when the Congregation of the Faith declares that it is impossible to admit women to the priesthood, then I have to argue against it and affirm from a dogmatic point of view that the priesthood of women is not impossible.'

30. *Glaube*, p. 229 (= Egan, pp. 187f).

31. *Glaube*, p. 91 (= Egan, p. 72). See too Rahner's interview in *Der Spiegel*, 'Im Beichtstuhl nach der Pille fragen?', Munich (1970), pp. 321–34. And also his contribution 'Die Papst-Erklärung – kein "letztes Wort" ' in H. Böckle (ed.) *Die Encyklika in Diskussion, Eine orientierende Dokumentation zu* 'Humanae Vitae', Zurich (1969), pp. 57–63.

32. *Glaube*, p. 198 (= Egan, p. 162) and see also: p. 216 (= pp. 176f); p. 234 (=Egan: missing); p. 237 (= Egan, p. 191).

33. *Glaube*, pp. 228f (= Egan, pp. 187f). See also pp. 238f (= Egan: missing).

Chapter 1 **Foundations of an Ecclesiology**

1. In what follows (and see Table of Abbreviations), *Foundations of Christian Faith* is referred to as *Foundations*, and *Handbuch der Pastoraltheologie* as *Handbook*. The latter was published in two volumes in 1964; in the third part of this first chapter (see 1.3), I present the *Handbook* in more detail.

2. 'I Believe', p. 100 (= p. 103).

3. Cf., 'Interpretation of the Dogma', pp. 215ff (= pp. 239ff). In the same year, 1951, Rahner produced a large manuscript of 393 pages, 'Problems of Contemporary Mariology', part of which is summarized in 'Interpretation of the Dogma'. Rahner's manuscript did not pass its censors and was never printed; cf., Vorgrimler, op. cit., especially pp. 88–90. Rahner's manuscript is at present being considered for posthumous publication.

4. 'I Believe', p. 101 (= p. 104).

5. Cf., ibid., p. 103 (= p. 105).

6. Cf., ibid., p. 104 (= p. 107): ' . . . if the message of God makes a fresh and unwonted impact on our minds, ill-prepared as they are for it, then this lack of prior dispositions on our part causes us to react with explicit hostility.'

7. Ibid., p. 106 (= p. 109).

8. Ibid., pp. 106f (= p. 109).

9. Cf., 'Piety', pp. 336ff (= pp. 249ff). See also, 'Some Theses on Prayer in the Name of the Church' in *TI* 5, p. 416 (= *ST* V, pp. 471ff).

10. 'I Believe', p. 108 (= p. 110).

11. Ibid.

12. Ibid., pp. 108f (= p. 111).

13. Ibid., p. 109 (= p. 111).

14. See 'Church as a Subject', pp. 188f (= p. 185). The original German title reads *Die Kirche als Ort der Geistsendung*; in the English translation the German '*Ort*' has become 'Subject', which is not the same as the true translation which is 'Sphere'!

15. 'I Believe', p. 109 (= p. 112).

16. Ibid., p. 111 (= p. 115).

17. Cf., 'Church as a Subject', pp. 190f (= p. 187).

18. 'Church of Sinners', pp. 253ff (= pp. 301ff).

19. This *sacramental* approach to the Church was patterned on Trent's teaching on the sacraments in general (cf., Tanner, pp. 684–5), a doctrine which Trent has duly emphasized against the Reformers. The sacraments work *ex opere operato*, whilst the fruitful receiving of sacramental grace by the subject is *ex opere operantis*. Rahner will come back to this easily misunderstood distinction on several occasions.

20. 'Church of Sinners', p. 259 (= pp. 307f). Again, Rahner takes Trent for granted insofar as he speaks of a sign 'containing' grace – another misunderstandable statement of Trent's doctrine on the

sacraments (cf., Tanner, p. 84, Canon 6 on the sacraments).

21. 'Sinful Church', p. 290 (= p. 343).
22. Cf., Tanner, p. 855. And see also *Lumen Gentium* 8: ' . . . the Church containing sinners in its own bosom, is at one and the same time holy and always in need of purification and it pursues unceasingly penance and renewal.'
23. 'Sinful Church', p. 290 (= p. 343). [My italics.]
24. Ibid., p. 291..
25. 'Church of Saints', p. 95 (p. 116).
26. 'Church of Sinners', p. 263 (= p. 312).
27. Cf., 'Church of Saints', pp. 103f (= pp. 125f):   ' . . . the Church is meant to be and to appear as the community of eschatological salvation.'
28. 'Membership', pp. 1ff (= pp. 7ff).
29. Cf., for example, 'Der prophetische Mensch und die Kirche' in *Katholischer Kirchenzeitung* 41 (1948), pp. 169f. See also: 'Peaceful Reflections on the Parochial Principle' in *TI* 2, pp. 283f (= *ST* II, pp. 399ff); and *Zeitschrift für katholische Theologie* (1948) 70, pp. 169ff.
30. In Egan, p. 52 (= *Glaube*, p. 63), Rahner expresses regret: ' . . . in the course of my theological activity defended out of genuine inner conviction many teachings of the Church. Of some of these I would now say that I can no longer see it that way. Perhaps I should have been able to size it up differently then. For example, I worked very hard to defend and to interpret the teaching on membership in the Church in Pius's encyclical *Mystici Corporis Christi* [1943]. I did this in a way I probably could no longer bring myself to do.' I am not sure to what this apparent 'regret' refers: to defending a papal encyclical at all or to Rahner's eventual interpretation.
31. See Cardinal König, 'Rahners theologisches Denken' in E. Klinger (ed.), *Glaube im Prozess*, Freiburg-im-Breisgau (1984), pp. 121–36. König chose Rahner to be his theologian at Vatican II and his article pinpoints some Rahnerian texts which are reflected by some decrees of the Council.
32. It is enough to recall the Donatist crisis and the rejection of the teachings of Wycliff and Hus on the Church and the ministering of the sacraments. See also Tanner, pp. 422–9 for the rejection of Wycliff and Hus at the Council of Konstanz.
33. 'Membership', p. 34 (= p. 40).
34. Rahner, in discussing his notion of 'anonymous Christian' in his

'wintry season', comes repeatedly to this conviction. For salvation, the fundamental option for God in a societal context ('rudimentary faith') or adherence to one's conscience is necessary. See Egan, p. 102 (= *Glaube*, p. 126): ' . . . explicitness and societal nature of the ultimate relationship to God are not simply any odd decisions left to human beings.' By 'decisions', Rahner means not an act of free will (*liberum arbitrium*), but a fundamental choice for life. When this is taken in faith, he continues, ' . . . then you can no longer say: "Christianity does not concern me,".'

35. Rahner qualifies this as a misunderstanding: ' . . . which has aroused real bewilderment among non-Catholic Christians.' See 'Membership', p. 37 (= p. 42).

36. Cf., Vass, Vol. 2, where the topic of salvation and God's universal salvific will in Rahner's writings was introduced, and also Vols 3 and 4 for the discussion that followed. It is useful to consult Rahner's contributions to *SM* V, pp. 405–9, 419–23 and 425–33. As for the history of this axiom, especially as regards Vatican II, consult the dissertation (with literature) of F. Cserháti, *Eingliederung in die Kirche um des Heiles willen*, Frankfurt (1984).

37. 'Membership', p. 50 (= p. 57); note Rahner's cautious conclusion, dotted with question marks!

38. Ibid., pp. 55ff (= pp. 63ff).

39. Cf., ibid., pp. 65–6 (= pp. 72–4); note also p. 84 (= pp. 66f) and p. 92 (= p. 73).

40. Cf., Tanner, p. 861. This is the classical statement of *Lumen Gentium* about the universal salvific will of God: though it does not speak explicitly of an 'orientation', it asserts the necessity of the Church to which Jews, Moslems, other religious believers and searchers of God may belong.

41. Cf., 'Membership', pp. 73ff (= pp. 80ff): 'Hence there can be, as in the case of the Sacraments, a twofold notion of the Church . . . Thus on the one hand, there is the notion of the Church as incarnate presence of Christ and his grace, together with Christ and his grace, and . . . the notion of the Church in as far as she must be essentially distinguished from this grace and inner divine union, without ceasing, however to be . . . a still valid Christian reality.' Also: ' . . . the Church as parallel notion to Sacrament understood as sign and grace, or . . . without an effect of grace.' This last complex sentence (and no doubt the crux of the translation) is buttressed by a note in

which Rahner's theory as regards penance is repeated: ' . . . the fruit of this sacrament is first and foremost reconciliation with the Church.'

42. Rahner suggests that the encyclical, in speaking of membership uses the first aspect of a composite sacramental reality. Cf., 'Membership', p. 74 (= p. 81). And he further remarks, in using the analogy of the Chalcedonian definition, ' . . . it would be a rationalistic error or see nothing more in the Church . . . than a purely juridical and social entity' – in fact, nothing but an ecclesiological Nestorianism. Cf., 'Membership', p. 70 (= p. 77). Likewise, to regard the Church only as a spiritual reality would be called an ecclesiological Monophysitism.

43. 'Membership', p. 75 (= p. 81).

44. Ibid., p. 87 (= p. 94).

45. Cf., ibid., p. 77 (= pp. 83f).

46. Ibid., p. 79 (= p. 85): 'Whatever may be the more exact explanation, there is, in fact, such a natural unity of all men which is the underlying *potentia oboedientialis* of God's saving work with regard to humanity.'

47. Ibid., p. 81 (= p. 88): 'The Incarnation . . . is a reality which belongs to the historical and visible dimension of reality which, as factual determination of the human race as a whole, is also a real ontological determination of the nature of each human being.'

48. Ibid., p. 84 (= p. 90).

49. Ibid., p. 75 (= p. 81). [My italics.]

50. Cf., *Hearers*, pp. 177–9 (= pp. 219–20). It is enough to quote here the conclusion of Rahner's philosophical theology: 'Let us assume that a man is convinced that it is part of the most essential basic attitude in life to seek decisive word of God's personal self-revelation somewhere in concrete here and now of human history . . . Such a man, we might suspect, . . . has already traversed the most essential part of the road to the Christian faith of the Catholic Church. . . . Anyone who takes unbiased account of these things will find it difficult not to recognise the Roman Catholic Church as the seat of genuine revelation of the living God.'

51. See 'Freedom', especially pp. 96ff (= pp. 102ff).

52. Cf., Vass, Vol. 1, pp. 68f and 81f.

53. 'Freedom', pp. 93f (= p. 100). Note here, however, that the English translation is misleading. Rahner would be careful of speaking of God as the 'object' of freedom: that is, one object among many

others. He rather speaks of God as a *woraufhin* – a purpose or meaning of our freedom.

54. Ibid., pp. 95f (= p. 102).
55. Ibid., p. 97 (= p. 104).
56. Ibid., p. 98 (= pp. 104f).
57. Cf., Vass, Vol. 2, pp. 68f and 81f.
58. 'Theology of Freedom', pp. 178ff (= pp. 215ff), especially p. 179 (= p. 216) where Rahner argues for a freedom of choice not for a categorial object, but for the very being of the self. This article was first published in 1964 as *Theologie der Freiheit*.
59. Ibid., p. 181 (= p. 218).
60. As Rahner puts it elsewhere: 'Freedom which in itself is infinite [that is, transcendental] can only be exercised within a limited sphere.' See 'Freedom and Manipulation in Society and the Church' in *Meditations*, pp. 33–71, especially, p. 41. This article was first published as *Freiheit und Manipulation in Gesellschaft und Kirche*, Munich (1970–71), see p. 15; and later published under the same title in Freiburg-im-Breisgau (1977), see pp. 67–104.
61. 'Theology of Freedom', p. 189 (= p. 225): 'The transcendental experience of God . . . is possible only in and through man who has *already* (in logical priority) experienced the human Thou by his intramundane transcendental experience [that is, of his *a priori* reference to the Thou] and by his categorial experience [that is, of his concrete encounter with the concrete Thou] and who only in this way can experience his reference to the absolute Mystery [that is, God]'. The word 'experience' in the above translation is *vollziehen* in the original German, which is more strictly 'perform'. Cf., 'Unity of the Love of Neighbour and the Love of God' in *TI* 6, p. 245 (= *ST* VI, p. 293).
62. See 'Theology of Freedom', p. 188 (= p. 227): 'The Christian ethos does not consist in the respecting of objective norms imposed by God on reality. All structures of things are lower than man. He can alter them, bend them as far as possible; he is their master and not their servant. The only ultimate structure of the person which manages to express it completely is the basic capacity of love, and this is without measure.
63. See 'One Mediator and many Mediations' in *TI* 9, p. 176 (= ST VIII, p. 226): 'Here too no one is alone; each one supports every other person. In the matter of salvation everyone is responsible and

significant for everyone else. The commandment to love one's neighbour . . . was given . . . to proclaim everyone's concern in everyone else's possibility of salvation.'

64. *Foundations,* especially p. 323 (= p. 314).

65. Ibid., p. 342 (= p. 332).

66. Ibid., p. 343 (= p. 332).

67. Ibid., p. 345 (= p. 315).

68. Ibid., p. 399 (= p. 386).

69. Ibid., p. 346 (= p. 335).

70. Ibid., p. 400 (= p. 386).

71. Cf., 'Piety', p. 352 (= p. 396)

72. Ibid., p. 340 (= p. 383)

73. The distinction employed here goes back to Augustine (Sermo 61, *de Verbis Domine*; in Tract. sup. Johannem) and used by Thomas Aquinas in *Summa Theologiae* II–II, q. 2, art. 2c.

74. Cf., Vass, Vol. 2, pp. 117ff. It should be noted here that Rahner does not follow strictly the classical distinctions: *credere in Deum; credere Deum; credere Deo.*

75. Cf., 'Piety', pp. 343f (= p. 387).

76. Ibid., p. 349 (= p. 392). And see also p. 347 (= p. 390).

77. Ibid., p. 348 (= p. 391)

78. Ibid., p. 351 (= pp. 394f)

79. Ibid., p. 345 (= p. 388).

80. Ibid., p. 346 (= p. 389).

81. Ibid., p. 350 (= p. 393).

82. Cf., ibid., p. 350 (= p. 394): 'This "I believe in You" which – within the Church – one person can, and indeed must, say to another must be based on the still more original "I believe in You" which God and man say to each other in the grace of "divine" faith.'

83. Cf., ibid., pp. 351f (= p. 396).

84. Ibid., p. 355 (= p. 400).

85. Cf., ibid., pp. 356f (= pp. 400f): ' . . . [the Church is] the vanguard, the sacramental sign, the historical tangibility of saving grace which goes beyond the sociologically tangible and the "visible" Church, i.e. the grade of anonymous Christianity which outside the Church has not yet come to itself, but "within" the Church is present to itself, not because it is simply not present outside but because, objectively speaking, it has not as yet reached full maturity there, and hence does not as yet understand itself in that

explicit way and reflex objectivity of the formulated profession of faith, of the sacramental objectification and of the sociological organisation which are found within the Church herself.'

86. Ibid., p. 361 (= p. 406). Rahner's argumentation here anticipates his 1961 thesis on the 'anonymous Christian'. This was finally formulated in 1964 – and discussed earlier in this series; see Vass, Vol. 4, Chapters 3 and 4. Rahner's argumentation continues, see p. 362 (= p. 406), to speak of the Church as the promise for the world 'in it becoming a church' (*der wachsenden Kirchenwerdung der Welt*), and its possibility to be saved by the Church in which mankind's acceptance of God's salvific will has become explicit.

87. Cf., 'Ideology and Christianity' in *TI* 6, pp. 43ff (= *ST* VI, pp. 59–76), especially p. 53 (= p. 71).

88. 'Church and Parousia' in *TI* 6, p. 305 (= *ST* VI, p. 359): 'In brief, the concrete history of the Church is the means by which the transcendental experience in faith and hope of grace as the divine life itself is objectified and so becomes in the concrete the object of man's saving decision.'

89. Cf., 'Church, Churches and Religions' in *TI* 10, pp. 30ff (= *ST* VIII, pp. 355ff). First published in 1966 as *Kirche, Kirchen und Religionen*, this whole essay is relevant here, but especially p. 40 (= p. 364).

90. Cf., 'Piety', p. 364 (= p. 364). As members we are looking for a Church in a way ' . . . that we experience our own faith as the faith of the Church and experience ourselves in this way as her members; the Church who is an object of faith because we believe in God.'

91. *Sendung und Gnade, Beitrage zur Pastoraltheologie zur gegenwartigen Situation der Christen*, Innsbruck (1959). The English translation, *Mission and Grace: Essays in Pastoral Theology*, was published in three volumes by Sheed & Ward, London and New York, NY, Vol I (1963), Vol II (1964), Vol III (1966).

92. Cf., Vorgrimler, op. cit., especially his Introduction, n. 2.

93. In this and the following chapters I translate the verb *vollziehen* and the noun *Vollzug* with 'to perform' and 'performance' respectively. This may sound odd, yet is closest to its German connotation. To 'perform' means 'to carry through an action to completion' which, I believe, corresponds best to the German. See also *Shorter Oxford Dictionary*, Oxford (1933), p. 1472.

242 A Pattern of Doctrines – Part III: A Man of the Church

94. At a preparatory stage Dr Scherer, the lector of Herder's publishing house raised such a difficulty in personal letter to the author, 24 August 1960.

95. *Handbook*, Vol. I, p. 118.

96. Definitions, both nominal and real, are normally given and asked for when a speaker or hearer is not certain or clear about a word that is being used or about something that is being mentioned. Real definitions can be understood as answers to 'What is . . . ' questions. See the treatment of H. Rikhof, *The Concept of the Church. A methodological inquiry into the Use of Metaphors in Ecclesiology*, London (1981), especially p. 211. Some theologians after Vatican II (including Congar, Hollböck, Semmelroth, Schmaus, Dulles) refused, as Rikhof notes (pp. 205–11), to give an essential definition of the 'mystery' which is the Church and resort to the use of metaphors. It remains to be seen whether Rahner has succeeded in his attempt. I shall return to Rikhof's book in the next chapter.

97. I prefer here to use the word 'unity'. This, I believe, is general enough to comprise the terms *coetus, communitas, communio, societas* and *koinonia*, as applied to the Church by *Lumen Gentium*. It is hard to assign corresponding words in German or English. As we shall see, Rahner will use mainly *Gesellschaft* (society) and *Gemeinschaft* (communion, or fellowship).

98. *Handbook*, Vol. I, pp. 118f. [My translation.]

99. We should not forget that this 'definition' was meant to ground a pastoral and missionary activity of the Church, albeit its theoretical elements. Just as in his Christology, Rahner does not acknowledge the distinction between essential and functional so in his ecclesiology. See Vass, Vol. 3, Chapter 4.

100. *Handbook*, Vol. I, p. 120.

101. Mark the parallelism between the supernatural existential, as dealt with earlier in the series (see Vass, Vol. 2, Chapter 3) and the historical, but *a priori* role of the Church. In fact, Rahner's study preparatory to this 'definition' implicitly connected the mystery of the Church with that of the supernatural existential.

102. One should consult here the German original (*Handbook*, Vol. I, p. 121). In introducing his sentence about the Church as a medium of salvation, Rahner emphasizes that she is *also* (*was sie auch*) presenting God on earth. This does not mean that the Church *is* God *present* on earth, which would be heretical – even if one is tempted

to think so. The sacrament 'presenting' God on earth *is not* God being 'present'.

103. *Handbook*, Vol. I, p. 122. As Rahner puts it: 'The Church confesses Christ the God-man, as the presence of God, because she understands man as someone who rejects all other deities.' [My translation.]

104. See Vass, Vol. 1, Chapter 7.

105. Cf., *Handbook*, Vol. I, p. 125.

106. See Vass, Vol. 3, section 2.2 and the corresponding reflections in section 3.3.

107. Cf., Tanner, p. 850 and the first chapter of *Lumen Gentium* as a whole.

108. This participation of God's Mystery, which the Church 'reflects' makes the Church herself a mystery – hence the recurring allusion of Rahner and post-Vatican theologians to the 'Mystery of the Church'.

109. Cf., *Lumen Gentium* 9: the first, and to my mind most important, allusion to the Church as a sacrament is here introduced in the chapter on the people of God. However, it is said that the Church was founded by Christ as a visible sacrament of unity and peace among those who in faith accept Christ's salvific deed for mankind. The word 'proto-sacrament' as such does not feature in the constitution of the Church.

110. Cf., *The Church and the Sacraments*, W. J. O'Hara (trs.), London (1967), pp. 6 and 18. Originally published in Germany as *Kirche und Sakramente*, Freiburg-im-Breisgau (1961).

111. Cf., *Handbook*, Vol. I, pp. 133ff.

112. *The Church and the Sacraments*, op. cit. Note that O'Hara rendered *Ursakrament* (p. 17) as 'fundamental sacrament'.

113. Cf., ibid., p. 19 (= p. 18).

114. The German verb used by Rahner is *sich vollziehen* and, as we shall later see, the sacraments are expressed as *Selbstvollzüge* of the Church – an expression which is hardly translatable.

115. *Handbook*, Vol. I, p. 134.

116. Cf., ibid., p. 135. Rahner stands by what he was trying to say in his 'Membership' article. See also this chapter (1.1.3) where this is more fully discussed.

117. Cf., ibid., p. 136.

118. Cf., *Summa Theologiae* I–II, q. 106, art. 1–2.

119. Cf., *Handbook*, Vol. I, p. 137.

120. Cf., ibid., p. 139, especially n. 18. The Church will not be substituted by another organ.
121. Ibid., p. 141.
122. *Handbook*, Vol. I, p. 145, n. 22: 'The essential difference between the Roman Catholic and Lutheran understanding of ministry is dependent on the question whether or not one can see the divine origin of the Church and, within it, that of the ministry.' I will examine this claim later.
123. *Handbook*, Vol. I, p. 147.

Chapter 2 Comments and Questions: Communion of the Faithful

1. See the brief summary of the 'History of Ecclesiology' in *SM* I, pp. 313–16, with literature.
2. Cf., H. Schuster, 'Karl Rahners Ansatz einer existentialen Ekklesiologie' in E. Klinger (ed.) *Wagnis Theologie, Erfahrungen mit der Theologie Rahners*, Freiburg-im-Breisgau (1979), pp. 370–86. Especially, p. 371.
3. Cf., Tanner, p. 808: 'Now reason, if it is enlightened by faith, does indeed when it seeks persistently, piously and soberly, achieve God's gift of some understanding, and most profitably, of the mysteries, whether by analogy from what it knows naturally, or from connection of these mysteries with one another and with the final end of humanity; but reason is never rendered capable of penetrating these mysteries in the way in which it penetrates those truths which form its proper object.'
4. Cf., M. Kehl, *Die Kirche. Eine katholische Ekklesiologie*, Würzburg (1993) p. 186. In his own ecclesiology, Kehl qualifies Rahner's concept, the people of God as 'a concept in transcendental theology which has not much to do with the biblical one.'
5. See the thorough examination of this method in E. Faruggia, *Aussage und Zusage. Zur Indirektheit der Methode Karl Rahners, veranschaulicht in seiner Christologie*, Rome (1985). Besides examining Rahner's Christology, Faruggia has some useful references to ecclesiology.
6. *Handbook*, Vol. I, p. 141. We should remember one of the properties or functions of the Church in Rahner's 'doctrinal ecclesiology' where he says, ' . . . she is in becoming: she becomes, because she

is and she can only be insofar as she becomes'. And, 'the Church in her very essence is historical'. See earlier, 1.3.3.

7. Concerning people leaving the Church, see Introduction, n. 9. And see also 1.1.1, where the Word of God and the word of the Church is discussed.

8. See 1.2.1.

9. See 1.2.2.

10. Ibid.

11. See Vass, Vol. 3, pp. 131ff.

12. Cf., M. Buber, *I and Thou*, Edinburgh (1958), especially Part Two and pp. 39ff. See also Ebner, *Das Wort und die geistigen Realitäten*, Munich (1980), especially fragment 10. For an analysis of the latter work, see B. Casper, *Das dialogische Denken*, Freiburg-im-Breisgau (1967), pp. 198–269.

13. See Vass, Vol. 1, pp. 84–7, for discussion of Rahner's concept of freedom; and, in Vol. 2, pp. 51–3 and Vol. 4, pp. 72–4 mainly for the notion of person. The main difference is that, whereas Rahner concentrates on freedom as consent to necessity, as against freedom of choice, I start and retain this latter as essential to freedom. In a similar way, I tie the emergence of 'person' to encounter and to what results from it. With Rahner, in many of his writings, 'person' is the highest quality of man's spirit – which I deny.

14. The unity of the three constituents of freedom is realized only in man who, alone, becomes and is a responsible person. This does not exclude speaking by means of analogy about freedom in non-human nature.

15. Cf., Kehl (1993), op. cit., p. 186. Here, Kehl uses Hegel in his description of an individual's relationship to institutions.

16. I shall leave this to Chapter 3. There, the Trinitarian, and especially the pneumatological background of the Church, will have to be emphasized. In anticipation, see Kehl (1993), op. cit., pp. 63–79. See also Jürgen Moltmann, *The Church in the Power of the Spirit: A Contribution to Messianic Ecclesiology*, London (1977), especially pp. 50–65, the English translation of *Kirche in der Kraft des Geistes*, Munich (1975). And a most inspiring book by the Orthodox bishop, J. D. Zizioulas, *Being as Communion: Studies in Personhood and the Church*, London and Crestwood, N.Y (1985). This latter, built on the author's remarkable patristic erudition, is concerned with the themes of personhood and the Church as communion.

17. See 1.1.3. See also 'Membership', p. 84 (= p. 90).
18. For this aspect, see Y. Congar, 'Ecclesia ab Abel' in M. Reding, *Abhandlungen über Theologie und Kirche*, Dusseldorf (1952), pp. 78–108.
19. J. Dullaart, *Kirche und Ekklesiologie*, Munich (1974), especially pp. 146–65. Also, M. Kehl, *Kirche und Institution. Zur theologischen Begründung des institutionellen Charakters der Kirch in der neueren deutschsprachigen katholischen Ekkesiologie*, Frankfurt (1976), especially pp. 171–238.
20. The two studies are by no means identical. Dullaart, it seems to me, remains in the same perspective of Rahner's *Hearers*, where he discovers the roots of Rahner's ecclesiology (p. 149). Kehl (1976) on the other hand, presents (pp. 190 and 220) Rahner's transcendental Church as disclosed not from the solitary reflection of the human subject, but rather from man's sociological dimensions. It is here that Kehl finds the underlying transcendental categorial scheme insufficient to harmonize Rahner's description of the Church. For Kehl, the Church is primarily a concrete historical subject, a reality outside ourselves which can only be experienced as an objective fact (p. 189). According to Dullaart, Rahner is 'hostile' to any institutionalisation (*Vergesellschaftung*) of the Church – in fact, Rahner seems to convert the apologetics of Vatican I, which argued from the visible structures of the Church to her credibility, in that he tends to justify the shortcomings of the visible Church by this transcendental prelude.
21. Thus in his concept of revelation. See Vass, Vol. 1, Chapter 6. And see also, the thesis of F. Senn, *Orthopraktische Ekklesiologie K. Rahners. Offenbarungsverständnis und seine ekklesiologische Konsequenzen*, Freiburg-im-Breisgau (1989). The 819 pages of this monumental thesis should be seen in company with the criticism of Neufeld published in 1990: cf., K. H. Neufeld, *Zeitschrift für katholische Theologie* 112, pp. 355f. As for the supernatural existential, see Vass, Vol. 2, Chapter 3. And for Rahner's theory of the symbol, see Vol. 3, section 4.3 in the context of Christology. For this latter investigation, too, consult A. Callahan, 'Karl Rahner's Thought of the Symbol: Basis for his Theology of the Church', *Irish Theology Quarterly*, 49 (1982), pp. 195–205.
22. Cf., Kehl (1976), op. cit., pp. 192f. A translation of his view amounts to: 'Rahner's attention goes to the general and ontological structure of salvation ... His thinking is always preoccupied [*gilt*]

with the ontological mediation of the unique and historical [i.e.] with its universal validity.'

23. *Handbook*, Vol. I, pp. 134f.

24. For discussion of the anonymous Christian, see Vass, Vol. 4, Chapters 3 and 4.

25. See Introduction.

26. Bonhoeffer. The translation follows the text of the first edition of Bonhoeffer's dissertation, submitted 1927. The dissertation itself was revised by Bonhoeffer and later corrected by advisers and colleagues; this material, along with publisher's notes, made up almost two-thirds of the volume which was eventually published as the 1930 edition.

27. Cf., ibid., especially Johann Gottlieb Fichte, Wilhelm F. Hegel, and their theological counterpart Friedrich Daniel Schleiermacher.

28. Max Scheler, *Formalism in Ethics and Non-formal Ethics of Values: A New Attempt toward the Foundation of an Ethical Personalism*, 5th Edition, Evanston, IL (1973). Max Weber, *Gesammelte Aufsätze zur Religionssoziologie*, three volumes, Tubingen (1920). An English translation of Vols 2 and 3 was published as *Essays in Sociology*, Oxford (1958). And see also Ernst Troeltsch, *The Social Teaching of the Christian Churches*, Louisville, KY and Westminster (1992).

29. Cf., Bonhoeffer, chapter 2, especially pp. 34–57 'The Christian Concept of Person and Concepts of Social-Basic-Relation'. Here, Bonhoeffer first of all distances himself from philosophical notions of individuum/person beginning with the Greeks and, especially, from German Idealism. Bonhoeffer's main objection is that the latter 'subsumes the person under the universal' – that is, man's immanent spirit, and: ' . . . it does not distinguish at all between a subject-object-relation and the I-Thou-relation; rather, the latter is subsumed under the former' (pp. 41f). This is, according to Bonhoeffer, unable to lead to the concept of society (p. 43). Although Rahner attempts to reach this notion of the person, he very often falls back to the ideas of German Idealism, by regarding the person as the highest peak of the human spirit.

30. Ibid.: 'The You sets the limit for the subject and by its own accord activates a will that impinges upon the other in such a way that this other will become the You for the I' (p. 51); ' . . . there would be no self-consciousness without community – or better, that self-consciousness arises concurrently with the consciousness of existing in

community' (p. 70); 'Thus the will, too, as actively arising from self-consciousness, is possible only in sociality . . . It is the nature of the will as activity to function in community' (p. 72); ' . . . human spirit in its entirety is woven into sociality on the basis of I and You . . . this is the essence of spirit to be oneself through being in the other' and 'here is where the openness of personal being becomes evident' (p. 73).

31. Ibid.: 'The person arises only in relation to a You, and yet, the person stands in complete isolation. Persons are unique and thus fundamentally separate and distinct from one another. In other words, one person cannot know the other, but can only acknowledge and 'believe' in the other' (p. 54); 'Thus the 'openness' of the person demands 'closedness' as a correlative, or one could not speak of openness at all' (p. 74); 'We must acknowledge that besides those acts that are only real through sociality, there are also purely inwardly directed acts' (p. 75). This leads Bonhoeffer to the reinterpretation of the 'collective person' (*Objektiver Geist* of the Idealists) see pp.77f; hence ' . . . one must articulate the similarity of structure of the collective person and the individual person in the eyes of the universal person of God (*Allperson Gottes*)' with a certain centre of activity, part of which are the divine persons (p. 79).

32. Ibid.', p. 78.

33. Ibid., p. 80.

34. See earlier, 1.1.3.

35. F. Tönnies, *Gemeinschaft und Gesellschaft: Grundbegriffe der reinen Soziologie*, Leipzig (1919). The English translation, *Community and Society*, was published in New York, NY (1963) and later reprinted (1988). In Chapter 3, I shall return to this, in my view, important book. Though it is not up-to-date in modern sociology, the ideas of Tönnies are, beyond doubt, useful for the understanding of the Church. Bonhoeffer, though with restrictions, lets himself be inspired by Tönnies: see Bonhoeffer, p. 87, n. 21 and [91]. In what follows I sum up Tönnies according to Bonhoeffer's presentation.

36. A family in itself, or a nation, cannot be qualified as a communion. Family, in itself, and nation, to a certain extent, are societal units (*Gesellschaft*) which presuppose the free will of humans for belonging together. That such a unit may become a communion (*Gemeinschaft*) is independent of human will: it 'occurs', it 'happens'.

37. Bonhoeffer, pp. 86–95.
38. The Church as a *societas perfecta* is nowadays hardly ever used.
39. Bonhoeffer, p. 101: 'If we describe the temporal intention of a communion (*Gemeinschaft*) as reaching the boundary of time (*grenzzeitlich*), that of a society (*Gesellschaft*) would be timebound (*zeitbegrenzt*) . . . ' In other words, for Bonhoeffer, communion is of an eschatological character.
40. Ibid., pp. 109ff.
41. Rikhof, op. cit.
42. Ibid., p. 204; and refer also to pp. 163ff.
43. See earlier, in Chapter 1.
44. I believe that, in a small Eucharistic community the universal Church is realized. The way, however, this small group experiences her communion has little or nothing to do with the universal Church. The first sentence is an interpretation of faith; the second is an immediate experience.
45. Rikhof, op. cit., pp. 230f.
46. Ibid., pp. 233ff.
47. Cf., Schuster, op. cit., pp. 372–3 for a short summary of Rahner's *termini* concerning the Church. See also Kehl (1976), op. cit., p. 220. Kehl's complaint is about the overemphasis of Rahner's transcendental approach

Chapter 3 **The Two-Faceted Church**

1. Rahner's *Löscht den Geist nicht aus* was first published in 1962 in *Münchener katholishe Kirchenzeitung* and later corrected and reformulated up to its publication as 'Do not stifle the Spirit!' in *TI* 7, pp. 72f (= *ST* VII, pp. 77f). Its main message in substance was published by *Die Furche* in Vienna that same year, as *Auch heute: Der Geist weht, wo er will*. It would be interesting to study the variants of these three publications.
2. Rahner's answer to their misgivings, 'Christ, yes; the Church, no.' For even in a loose, charismatic fellowship it ' . . . won't be very long before you have an institutional Church, that is an organized Church with legal structures.' Cf., 'Egan', p. 147 (= *Glaube* p. 180).

3. 'Der Einzelne in der Kirche', *Stimmen der Zeit* 139 (1946/47), pp. 260–76. See the English translation, 'The Individual in the Church' in *Nature and Grace*, London (1963), pp. 51–83. See also, *Gefahren im heutigen Katholizismus*, Einsideln (1950), pp. 11–38.

4. In *Stimmen der Zeit* 139, op. cit., p. 264 (= *Nature and Grace*, pp. 58ff). Although Rahner does not refer to the possible source of this distinction, it will accompany him up to his later doctrinal ecclesiology in *Handbook*. I shall use it in the same sense as Zizioulas, op. cit., especially pp. 27–65. Zizioulas speaks of man as an 'ecclesial' and as a 'biological hypostasis'.

5. Ibid., pp. 264ff (= *Nature and Grace*, pp. 59ff): 'The Church is the community of the redeemed bound together in the Spirit in Christ Jesus, and at the same time a visible organized [*rechtlich organisierte*] society with rules and founder's charter.' [My translation.]

6. It is later that Rahner reassumes this same topic. Cf., 'Principles and Prescriptions' in *Dynamic*, especially pp. 13–41. When Rahner says 'The Church does not administer all reality. Everything indeed belongs to the kingdom of God, but not to the Church that prepares the way for the kingdom,' (p. 27) he most likely refers to the institutional Church, which has only an 'indirect power' in matters of morality, whereas she leaves 'open in principle a domain within which several decisions are possible' (p. 26). These decisions are a matter of the individual's imperatives. Note the Kantian origin of the word which the translator happily renders as 'principle'. First published as 'Prinzipien und Imperative' in *Das Dynamische in Der Kirche*, Freiburg-im-Breisgau (1958), pp. 14–37.

7. Cf., 'Freedom and Manipulation in Society and the Church', in *Meditations*, pp. 33–71.

8. Ibid., p. 63 (= p. 95).

9. Ibid., p. 65 (= p. 97). Rahner seems to extend this 'sinful' manipulation even to the formal authority of the Magisterium. Its necessary acknowledgement does not happen 'by means of a pure, monotonous and repeated assertion . . . that there is such a formal authority,' but rather on the authority of the Church's witness: 'This must happen to such an extent that the formal teaching authority . . . appears as a secondary aspect of the whole of the Christian faith and as a part which does not itself sustain, but instead is sustained.'

10. Ibid., p. 60 (= p. 93): 'The history of the Church ought indeed to be

a history of freedom even in the social sphere of the Church, since the Church, as the universal sacrament of religious freedom, is radically committed to safeguard the social space of freedom itself, and if possible to extend it.' Rahner obviously refers to the Church as institution.

11. See *Lexikon für Theologie und Kirche* 5, pp. 714 where Rahner comments on *institutionalismus*. For him, however, an institution in the service of salvation (*dienende Mächte für das Heil des Menschen*) is no longer to be regarded as an institution in an everyday sense.

12. See 'Institution and Freedom' in *TI* 13, p. 107 (= *ST* X, p. 117).

13. Cf., ibid.

14. Cf., ibid., p. 110 (= p. 129). In this essay, Rahner's quarrel is with a kind of social anthropology which takes for granted the dilemma of N. Hartmann and J. P. Sartre: if there is freedom, then there is no God. Conversely, if there is God man is not free (*postulatorischer Atheismus*). Cf., Rahner's comments in the introduction, p. 105 (= p. 115).

15. Cf., ibid., p. 112 (= p. 122).

16. Ibid., p. 115 (= p. 126).

17. Ibid., p. 118 (= p. 29): 'Man . . . when he recognises, and accepts in a spirit of hope, a dimension of freedom which transcends this ambivalence inherent in the forms of freedom in which freedom is objectified.'

18. Ibid., p. 119 (= p. 131).

19. *The Shape of the Church to Come*, London (1974). This is the English translation of *Strukturwandel der Kirche als Aufgabe und Chance*, Freiburg-im-Breisgau (1972).

20. 'Structural Change in the Church of the Future' in *TI* 20, pp. 115ff (= *ST* XIV pp. 333ff). First published in 1977.

21. Without straying into the field of sociology, one should uphold a delicate distinction between these two terms. 'Institution' seems to be more apparent than 'social structures'. The first represents a pattern of value orientations, or interests, arising out of the intercommunication of the members of a society, whereas the second represents distinctive arrangements variably created and maintained among groups of a larger society which regulate the relationships of persons involved. Cf., J. Gould and W. Kolb (eds) *A Dictionary of Social Sciences*, London (1964), pp. 338f and pp. 668f. And compare T. Parsons, *The Social System*, Glencoe (1951)

with A. Gehlen, *Urmensch und Spätkultur*, 2nd Edition, Frankfurt-Bonn (1964).

22. 'Theological Justification of the Church's Development Work' in *TI* 20, pp. 65ff (= *ST* XIV, pp. 273ff). Published in 1976, this essay was originally a paper read before Misereor, the episcopal commission for the aid of developing countries.

23. Cf., 'Church's Responsibility', pp. 51ff (= pp. 248ff).

24. 'Toleration in the Church' in *Meditations*, pp. 75–115.

25. 'Church's Responsibility', p. 62 (= pp. 262f).

26. Consult, for example, M. J. Congar, 'Die Lehre der Kirche. Vom Abendländischen Schisma bis zur Gegenwart' in *Handbuch der Dogmengeschichte*, III Fasc 3d, Freiburg-im-Breisgau (1971), especially pp. 48ff.

27. To be a 'fruit of salvation' is not to be confounded by the ultimate end of human being. It is rather a category which *results* from the process of salvation anticipating the ultimate end. See 'Charismatic', pp. 81ff (= pp. 414ff).

28. See Rahner's contribution in *Lexikon für Theologie und Kirche* 2 (1958), pp. 1027–30. And see also, with no scriptural analysis, K. Rahner and H. Vorgrimler, *Dictionary of Theology*, New York, NY (1981), p. 64. Cf., the original German edition, *Kleines Theologisches Wörterbuch*, Freiburg-im-Breisgau (1961). Consult the ten-volume *Theologisches Wörterbuch zum Neuen Testament*, Stuttgart (1933), especially Vol. IX, pp. 393–7. A recommended reading is B. N. Wambacq, 'Le mot charisme' in *Nouvelle Revue Theologique*, Louvain (1975), pp. 345–50.

29. 'Charismatic', p. 85 (= p. 419): 'In the ecclesiology of former times [the official institutions] were concentrated upon almost to the exclusion of all else, and were at most regarded as also being the channels through which the charismata were mediated. Today on the other hand, the charismatic factor is felt in some sense to supply the institutional one with the motive force necessary for it.'

30. Cf., *Dynamic*. See Chapter 4.

31. Consult 'On the Question of a Formal Existential Ethics', in *TI* 2, pp. 217ff (= *ST* II, pp. 227ff).

32. Cf., Vass, Vol. 4, section 3.2.2.

33. *Dynamic*, p. 45 (= p. 49).

34. Ibid., p. 49 (= p. 44).

35. *Mystici Corporis Christi*, London (1938), pp. 13f and pp. 23f. See also *AAS*, pp. 200f.

36. *Dynamic*, p. 53 (= p. 47) and also pp. 54f (= pp. 48f) for Rahner's short scriptural argumentation, which is based on the doctrine of grace.

37. I do not believe that Rahner envisages here the complex notion of 'structures' in sociology. Cf., P. M. Blau (ed.), *Approaches to the Study of Social Structure*, London (1975).

38. *Dynamic*, p. 60 (= p. 53). Rahner takes here – among others – the example of the priestly ministry to which the obviously charismatic gift of celibacy is coupled by law. The official Church has the right to organize the charismatic element, because she is even in that respect charismatic.

39. Ibid., pp. 63f (= pp. 56f).

40. Ibid., pp. 82f (= p. 73). [My italics.]

41. See *Handbook*, especially '*Amt und freies Charisma*' in Vol. I, part 2, para 3, pp. 154–160.

42. Ibid., p. 155 and p. 159.

43. Ibid., pp. 159f. In a difficult sentence, Rahner speaks of the self-accomplishment of the Church in its entirety. This occurs in her faith, love and charity which is hardly under the control of the ministry.

44. Cf., 'Charismatic'.

45. It is not likely that Rahner knew, or studied, the more recent forms of sociological 'System-Theory'.

46. 'Charismatic', p. 89 (= p. 423).

47. Ibid., p. 97 (= p. 431). The 'most ultimate' in the original German is *das Eigentümlichste unter dem formalen Wesenszügen der Kirche*.

48. Ibid., p. 89 (= p. 423). [My italics.]

49. Ibid., p. 94 (= p. 428). By distinguishing between a closed and an open system and by trying to fit the relationship of the institutional to his own pattern of thought, Rahner arrives at a systematic viewpoint on the two-faceted Church.

50. Rahner's main argument, as we shall see in another context, is the principle of collegiality. He assumes, however, that collegiality is extended beyond the College of Bishops to the whole and (I guess) to her anonymous members. Cf., 'Charismatic', p. 93 (= pp. 425f). Thus, for example, for an infallible definition, pp. 90–3 (= pp. 424–7), the Pope is responsible not to God alone but to the whole of the Church; as history teaches, the important initiatives in the Church were not centrally geared. In short, in the Church there is

an in-built plurality at each and every level.

51. See Rahner's remarks in comparing revelation in Islamic and Christian contexts. Cf., 'Consecration in the Church', pp. 57ff (= pp. 113ff).

52. Cf., 'Structure', pp. 218ff (= pp. 519ff). The Church is an 'institutionalised group of individuals who bring into this institution something different from, and more than merely that which is recognised as belonging to the Church . . . ' and the Church's 'historical reality . . . is not simply identical with her nature.' In this essay, first published in 1970, Rahner distinguishes between the people of God, as a more generic term, and the people of the Church – which he identifies with the laity within her fold.

53. Ibid., p. 221 (= p. 561).

54. Cf., 'Consecration in the Church', p. 67 (= pp. 124f). Rahner here presupposes an intrinsic 'consecratedness' in every individual who is called to the Church. The sacraments of consecration (including not only ordination but also baptism) are 'the historical manifestation and the sociologically concretizing specification in the dimension of the visible Church of a holiness and consecratedness which always existed inescapably in that person in the form of an offer in virtue of God's salvific will.' That is, in virtue of the all-embracing supernatural existential.

55. Cf., among others, *Dynamic*, p. 71 (= p. 75).

56. *Foundations*, p. 325 (= p. 316).

57. Ibid., p. 332 (= p. 323).

58. Ibid., p. 333 (= p. 323).

59. Ibid., p. 335 (= p. 325).

60. Ibid., p. 334 (= p. 324).

61. Ibid., p. 341 (= p. 331).

62. Namely, Vögtle and Schnackenburg, especially in Rahner's 'The Church in the New Testament', briefly summarized in *Lexikon für Theologie und Kirche* 6, pp. 167–72.

63. *Foundations*, p. 342 (= p. 332).

64. Cf., 'Jus divinum', pp. 219ff (= pp. 249ff).

65. See Vatican I, 'concerning the primacy of the Pope' in Tanner, pp. 812ff; and Trent, 'concerning the doctrine on the sacraments' in Tanner, pp. 684ff, pp. 704ff, and p. 717. See also 'Canon 6, on divine law concerning the hierarchical order of the Church' in Tanner, pp. 742ff.

66. Cf., 'Jus divinum', p. 222 (= p. 252). For this, Rahner argues with

reference to his metaphysics of knowing: a notion can only be known via conversion *ad phantasmta*. That is, by an experienced 'image' in which a divine law is realized. One always starts with the 'historical'.

67. Ibid., pp. 222f (= p. 253), where Rahner speaks of a *Wesensidentität in Gestaltwandel*.

68. Ibid., p. 226 (= p. 257).

69. Cf. ibid., p. 230 (= p. 262). We should remember that for Rahner freedom is the 'the capacity for the eternal'.

70. Cf., Vass, Vol. 2, chapter 5. There it was pointed out that the dividing line for the ending of revelation is 'fluid'. Even in 'Jus divinum', p. 242 (= p. 274), Rahner is rather coy in drawing the line at which *fides ecclesiastica* – that is, teaching which relies on the infallible authority of the Church takes over from divine revelation – and he does not exclude the possibility of a post-apostolic revelation.

71. 'Jus divinum', p. 235 (= p. 267).

72. Ibid., p. 237 (= p. 270). Here, 'multivalent': insofar most of the time various possibilities or alternatives were available for the decision of the primitive Church.

73. Cf., ibid., p. 241 (= p. 275). Though Rahner emphasizes the possibility of a collegial government in the individual congregation which would equally had been chosen by the primitive Church.

74. Ibid., p. 243 (= pp. 276f).

75. Cf., 'Changeable', pp. 3ff (= pp. 241ff).

76. Ibid., p. 23 (= p. 261).

77. Cf. 'Structure', pp. 218ff (= pp. 558ff).

78. Ibid., pp. 221f (= p. 562).

79. Ibid., p. 226 (= p. 566). See also 'Opposition in the Church' in *TI* 17, pp. 127ff (= *ST* XII, pp. 469ff) where Rahner says: ' . . . the person who takes the absolute character of his believing commitment to God in Jesus Christ with radical seriousness will not view a withdrawal of this commitment as being for him a real, inner possibility. Insofar as he then makes this "Yes" to the Church part of his absolute commitment, he can and will quite unequivocally understand opposition to and criticism of it only within the context of the Church itself.'

80. 'Lay Apostolate', pp. 319ff (= pp. 339ff).

81. Note that the same approach was taken over by the New Code of Common Law. Cf., *CIC*, pp. 204–6.

82. Cf., 'Lay Apostolate', pp. 323f (= p. 344).
83. Cf., 'Consecration of the Layman', pp. 263ff (= pp. 313ff).
84. Ibid. In this essay, however, Rahner's interest is not so much in the structures emerging from these commissions within the visible Church, but rather in the anthropological possibility of one person's care for another's free and responsible decision. This responsibility, being exclusively personal, cannot be interfered with. The only way of standing by the other person is through the love of God, which can develop into a communion of persons based on mutual love. Thus, the 'care of souls' does not happen by announcing general principles, but can only be mediated through the love of God to which each person is called.
85. Cf., ibid., p. 57 (= p. 113). Rahner speaks of a grace which 'must be understood as an intrinsic existential of the history of humanity' present always and everywhere as in the form of an offer.
86. Ibid., p. 67 (= p. 124). This line of thought will shape Rahner's approach to the sacraments of the Church, to which I shall return.
87. Cf., ibid., p. 68 (= p. 125).
88. Cf., 'Pastoral Ministries', especially, pp. 79f (= p. 139). Vatican II, in addition to Trent's concept, emphasized community leadership as a function of ministerial priesthood: 'If someone as pastoral assistant is in fact appointed community leader, he is granted in this capacity the basic nature of the priest and at the same time refused sacramental powers that flow from this basic nature. Is this theologically consistent?'
89. Cf., 'Consecration in the Church', p. 71 (= pp. 129f). The meaning of 'Protestantization' is obscure.
90. Ibid., p. 69 (= p. 127).
91. 'Pastoral Ministries', p. 75 (= pp. 133f).
92. 'The Position of Woman', pp. 75ff (= *ST* VII, pp. 351).
93. Cf., ibid., pp. 88ff (= pp. 362ff).
94. Ibid., p. 82 (= pp. 357).
95. See 'Women and the Priesthood' in *TI* 20, pp. 35ff (= *ST* VII, pp. 208ff). Rahner says: 'It does not seem to be proved that the actual behaviour of Jesus and the Apostles implies a norm of divine revelation in the strict sense of the term. . . . This practice . . . can certainly be understood as "human" tradition . . . which was once unquestioned, had existed for a long time and nevertheless became obsolete as a result of sociological change.' Note that Rahner also argues against Pope Paul VI's decree by referring to the 'extended'

task of community leaders.
96. *Handbook*, Vol. II/I, p. 231. [My translation.]
97. Ibid., p. 262.
98. 'Position of Woman', p. 81 (= p. 356).
99. *ST* XVI, p. 196, 'Südamerikanische Basisgemeinden in einer europäischen Kirche?' There is no English translation.
100. *ST* XVI, pp. 160ff; here p. 162, *Über die Zukunft der Gemeinden*. [My translation.]
101. Cf., 'Hierarchy', pp. 65–81.
102. Cf., ibid., p. 66.
103. Ibid., p. 70: 'Hierarchical ministry of the Church is within the earthly and social dimension of the community. They are the authoritative guards of the uniform witness of the Church for the world.' [My translation.]
104. Ibid., p. 75: 'The hierarchical structure of the meaning and purpose of a society and the hierarchical structure of a societal organisation of the same are different.'
105. Cf., 'On The Trinity' translated from *Mysterium Salutis*, II. As presented and analysed in Vass, Vol. 3, pp. 17–37.
106. Cf., 'Hierarchy', pp. 73ff.
107. Cf., Ibid., p. 79.
108. *Handbook*, Vol. II/1, pp. 56f. This basic distinction will have some importance in Rahner's sacramental theology.
109. Though they are not the only such references, the following lectures were published roughly about the same time: 'Priesthood' (1968/69); 'Priestly Image' (1968/69); 'Priestly Ministry' (1969). Also 'Diaconate', a paper read in 1968.
110. Cf., 'Priestly Existence', pp. 239ff (= pp. 285ff). This essay was published in 1942.
111. 'Priestly Image', pp. 40f (= p. 375).
112. 'Priestly Existence', p. 247 (= pp. 294f).
113. Ibid., pp. 244f (= p. 290).
114. Ibid.: ' . . . the sign which makes present [in historical visibility] for us what exists in itself.' This experience, however, which in his 'Priestly Existence' is strictly supernatural ('Not immediately accessible to the grasp of human experience in its inner self,') will soon become in Rahner's further reflection the experience of grace due to the *supernatural existential*. See Vass, Vol. 2, pp. 59ff.
115. Rahner's argumentation here relies on *Hearers* – with which I shall not complicate my presentation.

258 A Pattern of Doctrines – Part III: A Man of the Church

116. 'Priestly Existence', p. 250 (= p. 298).
117. Ibid., p. 248 (= pp. 295f).
118. 'Priesthood', p. 33 (= p. 368).
119. As we shall see, the whole doctrine of Trent about the Eucharist and the Mass concentrates on the idea of sacrifice; cf., Tanner, pp. 732f, especially p. 34 and the corresponding Canon 2, p. 734, and the sacrament of order Canon 1, p. 743.
120. Cf., 'Priestly Existence', p. 249 (= p. 297). [My italics.]
121. Ibid. [My italics.]
122. Cf., ibid., p. 252 (= pp. 300f).
123. Ibid., pp. 253ff (= pp. 302ff). For discussion on Trent, see Tanner, p. 744.
124. 'Priestly Existence', pp. 254ff (pp. 302f).
125. In his later writings Rahner does not deal much with the same topic, yet he will briefly face it again in 1969 in discussing the pros and cons of his suggested 'priesthood for time'. I shall have to refer to the same topic in dealing with the sacraments.
126. It seems that in 1942 in searching for an *existential* meaning we can hear an echo of Rahner's own *Hearers*: the truth about the powers conferred by ordination is measured by a 'degree of inwardness', of being present to oneself (*Beisichsein*) 'therefore existentiality is required in grasping the true meaning of this double power resulting from the sacrament.' Cf., 'Priestly Existence', p. 259 (= p. 308).
127. 'Priestly Existence', p. 254 (= p. 302).
128. Ibid., p. 257 (= p. 306). Rahner maintains this approach also in his later writings. In his essay 'Diaconate', p. 62 (= p. 396), he writes: 'It is clear that which constitutes the essence of the [priestly] office does not consist in any immediately apprehensible sense in sacramental powers of specifically sacerdotal kind, or . . . in any special powers exercised in the community's celebration of the Eucharist.'
129. Ibid., p. 260 (= p.309).
130. Later, when Rahner assumes the difference between the *Volkskirche* and the confessing Church, he will admit that in future there will be a remnant of 'nominal' Christians, less committed to the word, yet asking for some cultic services from her ministers (for example, baptism, wedding, burial). He asserts: 'People still come to the Church even when we badly preach,' but on the next page he adds: 'the success of our work will depend on the vitality of our own personal religious lives . . . upon the question whether [the priest] is

really a man who lives from the heart and centre of his own personal existence . . . '. In 'Priestly Image', pp. 56f (pp. 391f).

131. 'Priestly Existence', p. 261 (= p. 311).
132. 'Priesthood', p. 36 (= pp. 370f).
133. 'Priestly Ministry' p. 208 (= p. 454). [My italics.]
134. 'Diaconate', p. 64 (= p. 399). See also *Handbook* I, pp. 160ff and, again: ' . . . variations within the single official ministry, in accordance with the needs of a particular age . . . of cultural milieu, etc., without prejudice to the sacramentality of the process by which offices are conferred.' Cf., 'Priestly Ministry', p. 209 (p. 456) and also 'Priesthood', p. 35 (= p. 356).
135. Although tradition prefers to speak of cultic function (Eucharist, penance, etc.). See 'Priesthood', p. 35 (= pp. 369f): 'But this does not invalidate the point that the Church is free to choose between a wide range of possibilities, or that she can exercise her own free judgement as to how best to divide up this *single* office between various functionaries according to the requirements of the situation at any given time . . . as determined by the very nature of the Church.' See also 'Priestly Image', p. 44 (= p. 378): 'We should take as our starting point a concept of the Church . . . and achieve an understanding of what is special in the function which the presbyters in the Church take upon themselves in the light of the nature of the Church.'
136. 'Priestly Image', p. 59 (=p. 393).
137. Ibid., p. 57 (= p. 391).
138. Ibid., 'Priestly Ministry', p. 216 (= p. 463).
139. For discussion of Vatican II's *Lumen Gentium* 29 on the Church, cf., Tanner, p. 874; for *Lumen Gentium* 16 on the Missions, p. 1026; and for *Lumen Gentium* 16 on the Eastern Churches, p. 905.
140. See the supplement to *Lexikon für Theologie und Kirche* 1, pp. 256ff, concerning the decree on the diaconate by Rahner's pupil, H. Vorgrimler. See also, P. Winniger, *Le diacre dans l'Èglise et le monde d'aujourd'hui*, Y. Congar (ed.), Paris (1966) in which Rahner's article, 'Teaching of the Second Vatican Council on the Diaconate', was published. It was later reprinted in *TI* 10, pp. 222ff (= *ST* VIII, pp. 541ff).
141. Ibid., p. 232 (= pp. 551f).
142. Cf., 'Diaconate', p. 66 (= p. 400). And p. 72 (= p. 406): 'In the present situation of the Church . . . [many] functions should be left to laymen, and should be regarded as functions which are not so

important in themselves that they need to constitute a specific office in the Church today.'

143. Ibid., p. 67 (= p. 401).

144. Ibid., pp. 69f (= p. 403): ' . . . this subdivision can and must be conditioned by the concrete situation in which the Church fulfils her task through her official ministry.' That is to say, this concrete situation is an essential element in Rahner's line of argument.

145. Cf., ibid., pp. 298f (= *ST* V, p. 337).

146. Ibid., p. 75 (= p. 409).

147. Cf., 'Practical Theology and Social Work in the Church' in *TI* 10, pp. 349ff (= *ST* VIII, pp. 667ff).

148. Thus, Rahner's early articles on primacy and the episcopate, *Primat und Episkopat, Einige überlegungen über die Verfassungsprinzipien der Kirche*, were published in *Stimmen der Zeit* 161 (1956/57), pp. 321ff. They were to be overtaken by the fourth volume of *Quaestiones Disputatae*, published in Freiburg-im-Breisgau (1961) as *Episkopat und Primat* in collaboration with Rahner's, then, friend and colleague Josef Ratzinger and later on published in its first part as *The Episcopate and the Primacy* London (1962). Cf., 'Episcopate'.

149. Thus, for example, Rahner in *Commentary*, pp. 216–46.

150. Not all of Rahner's references can be listed here, but for a representative selection see: 'Office'; 'Past and Present Forms'; 'Episcopacy'; and 'Aspects'.

151. 'Episcopate', p. 16 (= p. 17).

152. Ibid., p. 22 (= p. 23).

153. Ibid., p. 25 (= p. 26).

154. Ibid., p. 27 (= p. 28).

155. Ibid., p. 36 (= p. 35). Rahner adds: 'Part of her self is the Spirit [*zu ihr selbst gehört der Geist*] who alone can guarantee the unity of the Church.'

156. Although, as Rahner admits in a footnote, the Church can distribute this power 'by the will of her Founder, in that measure which she finds appropriate at any given time.' See 'Episcopate', pp. 69f (= p. 65), n. 4.

157. Cf., 'Episcopate', p. 69f (= pp. 64f).

158. Ibid., p. 73 (= p. 69).

159. Cf., ibid., p. 74 (= p. 67). To which he adds: ' . . . the episcopate is obviously subject of these divine rights only insofar as it is unified in the bishop of Rome . . . '. This will be of significance concern-

ing the relationship of the papacy and the episcopate.

160. I shall return to this argument in the next section.

161. For discussion on *Lumen Gentium* 3, art. 18–28, see Tanner, pp. 862–74.

162. A doctrine already introduced in *Lumen Gentium* 10: 'The ministerial priest, through the sacred power [*potestate sacra*] that he enjoys forms and governs the priestly people . . .'

163. *Commentary*, p. 193.

164. Ibid., p. 187.

165. Ibid., p. 194. See also 'Episcopacy', p. 363 (= p. 425): ' . . . but the fact that the Council finds a sacramental and therefore pneumatic basis for the transmission of every office is of incalculable significance for juridical *praxis* in the Church . . . [as well as] . . . the very fact that the law is rooted in the Pneuma makes it unmistakably clear that in the Church the law is no worldly law but a law which is holy and sustained by the Spirit . . . and it is put into effect and applied in accordance with the will of Christ [and] is inspired and sustained by this Spirit, of the will to serve, of fraternity, of respect for every person and his conscience, of self-criticism, etc.'

166. Cf., *Commentary*, p. 300. To speak of the episcopate on the sacramental level, as the much debated 'Preliminary explanatory note' argues, refers to the 'ontological participation in the sacred functions' and not in practicable powers (*munus* and not *potestas juridica*). The bishop through his office (*munus*) is entrusted with these functions, it does not mean that his office is ready for action (*actu expedito*). Cf., Tanner, p. 899. And, as J. Ratzinger in his corresponding interpretation remarks, the final text, contrary to the preparatory schema, speaks of a sacramental and not of juridical principle.

167. 'Past and Present Forms' in *TI* 6, p. 377 (= *ST* VI, p. 440). Rahner argues from the apparently parallel case of the Christian obligation of neighbourly love, which has to find its concrete expression beyond being a mere formality: the local ordinary has to express his duty as regards the neighbouring diocese.

168. Ibid.

169. Twenty years on, the new Code of Canon Law has not followed suit: cf., *CIC*, Canon 455 which still seems to require the interference of Rome. The decisions of the conference are restricted to the requirements of universal Church law, they have to be decided by a two-thirds majority and subjected to the supervision of Rome.

The head of the conference has no right to overrule the individual bishops.

170. This article first appeared in *Stimmen der Zeit* 69 (1963/64), pp. 161ff, and was reprinted in 1965 in the sixth volume of *Schriften für Theologie*, p. 369, under the title *Über das Episkopat* with an additional note at its beginning, pp. 369–73 (= pp. 369–75). In it, Rahner defended his views against the criticism of D. T. Strottmann. For the English translation see 'Office'.

171. 'Office', p. 345 (= pp. 405f).

172. Cf., ibid., pp. 322f (= pp. 379f).

173. Cf., ibid., pp. 325–8 (= pp. 383–6).

174. Ibid., pp. 340f (= pp. 400f). The quotation is, in part, my own translation ('at the disposal of . . . ') as the English version of the same is misleading. To this complicated sentence there is a footnote attached in which Rahner tries to explain how far this statement can be underscored by divine right.

175. Ibid., see his practical suggestions concerning: the College of Cardinals (pp. 325ff); Titular Bishops (pp. 328ff); Relative and Absolute Ordination (pp. 330ff); The Nature of the Diocese (pp. 333ff); The Patriarchate (pp. 339ff); The Bishop and his Priests (pp. 340ff), within which also the role of the *presbyterium* is delineated.

176. D. T. Strottmann, 'Primauté et Céphalisation: A propos d'une étude de P. Karl Rahner', *Irénicon* 38 (1964), pp. 187ff. Additional to these latter pages are those attached to the mentioned reprint of 'Office' in *ST* VI.

177. Cf., 'Episcopacy', p. 366 (= p. 429).

178. Cf., 'Synod', p. 129 (= p. 371). See also 'Aspects', p. 194 (= p. 439).

179. Cf., 'The Congregation of the Faith and the Commission of Theologians' in *TI* 14, pp. 98ff (=*ST* X, pp. 338ff).

180. 'Synod', pp. 121f (= p. 365).

181. Ibid., p. 120 (= p. 360). See Rahner's remark on the working paper for the German Synod imposed by Rome. Though Vatican II acknowledged a sort of pluralism it did not determine how it should be reconciled with the authority of the Pope and the unity of the Church. The Vatican's working paper for the German Synod hardly goes 'beyond a vague and uncommitted statement on the kind of pluralism within the Church that is justified', ibid., p. 119 (= p. 361).

182. Cf., ibid., p. 126 (= p. 368).

183. Cf., ibid., pp. 127f (= pp. 369f).

184. Ibid., p. 131 (= p. 373).

185. Cf., J. G. Gerhartz, 'Keine Mitentscheidung von Laien auf der Synode?', in *Stimmen der Zeit* 184 (1969), pp. 145ff.

186. 'Aspects', p. 194 (= p. 430).

187. Ibid., p. 197 (= pp. 442).

188. Ibid., pp. 197f (= p. 442).

189. Cf., ibid. Towards the end of 'Aspects', Rahner peers ahead into the future shape of the Church – in a situation of permanent diaspora, instead of the vanishing *Volkskirche*, a Church of free believers – and concludes: 'The focal point for the Church to discharge its functions, to achieve credibility and to perform its task of preaching the gospel . . . now to be found in the local community at the roots of society, for it is here that its encounter with the special social situation is achieved, here that faith must emerge ever afresh. . . . ' This is aimed at the solidarity with the struggle of the socially marginal groups. Rahner continues, ibid., p. 199 (= p. 449): ' . . . the life of the Church today is primarily lived in a "integrated community".'

190. *The Shape of the Church to Come*, op. cit., p. 52.

191. Ibid., p. 53.

192. 'Episcopate'.

193. *Commentary*, p. 196.

194. Ibid.

195. Cf., the *nota explicativa* in Tanner, p. 899.

196. It was a suggestion later to be realized in the form of the periodical assembly of the world episcopate convoked and headed by the Pope.

197. See the rather laborious essay, 'Pope and Bishops' which was designed for the *Festschrift* in honour of Archbishop (later Cardinal) P. Parente, whose view at the Council was similar to that of Rahner. However, because of the opposition to its thesis, publication was delayed.

198. Ibid., p. 53 (= pp. 378f).

199. Ibid., p. 54 (= p. 378).

200. Ibid., p. 55 (= p. 379).

201. Cf., Tanner, p. 899.

202. 'Pope and Bishops', p. 56 (= p. 380). [My italics.] And, again, p. 63 (= p. 386): 'This one subject must be conceived in such a way that it includes, from the outset and of its own nature, both these

entities. . . . This means: whether we say 'pope' or 'college of bishops' our conceptions of both these entities must be such that each implies the other.'

203. Ibid., p. 58 (= p. 382). [My italics.] And p. 64 (= p. 387).

204. Ibid., p. 65 (= p. 388).

205. Cf., ibid., pp. 65–6 (= pp. 389–90).

206. *Dynamic*, p. 45 (= p. 41). But see also the original German.

207. Ibid.

208. Cf., Rahner and Vorgrimler, *Dictionary of Theology*, op, cit., p. 395.

209. 'Authority', pp. 61ff (= pp. 326ff).

210. Ibid., p. 61 (= p. 326).

211. Ibid., p. 69 (= p. 334).

212. Ibid. Here, 'justified capacity' corresponds to *Befähigung.*

213. Ibid., p. 70 (= p. 335). Cf., p. 71 (= p. 336).

214. Ibid., p. 75 (= p. 341).

215. Ibid., p. 77 (= pp. 342f). The main premise of Rahner's argument is 'socialization' (*Vergesellschaftung*).

216. Ibid., p. 79 (= p. 344).

217. Ibid, p. 79 (= p. 345).

218. Cf. ibid., pp. 80f (= pp. 346f).

219. Ibid., p. 81 (= p. 347).

220. Ibid., p. 82 (= p. 348); that is, the coercive power is restricted to what is necessarily implied in the exercise of authority. Rahner adds: ' . . . which in concrete cases can have a very considerable impact, as, e.g., when the bearers of church authority withdraw a person's ecclesiastical teaching license.' This latter is a problem I shall face in the next section.

221. Ibid., p. 83 (= p. 349).

222. 'The Perennial Actuality of the Papacy' in *TI* 22, pp. 191ff (= *ST* XVI pp. 249ff).

223. Ibid., p. 203 (= p. 264).

224. Ibid., p. 201 (= p. 262).

225. Ibid., p. 204 (= p. 266).

226. Ibid., p. 203 (= pp. 264f).

227. Ibid., p. 203 (= p. 265).

228. Cf. 'Christianity's Absolute Claim' in *TI* 21, pp. 171ff (=*ST* XV, pp. 171ff).

229. For example, 'Assent', p. 158 (= p. 495).

230. On the hierarchy and its meaning see this chapter, Section 3.2.2.

231. 'Authority', p. 84 (= p. 349).
232. *Lexikon für Theologie und Kirche* 6, pp. 884–90. And see also, *SM* Vol. 3, pp. 351–8. The latter corresponds to 'Lehramt', pp. 177–93. Cf. 'Magisterium'. I shall quote the first as 'Magisterium' without giving its parallel German.
233. Cf. 'Magisterium', p. 352a. See also Imhof and Biallowons, op. cit.
234. Cf. 'Faith and Doctrine'; here p. 44 (= p. 383).
235. 'Magisterium', p. 352b.
236. Ibid.
237. Ibid., p. 355b.
238. Ibid., p. 354b.
239. See Tanner, p. 869. See also, 'Crisis of Authority', especially p. 4 (= p. 342).
240. To which Rahner adds, in *Commentary*, p. 213, commenting upon *Lumen Gentium* 25: 'The "irreformable" nature of the definition clearly excludes only error in faith. It does not affirm that the dogmatic definition . . . corresponds fully to the justifiable demands of the mentality of a given age, or that it may not be replaced later by a better formulation. In this sense, it is always "reformable".'
241. In 'Lehramt', p. 57 (= p. 72).
242. Ibid.
243. 'Authority', p. 84 (= p. 349).
244. 'Magisterium' p. 358a.
245. Ibid.: 'The faithful must . . . be able to see clearly . . . that the Magisterium . . . tries to bring them into contact with the very reality of salvation precisely through its decisions and pronouncements. And in doing so the Magisterium must make every effort to explain intelligibly to the educated faithful, how its decisions and pronouncements have come about.'
246. 'Authority', p. 84 (= p. 350). And see Rahner's repeated statements elsewhere: for example, in 'Situation', pp. 18–20 (= pp. 26–32).
247. 'Situation', especially pp. 18ff. See also 'Certainties?', p. 51 (= p. 290).
248. 'Assent', p. 148 (= p. 485).
249. Cf., ibid., p. 150 (= p. 487).
250. Ibid., p. 154 (= p. 492).
251. Ibid., p. 155 (= p. 492).
252. Ibid., p. 154 (= p. 492).
253. Ibid., p. 155 (= p. 492). See also 'Magisterium', p. 353b.
254. 'Courage for an Ecclesial Christianity' in *TI* 20, pp. 3ff (= *ST* XIV,

pp. 11f). Translated from the original German edition; cf., W. Jens (ed.) *Warum ich Christ bin?*, Munich (1979), pp. 296ff.

255. Ibid.
256. See Tanner, p. 974 and p. 975. See also Rahner's 'Theology and the Church's Teaching Authority after the Council' in *TI* 9, pp. 83ff (= *ST* VIII, pp. 111ff) where he comments upon a rescript from Cardinal Ottaviani, Pro-prefect of the Congregation of the Faith (that is, the Holy Office and not as in the English translation, 'propagation of the faith'). Ottaviani's rescript was published in 1966 in *AAS*, pp. 659ff. In the latter, Rahner pays attention to a distinction brought by Ottaviani himself between the deposit and opinions about it. Ottaviani's complaint is that some of the theological opinions affect dogma (here in the sense of deposit) and are 'no longer keeping within the limits of legitimate freedom of opinion.'
257. 'Crisis of Authority', p. 8 (= p. 344).
258. See 'Official Teaching', p. 169 (= p. 233).
259. See, 'Certainties?', p. 48 (= pp. 288f).
260. Ibid., p. 50 (= p. 289).
261. Cf., ibid., p. 52 (= p. 291), to which Rahner adds 'in which reason and freedom and the divine grace that liberates constitute a unity.'
262. Ibid., p. 54 (= p. 293).
263. Ibid., p. 55 (= pp. 293f).
264. Ibid., p. 57 (= p. 296).
265. Ibid., p. 59 (= p. 299).
266. Ibid., p. 60 (= p. 300).
267. See, for example, 'Changeable', p. 9 (= p. 246).
268. Cf., in 'Faith and Doctrine'.
269. Ibid., p. 39 (= pp. 277f).
270. Cf., ibid., pp. 39–40 (= pp. 278f). Rahner aptly illustrates the historicity of objective and subjective hierarchy of truths to the relationship of phylogenesis and ontogenesis.
271. Cf., 'Changeable', p. 10 (= p. 248).
272. Ibid., p. 12 (= p. 250).
273. Cf., 'Faith and Doctrine', p. 38 (= pp. 276f).
274. H. Küng, *Infallible? An Inquiry*, London and New York, NY (1971) and (paperback) London (1972). German original, *Unfehlbar? Eine Anfrage*, Einsiedeln (1970).
275. Reactions included: W. Kasper, *Glaube und Geschichte*, Mainz (1970); and Y. Congar 'Infallibilité et indéfectibilité' in *Ministères*

et communion ecclésiale, Paris (1971), pp. 141–165. And see 'Zum Problem Unfehlbarkeit. Antworten auf die Anfrage von Hans Küng' in *Quaestiones Disputatae* 54, Freiburg-im-Breisgau (1972).

276. 'On *Humanae Vitae*', pp. 193–210 (= pp. 276ff). See also the infamous interview with Rahner: 'Im Beichtstuhl nach der Pille fragen?', *Der Spiegel* 39 (1968), p. 22.

277. Hans Küng repeated his radical attack against the principle of infallibility in 1995 on the occasion of the Holy Office's rescript about the ordination of women attributing their exclusion to the infallible teaching of the Church: that women are incapable of being ordained in the priesthood belongs to the unchangeable deposit of faith. Cf., 'Waiting for Vatican III', *The Tablet*, 16 December 1995, pp. 1616ff.

278. 'Certainties?', p. 47 (= p. 286). [My italics.]

279. Rahner justly remarks that the selection of magisterial errors by Küng is rather tendentious. [My translation has 'tendentious' for *frisiert* – though *frisiert* is not really translatable and can mean 'artificially distorts'.] See also 'Kritik'.

280. 'Kritik', p. 31. [My translation.]

281. Ibid., p. 39. [My translation.] See also, p. 69.

282. See 'Replik. Bemerkungen zu Hans Küng, im Interesse ser Sache' in *Quaestiones Disputatae* 54, Freiburg-im-Breisgau (1971), pp. 49ff. There is no English translation.

283. Cf., ibid., p. 63.

284. 'Infallibility', p. 79 (= p. 319).

285. Ibid., p. 67 (= p. 306).

286. Ibid., p. 68 (= p. 307). [My italics.]

287. Cf., ibid., pp. 70f (= pp. 309f).

288. Ibid., p. 77 (= p. 316).

289. Ibid.

290. See 'Dispute Concerning the Church's Teaching Office' in *TI* 14, pp. 85ff (= *ST* X, p. 324); here, p. 95 (= p. 335).

291. Cf., 'Infallibility', p. 79 (= p. 319).

292. Cf., ibid., especially note 2, pp. 71f (= pp. 310f).

293. True enough, Pope Paul VI in his sermon concluding the Council emphatically named Mary the 'Mother of the Church', but few took this as an *ex cathedra* definition. See also 'The Interpretation of the Dogma of the Assumption' in *TI* 1, pp. 215ff (= *ST* I, pp. 239ff).

294. Cf., 'Infallibility', p. 74 (= p. 313).

295. Ibid., pp. 81f (= p. 320).
296. Cf., ibid., p 83 (= pp. 320f). Incidentally, Rahner illustrates this state of affairs with the following hypothesis: if the pope had dogmatized the rejection of artificial means of contraception, as in *Humanae Vitae* (which Pope Paul VI never did, yet John Paul II was very near to doing so), then such a new dogmatic formula when put forward would not exclude other possible interpretations of the same. Remember: 'new' dogmatic statements are no longer capable of being true or false(!).
297. Ibid., p. 74 (= pp. 313f).
298. 'On *Humanae Vitae*', especially p. 265 (= pp. 278f).
299. Ibid., p. 270 (= p. 283) and *passim*: ' . . . the papal encyclical clearly falls under the heading of the kind of doctrinal pronouncements of the Church . . . , namely doctrinal pronouncements which are authentic but non-definitorial in character, and so at least in principle susceptible of revision.' See also 'Mysterium Ecclesiae', especially pp. 140 (= pp. 485ff).
300. See 'Lehramt', p. 58 (= p. 73).
301. Ibid., p. 59 (= p. 75).
302. Ibid., p. 60 (= p. 75).
303. Cf., ibid., p. 59–60 (= pp. 73–5).
304. Ibid., p. 61 (= p. 76).
305. Cf., ibid., p. 63 (= pp. 79f).
306. Ibid., p. 64 (= p. 81). See also 'Mysterium Ecclesiae', especially here p. 144 (= p. 485). This essay was written in reaction to the declaration of the Holy Office with the same title.
307. Cf., '*Das Römische*: Theology and the Roman Magisterium' in *TI* 22, pp. 176ff (= *ST* XVI, pp. 231ff) (1980).
308. Ibid., p. 181 (= p. 237).
309. Ibid., p. 184 (= p. 241).
310. Ibid., p. 189 (= p. 247): 'Yet I must say that the number of cases of unjustified curtailment of freedom that I have seen inflicted on theologians during my lifetime is considerable.'
311. Ibid., p. 188 (= p. 247).
312. See 'Pluralism in Theology and the Unity of the Creed in the Church' in *TI* 11, pp. 3ff (= *ST* IX, pp. 11ff) (1969), especially p. 11 (= p.15).
313. Ibid., p. 7 (= p. 15).
314. Ibid., p. 14 (= p. 22).
315. Cf., 'Official Teaching', p. 167 (= p. 219).

316. Ibid., p. 169 (= p. 223). [My italics.]
317. Ibid.
318. Cf., ibid., p. 171 (= pp. 224f).
319. Ibid., p. 172 (= p. 226).
320. Ibid., p. 173 (= p. 228).

Chapter 4 Comments and Questions: The Church in the Power of the Spirit

1. Moltmann, op. cit., here p. 33.
2. Bonhoeffer. See also Kehl (1976), op. cit., especially pp. 132ff under the title 'Die sozialphilosophische Analogie: Communio durch Kommunikation'.
3. See Kehl (1976) for references to J. Habermas, *Theory of Communicative Action*, Cambridge (1987), p. 138, n. 7.
4. Cf., 'Bonhoeffer, p. 33.
5. Cf., Kehl (1976), op. cit., p. 137.
6. Ibid., pp. 138–46. Kehl sums up the social philosophy implied in the theory of 'communicative action' as a model and then (pp. 147–59) applies the distinguishing marks of the same to our faith in the Church (pp. 147–59). See especially the summary (p. 159).
7. The access to the Church according to her double aspect is parallel to Tillich's ecclesiology speaking of the 'Spiritual Presence . . . in the Spiritual Community': cf., P. Tillich, 'Spiritual Presence in the Spiritual Community' in *Systematic Theology III*, Chicago, IL (1963), pp. 159–72. So is Tillich's approach to the relationship of sociology and ecclesiology: 'Every church is a sociological reality. As such it is subject to the laws which determine the life of social groups with all their ambiguities . . . ' And, he continues (pp. 176ff): 'The other view of the churches is the theological. It does not refuse to recognise the sociological aspect, but it does deny its exclusive validity . . . '. See, incidentally, Tillich's understanding of the Roman Church (pp. 177ff).
8. 'Charismatic', p. 97 (= p. 431).
9. See Kehl (1976), op. cit., pp. 68ff: 'The Holy Spirit is the space [*Raum*] for the Church.'
10. Y. Congar, *The Word and the Spirit*, London (1984). English trans-

lation of *La parole et le Souffle*, Paris (1984), chapter 7, pp. 101f. See especially pp. 113f where Lossky is quoted. Cf. V. Lossky, 'Christomonism dans la tradition latine?' in *Ecclesia a Spiritu Sancto edocta*, Paris (1970), pp. 42–63.

11. Cf., Vass, Vol. 3, sections 3.3. and 3.4. There, discussing the image of the Trinitarian God, I emphasized the priority of the 'personal being' which posits its 'substantive being' common to all three Persons, the priority of relations ('processions') to the common substantial being of the one God. Thus, when I propose an *ontological difference* I refer to the relationality of the *personal beings* of the Son and the Spirit and not to their common divine nature.

12. Moltmann, op. cit., p. 36. His formulation 'The Holy Spirit is the divine Subject of the history of Jesus' is not easily reconcilable with the Chalcedonian definition. According to this latter it is, strictly speaking, the Logos who is the divine subject in the history of Jesus. In other words, the Son would be the sole agent in the earthly life of Jesus and somehow the Spirit would stand by him. There is nothing nearer to a hidden monophysitism than this last statement – a feature characteristic of post-Chalcedonian orthodoxy in the West which also made a *pneumatological* Christology superfluous.

13. Zizioulas, op. cit., pp. 127f.

14. H. U. von Balthasar, *Theo-Drama, Theological Dramatic Theory, III. Dramatis Personae: Persons in Christ*, San Francisco, CA (1992), pp. 183–91. English translation of *Theodramatik II Die Personen des Spieles 2. Personen in Christus*, Einsiedeln (1978).

15. Cf. Vass, Vol. 3, section 2.2, especially pp. 227f.

16. Zizioulas, op. cit., especially pp. 128ff. In this very inspiring essay, Zizioulas argues for the precedence of the Spirit through the difference in the liturgical rites of baptism and confirmation and illustrates thus the different work of the Spirit from that of the Son: whilst the Son in the incarnation *becomes history*, the Spirit raising him from the dead raises him *beyond* history. Though the Spirit does not *become* history, his work is equally in history, that is, always with a reference to history's eschatological fulfilment.

17. It is already the view of Augustine: the Spirit is *ineffabilis quaedam communio Patris et Filii*. Cf. *De Trinitate* V, pp. 11–12.

18. See *Lumen Gentium* 7. [My italics.]

19. Zizioulas, op. cit., p. 132.

20. See the definition of the new *Encyclopaedia Britannica*, Vol. III, pp. 567f. Constitution is 'the body of doctrines and practices that form the fundamental organising principles of political state.' It is, however, added that in some states such as the United Kingdom and the United States of America the constitution is not a written document, but a collection of statutes and traditional practices, generally acceptable. The Church as a society, too, is similarly without a written constitution.

21. With this Rahner has implicitly come to my conclusion according to which the theological essence of the Church is the Spirit.

22. For this description I am indebted to a small book published in Hungarian about institution and charisma. Cf. F. Tomka, *Intézmény és karizma az egyházban. Vázlatok a katolikus egyház szociológiájához*, Budapest (1991); here, pp. 38f.

23. See this chapter, Section 2.1.1. See also, K. Rahner, 'Freedom and Manipulation in Society' in *Meditations*.

24. See Section 3.1.1 referring to *Meditations*.

25. Cf., Rahner's 'Theology of Power' in *TI* 4, pp. 391ff (= *ST* IV, pp. 485ff). In reading this article, which was first published in 1960, one can easily substitute the function of institutions for power.

26. See K. Mörsdorf, *SM* III, p. 27a. [In my translation slightly corrected.]

27. The reference is to the two works of an unknown author on the turning of fifth century, Denis, the Areopagite. With a Neoplatonic inspiration Denis constructs the 'hierarchy' of the angels (*De coelesti hierarchia*) imitated by the ministry of the Church (*De ecclesiastica hierarchia*); see, for example, his Chapter V, paragraph 6.

28. See Kehl (1976), op. cit., p. 115. See also H. Dombois, *Hierarchie: Grund und Grenze einer umsritten Struktur*, Freiburg-im-Breisgau (1971).

29. Kehl (1976), op. cit., Chapter 2, pp. 23ff. It is a pity that Kehl does not try to tease out elements of this merely secular sociology in Rahner's concept of churchly institutions.

30. Tomka, op. cit., pp. 38f.

31. For this consult P. Beger and T. Luckman, *The Social Construction of Reality: A Treatise in the Sociology of Knowledge*, London (1966) and (paperback) New York, NY (1967), especially pp. 53ff. To use the terms of Berger and Luckmann, the fresh beliefs and customs of the early Church were once 'externalised' and their

heirs will encounter these in their 'objectivised' facticity which will be 'internalised' by subsequent ones. Or, as Mary Douglas would say, institutions are 'thinking and acting' and thus they are a demand to freedom's acceptance. Cf., Mary Douglas, *How Institutions Think*, Syracuse (1986). Later, published in Germany as *Wie Institutionen denken*, Frankfurt (1991).

32. See Gehlen, op. cit., especially pp. 42ff. See also F. Jonas, *Die Institutionslehre von A. Gehlen*, Tübingen (1966). Gehlen deduces the necessity of institutions directly from the necessity of human culture.

33. For example, N. Luhmann, *The Differentiation of Society*, New York, NY (1982), pp. 84ff. See also N. Luhmann, 'Institutionalisierung: Funktion und Mechanismus im sozialen System' in H. Schelsky (ed.), *Zur Theorie der Institution*, Dusseldorf (1970), pp. 27–41, especially pp. 36ff.

34. See M. Weber, *Die charismatische Herrschaft und ihre Umbildung*, as quoted by Tomka, op. cit., p. 72, n. 1.

35. It is worth while returning to Rahner's analogy of the chess club and the Church. The chess players can freely determine or freely accept further institutionalization in their group. To decide, however, what the club is about is no longer their free decision and/or acceptance.

36. A typical example for this is René Girard's theory of mimetism and of the scapegoat: human associations originate by people trying to overcome violence which is an inevitable consequence of mimesis. The means for this is religious – that is, by projecting the cause of violence on to a scapegoat to be sacrificed and later 'adored' in its 'transcendence'. Unity among humans is only possible through sacrifice – that is, by the sacred. Note, however, that for Girard sacrifice and the sacred are used in a pejorative sense. Their ubiquitous efficience is only broken by the gospel of Jesus Christ. See, Girard's three main works: *La violence et le sacré*, Paris (1972), pp. 444; *Des choses cachées depuis la fondation du monde*, Paris (1978), pp. 33ff; and *Le bouc émissair*, Paris (1982).

37. W. G. Kümmel, 'Jesus und die Anfänge der Kirche' in *Heilsgeschehen und Geschichte: Gesammelte Aufsätze* Marburg (1965), pp. 289–309, especially pp. 308f.

38. For some exegetes the fact that nowhere else does Jesus speak of 'my church' suggests that he never thought of instituting one. In Matthew 18:17, the *ekklesia* refers to an established *praxis* of

reconciliation in the *kahal*.

39. Cf. O. Luz, *Evangelisch-Katholischer Kommentar zum Matthäusevangelium*, Zurich (1990), p. 462.

40. See K. Kertelege, *Gemeinde und Amt im Neuen Testament*, Munich (1972), pp. 40ff. Both Luz and Kertelege give a summary of the most important literature concerning our present question.

41. For this argumentation I am indebted to A. Vögtle, 'Jesus und die Kirche' in M. Roesle (ed.) and O. Culmann, *Begegnung der Christen*, Frankfurt (1958), pp. 54–81.

42. Cf. Tillich, op. cit., pp. 160ff. Tillich, very correctly, compares the confession of Peter in Matthew 16 with the event of Pentecost. Just as Peter was grasped (as our Lord there says) by this spiritual presence, so were the assembled disciples of Jesus.

43. Tillich's ecclesiology, however, does not manage to integrate the visible, institutional side of the Church. Cf., W. Pannenberg. *Systematic Theology III*, Edinburgh (1998), pp. 131f and notes. English translation of *Systhematische Theologie* III, Goettingen (1993).

44. Zizioulas, op. cit., 'Apostolic Continuity and Succession', especially pp. 171ff, and his other suggestions in this book of collected essays.

45. Ibid., especially 'Eucharist and Catholicity', pp. 143ff. See also J. D. Zizioulas, 'The Unity of the Church in the Eucharist and the Bishop in the First Three Centuries', Athens (1965). This latter thesis is, unfortunately, only published in Greek.

46. Or, in order to avoid the use of the word 'analogy' which, in Section 2.4.1, I have preferred to call 'parallelism through dialogue'. This, I believe, corresponds better to 'analogy of correlation'.

47. Cf., Zizioulas, op. cit., pp. 210ff: 'There is no ministry in the Church other than Christ's ministry.' I took over his scriptural references and refer the reader for the patristic evidence he quotes. See also T. F. Torrance, 'Consecration and Ordination', *Scottish Journal of Theology* 11 (1958) , pp. 225ff: 'Just as we are given to share in his [Christ's] Sonship, so we are given to share in his Priesthood.

48. See 'Consecration in the Church', p. 67 (= p.125).

49. Something similar could be said of sacramental marriage through which the smallest cell of Christian community comes to be, *ad intra*, however with the task of witnessing their indissoluble love

in Jesus the Christ to the world, *ad extra*.

50. In his 1936 article 'Consecration in the Church' he still speaks of the sacrament of baptism as a cause; and in 1976 consecration of the individual is due to God's universal will to save. It is not clear whether this latter is a 'cause' of the supernatural existential or an existential fact.

51. In fact, the nearest we could come to the understanding of someone becoming a member of the Church, if we here reassumed a certain doctrine of divine election which, though primarily refers to the community of the Church and rebounds in the election of the individual. See, with due precautions, Pannenberg, op. cit., pp. 435ff.

52. Belonging to, or finding oneself a member of, the Church points to the fact that a great majority of Christians are without this awareness. Nonetheless, we have to justify their place among the structures of the Church.

53. See H. Denzinger, *Enchiridion Symbolorum*, A. Schönmetzer (ed.), Freiburg-im-Breisgau (1962), pp. 1776. See also Tanner, p. 744, for an insistence on the divine origin of the hierarchy against Luther who regarded it as introduced by human right only. However, Trent never defines that each of the three traditional grades as such are of divine right, yet theirs is a graded difference. See Pannenberg, op. cit., pp. 416, n. 966, who interprets the approach of *Lumen Gentium*, coining the expression *'unterschiedliche Wahrnehmungsweisen des einen Amtes'*; that is, 'the three different forms of perceiving the one ministry'.

54. Thus, the sanctification (consecration) and mission of Jesus are applied in turn in different senses to the general priesthood of all the faithful and to the special office of the consecrated priests. Cf., *Commentary*, pp. 220f.

55. This is also Rahner's view concerning the origin of the visible Church with her institutions. Likewise, Grillmeier in *Commentary*, p. 221: 'One must always begin with this original fullness and unity of the office if one is to recognise that the Church has received . . . the authority to introduce a graded participation and distribution of the priestly ministry or to alter this in course of time.' [My italics.]

56. Cf., Zizioulas, op. cit., p. 210; see too, *passim*, especially his essay, 'Apostolic Continuity and Succession', pp. 171–208 where Zizioulas explains his distinction in detail between a historical and eschatological approach to the mystery and reality of the Church.